HRAJUKU
STREET
TOKYO
BREAK
EVERYDAY
EVERYTIME
REXON
HENKA
24K

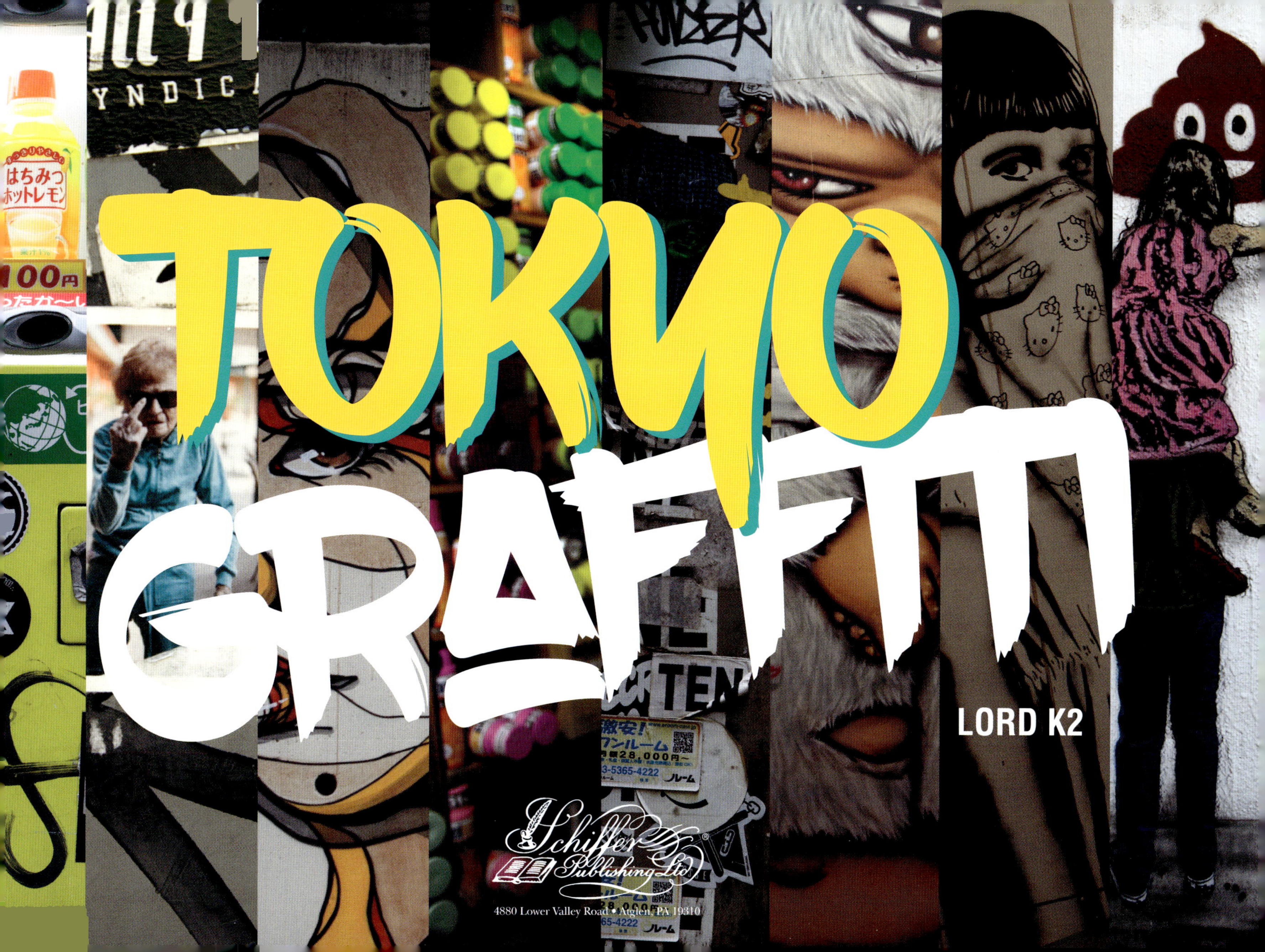

TOKYO GRAFFITI

LORD K2

Schiffer Publishing Ltd
4880 Lower Valley Road • Atglen, PA 19310

This book is dedicated to Oscar and Ely.

Library of Congress Control Number: 2017951905

Photography: Lord K2
Text: Little Pink Pills (Mika Revell)

Type set in Century Gothic

ISBN: 978-0-7643-5473-1
Printed in China

Published by Schiffer Publishing, Ltd.
4880 Lower Valley Road
Atglen, PA 19310
Phone: (610) 593-1777; Fax: (610) 593-2002
E-mail: Info@schifferbooks.com
Web: www.schifferbooks.com

For our complete selection of fine books on this and related subjects, please visit www.schifferbooks.com. You may also write for a free catalog.

Schiffer Publishing's titles are available at special discounts for bulk purchases for sales promotions or premiums. Special editions, including personalized covers, corporate imprints, and excerpts, can be created in large quantities for special needs. For more information, contact the publisher.

We are always looking for people to write books on new and related subjects. If you have an idea for a book, please contact us at proposals@schifferbooks.com.

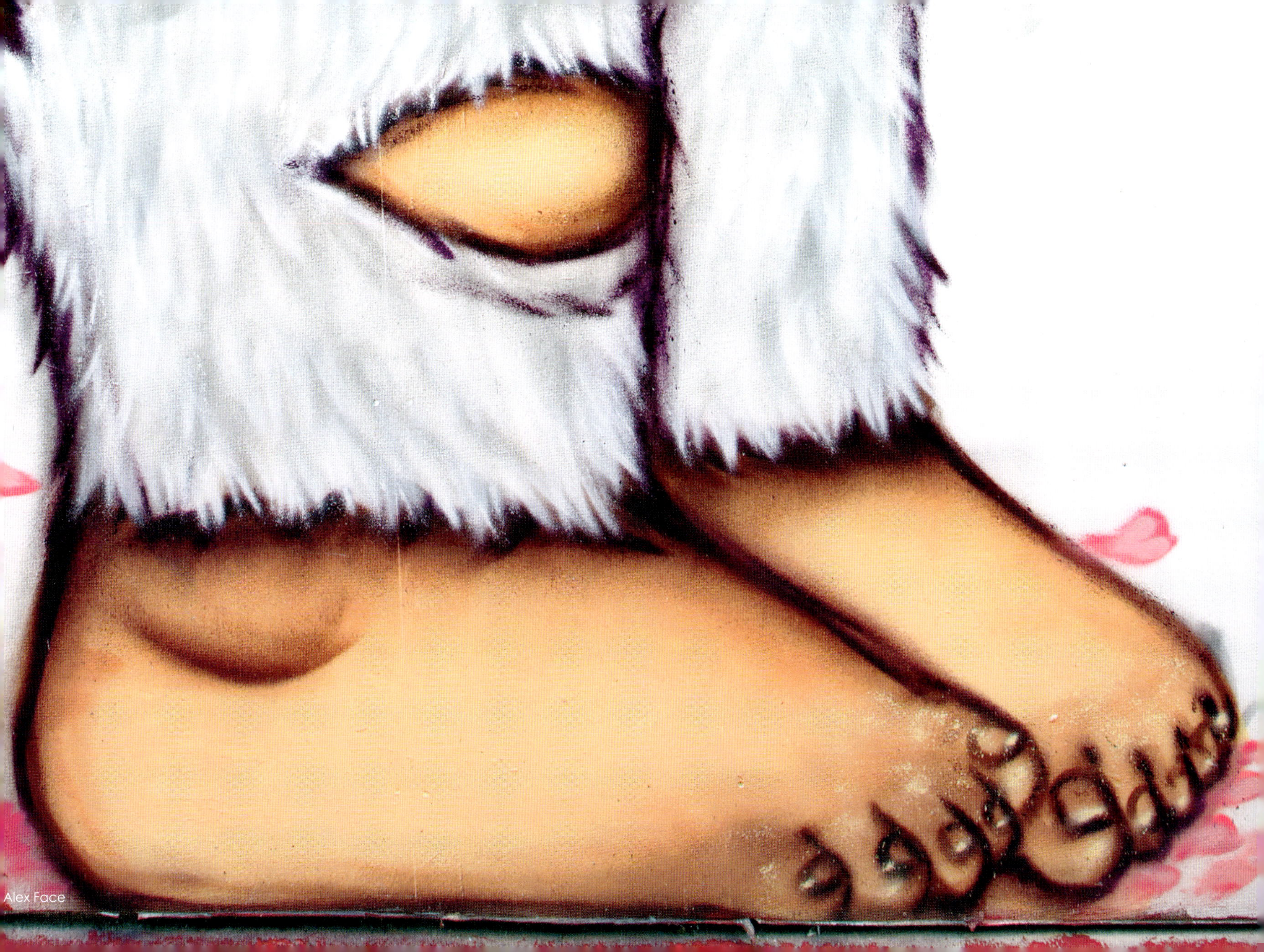
Alex Face

Contents

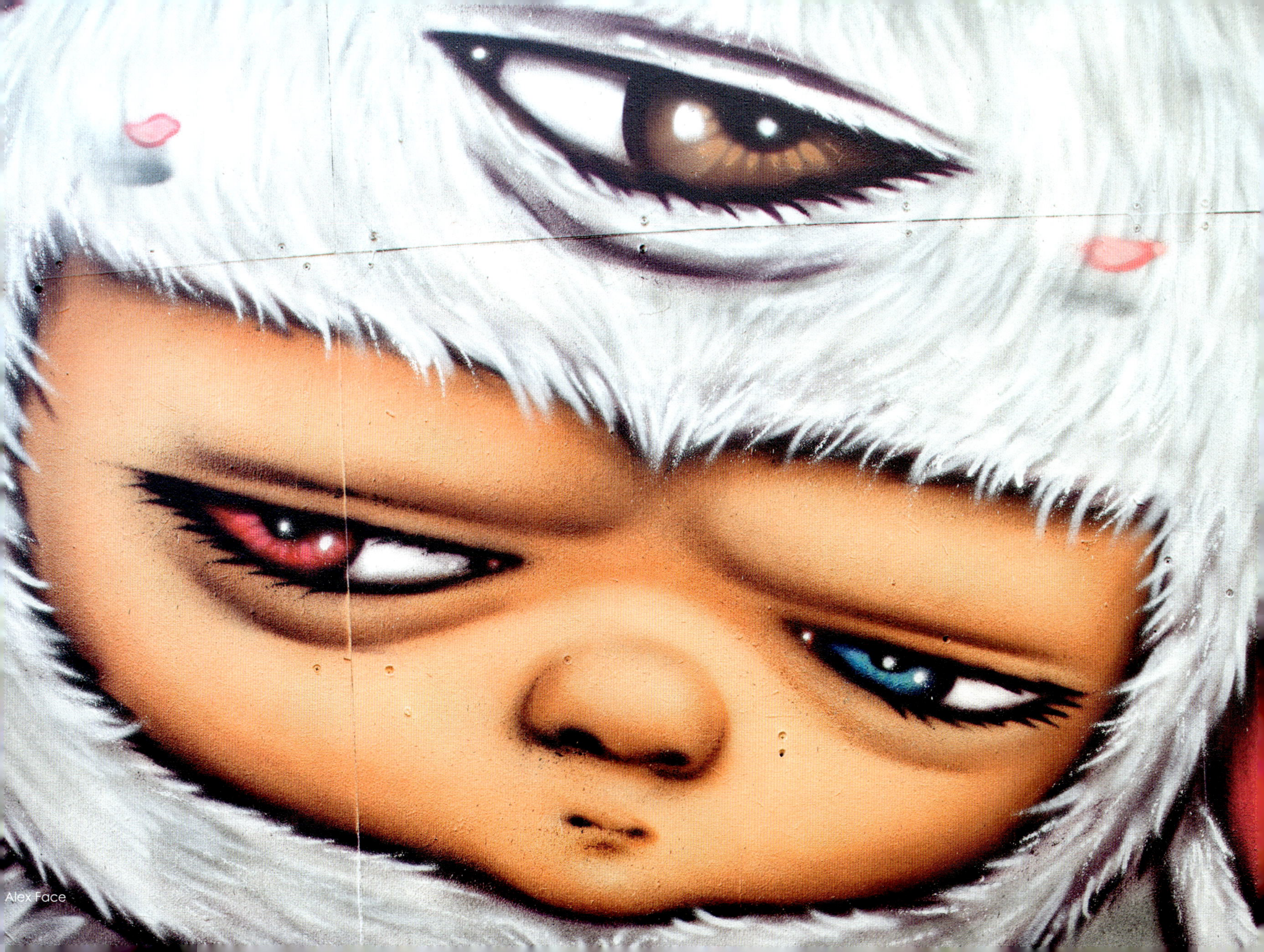
Alex Face

Preface

When I first started asking where in Tokyo I could find street art, the standard response was, "There is no street art in Tokyo." So I began to cycle around the city to see if this was in fact true. What I discovered were pockets of urban art spread throughout the city. Each neighborhood showcased a different variety of art dependent on unspoken constraints and brought to light a world of urban art hidden in plain sight. As I explored, documenting what I saw, it dawned on me to accept the challenge and produce a book in the city where "There is no graffiti." It is not possible to walk around the swelling metropolis of Tokyo and effortlessly encounter art. So I embarked on an expedition to find all that I could and expose the secrets of Tokyo's street culture.

The first thing you notice when searching for graffiti in Tokyo are the stickers! Particularly around the trendy fashion districts of Shibuya and Harajuku, stickers seem to smother the backs of signs, surfaces, undersides, and out-of-reach nooks. Due to strict laws prohibiting vandalism, artists will not stand around painting freely on the streets for any prolonged period of time without permission. Therefore, stickers are the solution. Due to the slim chance of being caught, one can slap up their calling card and quickly sink back into the crowd. When walking through the neighborhoods and streets, it's almost as if there is no rubbish, no disorder, but just around the corner, brightly colored vinyl and stickers from all over the world seem to creep up from behind.

Bombing, or quick throw ups of tags and crew names, is the second most visible form of urban art found in the city. These simple signatures can be achieved in seconds or a few minutes with a can of spray paint, but must be done covertly and often in the middle of the night. Using spray paint in an environment with high pedestrian traffic is not only an immediate way to draw unwanted attention, it is also a highly disgraceful and stigmatized act in Japan. Artists need permission to paint on the streets, and obtaining permission in Tokyo is no easy feat. Graffiti artists and "taggers" take a considerable risk when painting like this and must be swift and stealthy. The more common, decorative forms of arts which usually appear in the open streets of major international cities are few and far between in Japan.

However, organizations are beginning to test the waters of Tokyo, arranging street art events and gaining permission for commissioned walls and large-scale murals. The global network of artists now known as POW! WOW! Worldwide, and headed by Kamea Hadar, arrived from Hawaii during my tour of Tokyo. Their mission to change conservative attitudes towards urban art invaded the streets of

Tokyo in an eruption of painting. Local and international artists were able to paint openly for a month in a couple locations throughout the city. This festival of arts, music, and community stimulated the city to an unprecedented result highlighted in these pages.

After extensive hunting, my quest for street art was rewarded and my overlap with POW! WOW! was nothing but serendipitous. With my collection of photographs complete, I was perplexed by how to narrate this experience of Tokyo's underground art world. I began by conducting interviews with the graffiti elite but quickly found my efforts were futile. Any probing questions were deflected with, "I don't know," or a cautious reply followed with, "Don't quote me, I don't want to get into trouble." The street art scene in Tokyo is unlike any I have experienced elsewhere. The close-knit communities of well acquainted friends or enemies were nowhere to be found here. As many Japanese traditionally keep to themselves, this demeanor runs over into the street art world. Hence, there is not yet an evolved scene to speak of. During my trip I was introduced to artist Mika Revell, who was painting on the streets and researching the scene while on an arts residency. Her thorough investigation of Japanese culture and the Tokyo street art scene surpassed my knowledge and it soon became apparent that Mika could provide a commentary that would do justice to the artwork, the city, and the photography in this book.

I am pleased to present to you *Tokyo Graffiti*.

Lord K2

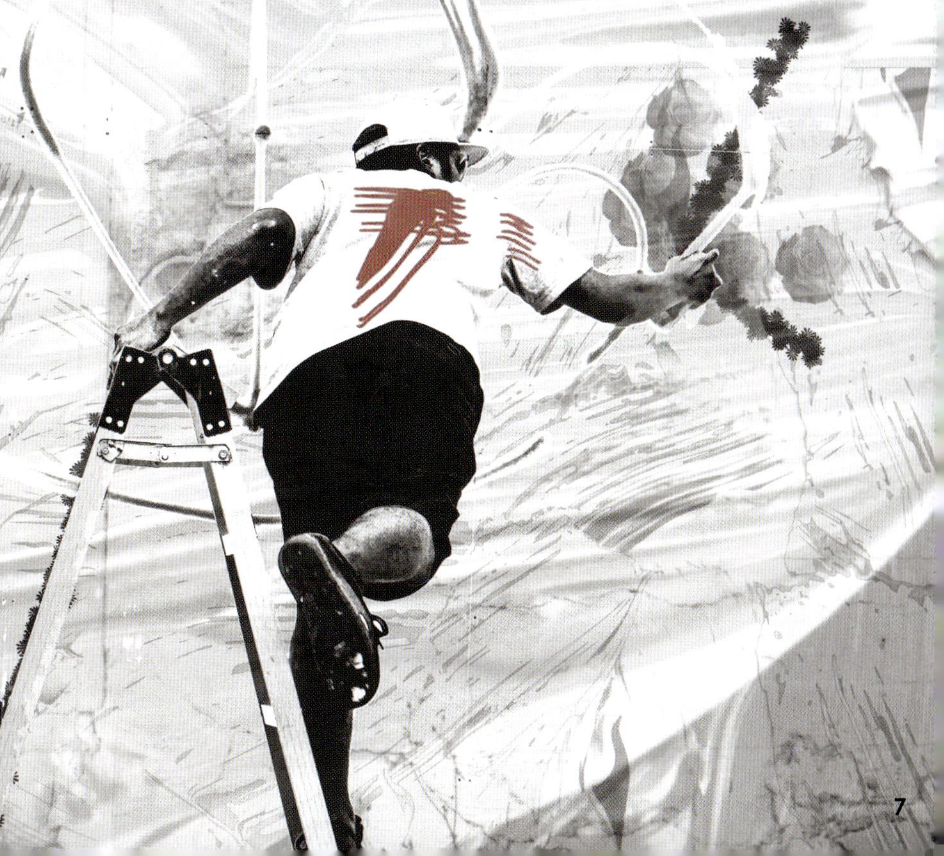

Alex Face

Introduction

The earliest written mention of Japan is found in Chinese historical texts dating back to the first century AD. Now, more than 2,000 years later, one of the greatest cities in the world continues to barrel forward at light speed, leaving behind a trail of fascinating visual history. It takes approximately two hours in Tokyo to become charged with an electrifying current that will invade your sleep. Stepping onto a train filled with downcast, phone-lit faces you launch through a time-lapse of neon lit architecture from the 40s to present. Speckled with temples, monumental sculpture, sky scrapers, shrines, and shacks, Tokyo's urban cityscape is interlaced with street art, sticker art, graffiti, and murals; you just have to look closely.

At first glance, Tokyo is one of the cleanest and most efficient cities to visit. The streets and train stations convey a manicured, respectful, and somehow futuristic vibe. It's easy to acquire polite gestures, habits, and greetings by the hour. Unlike New York or Berlin, graffiti is not visible on every brick wall, nor is there spray paint on many signs or stencils on the sidewalks. There is a palpable adherence to tradition and a strong sense of respect for the country of Japan amongst its inhabitants. Perhaps derived from generations of a feudal system, Buddhism, and Shintoism, the lack of litter, silence on the trains, and absence of street art seem to be a communal response to the environment.

We all know the origins of mark making extend back to the beginnings of mankind. Nowadays, we can visually trace when certain elements of what has become the all encompassing term "street art" began to creep its way into the main stream. The gestural streaks of spray paint, the dripping markers, and high-contrast stencil techniques rapidly spread across continents and cultures, from the streets, to the galleries, and into the public. Although the content, conscience, and context of street art has changed constantly over time, the basic impetus has remained the same. Artists are compelled to create, sometimes for the aim of self expression; to reclaim the urban environment; and, sometimes, to criticize the current political or cultural norm. The desire to invade the public space, produce something new, and fascinate the viewer remain at the core of the urban art movement.

When you walk the streets of Tokyo you embark on a course compounded with cultural importance and moments of the surreal. Rivers dappled with cherry blossoms or flags and paper lanterns signify holidays, new seasons, or the type of business you will find inside. Finding street art may seem difficult at first, but once in the heart of areas like Shibuya, Shinjuku, or Harajuku, it is hard to miss. Street art is mostly localized to these busier, more international areas of commerce near large train stations and with high visibility. In these spots, one can find thousands of stickers, quick tags, and the works of internationally respected artists like Space Invader, Andre, Rone, and Buff Monster.

Although individual artists have different reasons for working in the streets, the desire to have your work seen is primary. Locations that are risky to get to, tread by famous artists, or that are capitals of activity are highly sought after. Tokyo presents an interesting challenge because of its laws, standards of cleanliness, and cultural heritage. However, this won't stop the creativity and dedication of many. Like the cultural collage that is modern day Japan, the street art of Tokyo suggests a harmonious balance of incongruous elements. The use of calligraphic-style fonts, seventeenth-century traditional imagery, or the appropriation of Western graffiti styles all perpetuate a vibrant, innovative, and vital component of the Japanese and communal world view.

At the turn of the nineteenth century, the term avant-garde became used to describe those experimental individuals pushing the boundaries of society and intellect. Often preceding the philosophies, revolutions, and reforms of the era, the artists, authors, and free thinkers of a civilization led the way. Exploration, experimentation, and the violation of rules often comes with the territory. In Japan, many practices often seem bizarre or unnecessary yet are entrenched with deep significance. For a new generation, influenced by the outside world and more connected than ever before, it is a perplexing map to navigate. To uncover the mysteries of your own heritage while finding significance, purpose, and position amongst humanity seems a daunting task. Secretly painting in and out of plain sight, the new avant-garde are chipping away at those antiquated ideals, social injustices, and unnecessary regulations. The street artists of today's Tokyo and other places around the globe are attacking the walls and perhaps the very foundations upon which they're built.

Little Pink Pills (Mika Revell)

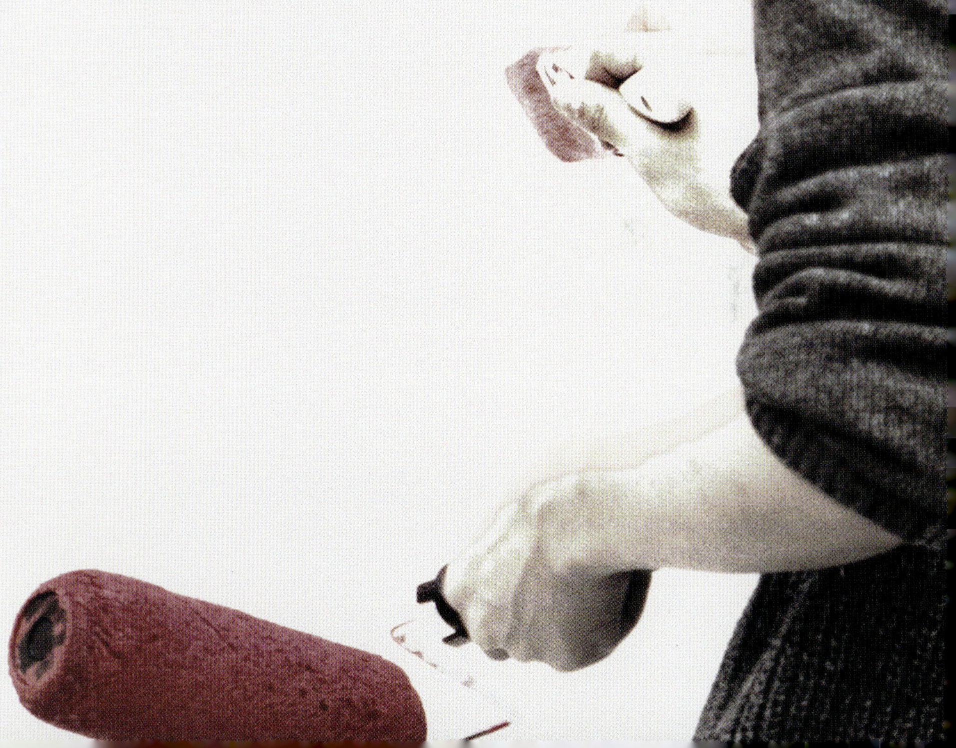

A Brief History

The roots of Tokyo's street-art and graffiti scene are not hard to trace nor do they appear to reach very deep into Japan's own history. Although elements of traditional Japanese art are present in today's murals and writing styles, graffiti, or *rakugaki*, was acquired from America. In 1980s New York City, a battle was taking place on the streets in response to socioeconomic and environmental realities. Graffiti became a method of marking one's territory, and "bombing" subway cars with the writer's name and crews became prevalent. Hip-hop culture emerged through dance, music, fashion, and film and began to spread all over the world.

In 1983, the release of the film *Wild Style* announced the arrival of hip-hop culture in Tokyo. A group of popular musicians, break dancers, and graffiti artists performed in a local shopping mall to promote the film's debut and shocked their young audience. The success of the film and the popularity of other documentaries paved the way for street culture in Tokyo and eventually for Japanese graffiti and street art. While the "writers" and artists of New York City were fighting a fight for recognition and a place in their society, the youth of Japan were discovering this form of self expression through art and culture for the first time.

As the worldwide fascination with American street culture spread, Tokyo embraced it! Break dancing was the first art form to be adapted by young people in Tokyo. On Sundays, groups of young dancers began to gather in Yoyogi Park to break dance and DJ, a tradition that continues to this day. The oversized, vibrant fashions of rappers and artists in the US quickly caught on and morphed into Japan's own version of street style. Skateboarding was another form of American life that was introduced and popularized at this time. In the years following the release of *Wild Style*, Tokyo began to develop and add its own voice to the international hip-hop scene.

By the early 90s, Japanese musicians had invented their own rap styles. Due to the significant linguistic differences between English and Japanese, it took Japanese artists time to develop a rap method that maintained the rhyme and rhythm similar to their Western role models. As a result, Japanese rappers developed a blend of English phrases and Japanese to find a structure that eventually achieved acclaim through J-rap in the mid 90s. Major cultural differences also led Japanese rappers to create a form of hip-hop that rarely references misogyny, guns, or hard drugs. Rather, the individualistic ideals of America seemed to catch on and a resistance to Japanese tradition was cultivated. MC Shiro of Rhymester described contemporary Japanese hip-hop lifestyle as "in defiance of the mainstream Japanese society, a culture of the first person singular."

Graffiti was the last aspect of hip-hop culture to break through in Japan. In fact, Japanese graffiti is still young and developing its style. Tagging became popular throughout the late 90s but took another decade to fully catch on. This desire for self assertion and stylistic rebellion was not common in traditional Japanese culture, yet the underground scene was growing. In 2004, Japanese writer WANTO travelled to the US and began to work with the internationally famous American crew MSK. In 2008, WANTO created his own crew, 246, distinguishing himself as a leader and trailblazer in the Japanese graffiti world. 246, named after a major traffic way in Tokyo, is now the most well-known crew, with members from the US, Japan, Mexico, and Taiwan. Today you will see the names of writers from all over the world covering shutters and store fronts with their unique and rebellious ingenuity.

In the past two decades, street art seems to have taken over the Western art world and become a socially acceptable, marketable, and mass-produced art form. In Japan, several legal graffiti walls have become popular, from the Yokohama Wall of Fame, the Sakuragicho Station Wall, "The Ghetto" in Shinjuku, and along the Yamanote train line. Japanese artists have begun to incorporate their own styles, including historical influences from Japanese *kanji*, calligraphy, anime, and manga characters. Although these more elaborate murals and works are now more mainstream, there is still a battle with traditional taggers over walls and territory.

In 2005, a major contemporary art museum presented an exhibit at the Art Tower Mito dedicated to showing Japanese graffiti writers. Entitled X-COLOR Graffiti in Japan, this show was the first of its kind, and called a "beautiful deviation," by its curator, Kenji Kubota. Writers from all over Japan were invited to tag the walls of the museum and create works throughout the city. The viewer was presented with this groundbreaking idea of "graffiti as art" in this never-before-seen kind of exhibition.

Although Japan's inner city youth do not suffer from the same social issues as young people in America, they have utilized graffiti, street art, and culture to exorcise their sense of alienation and experience of the urban landscape. Tokyo is famous for its hyper-consumerism, cultural homogeneity, and adherence to tradition. Presently, the young artists of Tokyo are continuing to evolve with this "self-aware and self-affirmative movement." Street art, although still in its adolescent stages, has become an integral part of Japanese hip-hop culture. Grounded in the streets of New York, this innovative art form has grown into the contemporary culture and visual art of Japanese life.

Little Pink Pills (Mika Revell)

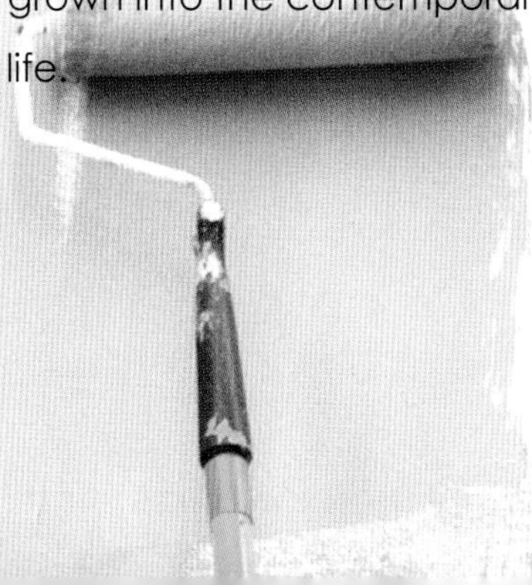

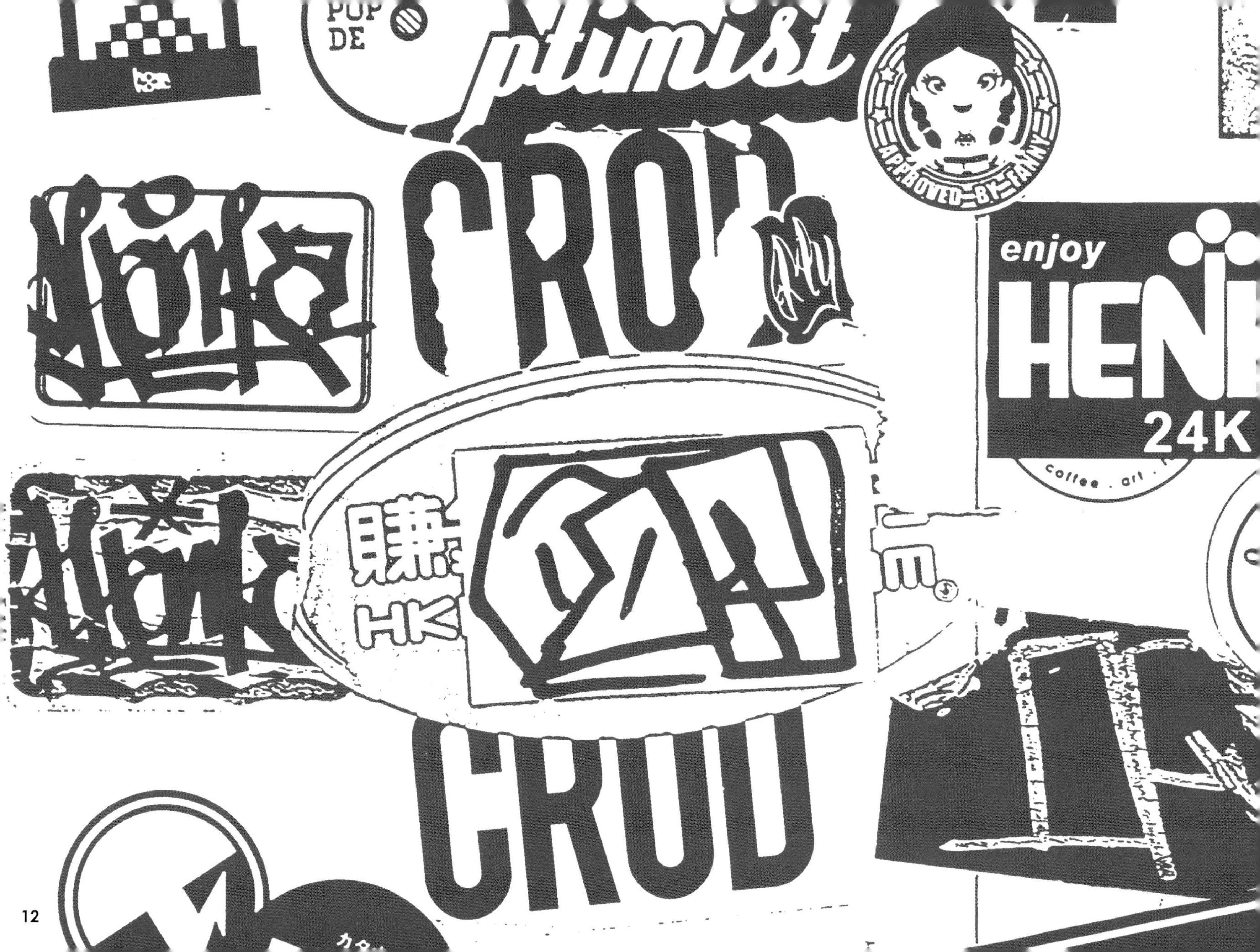
PUP
DE
ptimist
enjoy
24K
coffee . art .

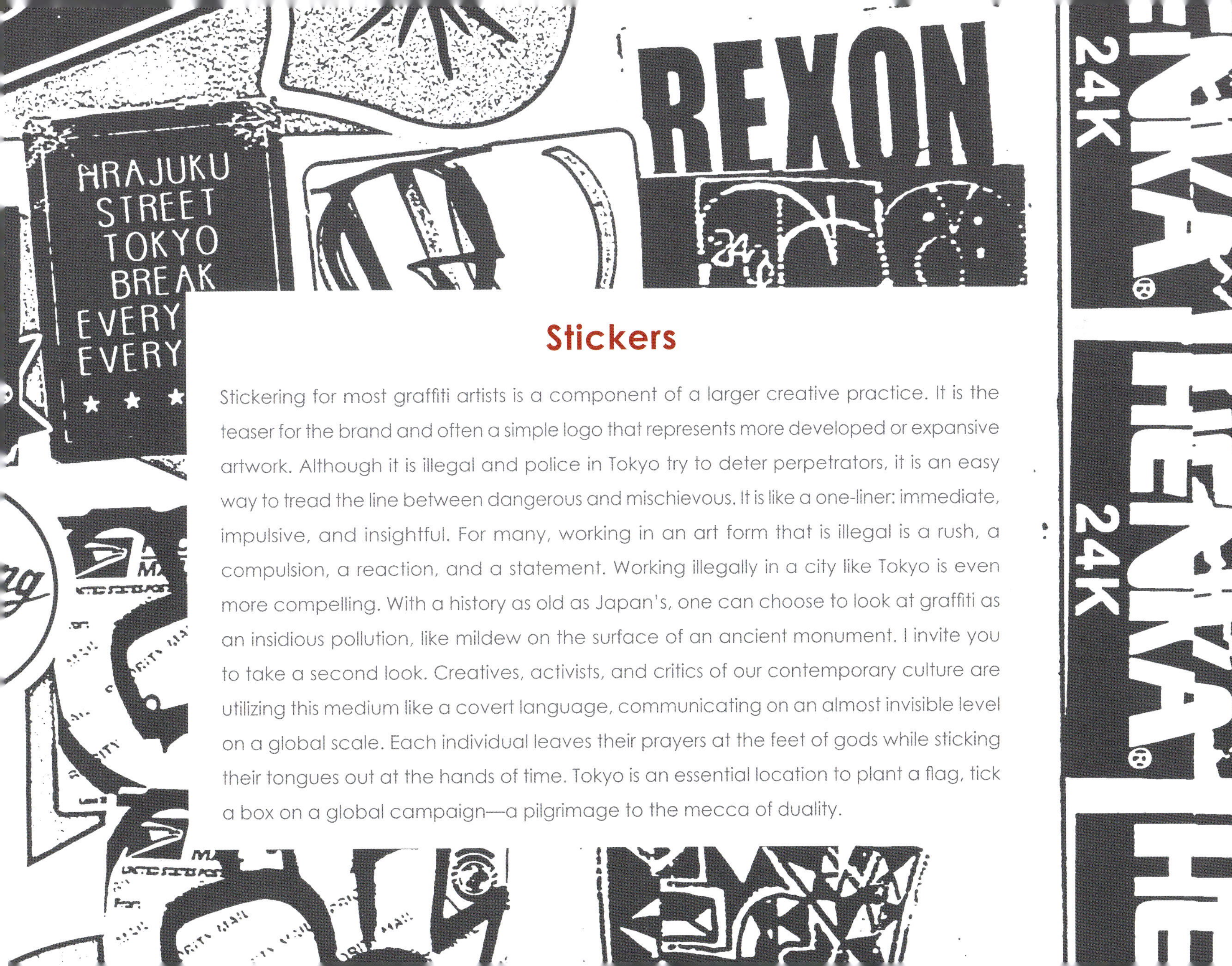

Stickers

Stickering for most graffiti artists is a component of a larger creative practice. It is the teaser for the brand and often a simple logo that represents more developed or expansive artwork. Although it is illegal and police in Tokyo try to deter perpetrators, it is an easy way to tread the line between dangerous and mischievous. It is like a one-liner: immediate, impulsive, and insightful. For many, working in an art form that is illegal is a rush, a compulsion, a reaction, and a statement. Working illegally in a city like Tokyo is even more compelling. With a history as old as Japan's, one can choose to look at graffiti as an insidious pollution, like mildew on the surface of an ancient monument. I invite you to take a second look. Creatives, activists, and critics of our contemporary culture are utilizing this medium like a covert language, communicating on an almost invisible level on a global scale. Each individual leaves their prayers at the feet of gods while sticking their tongues out at the hands of time. Tokyo is an essential location to plant a flag, tick a box on a global campaign—a pilgrimage to the mecca of duality.

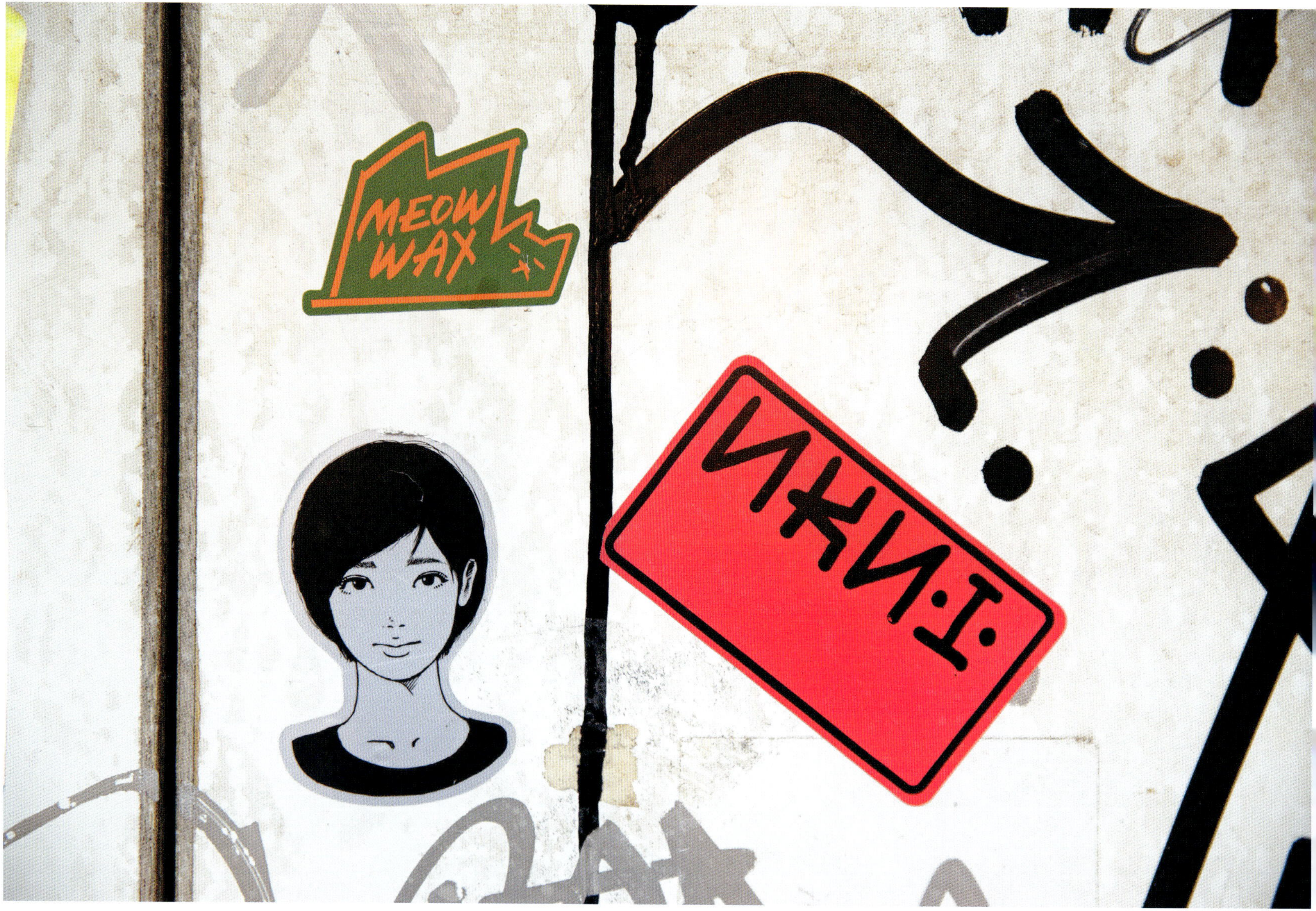

Kyne

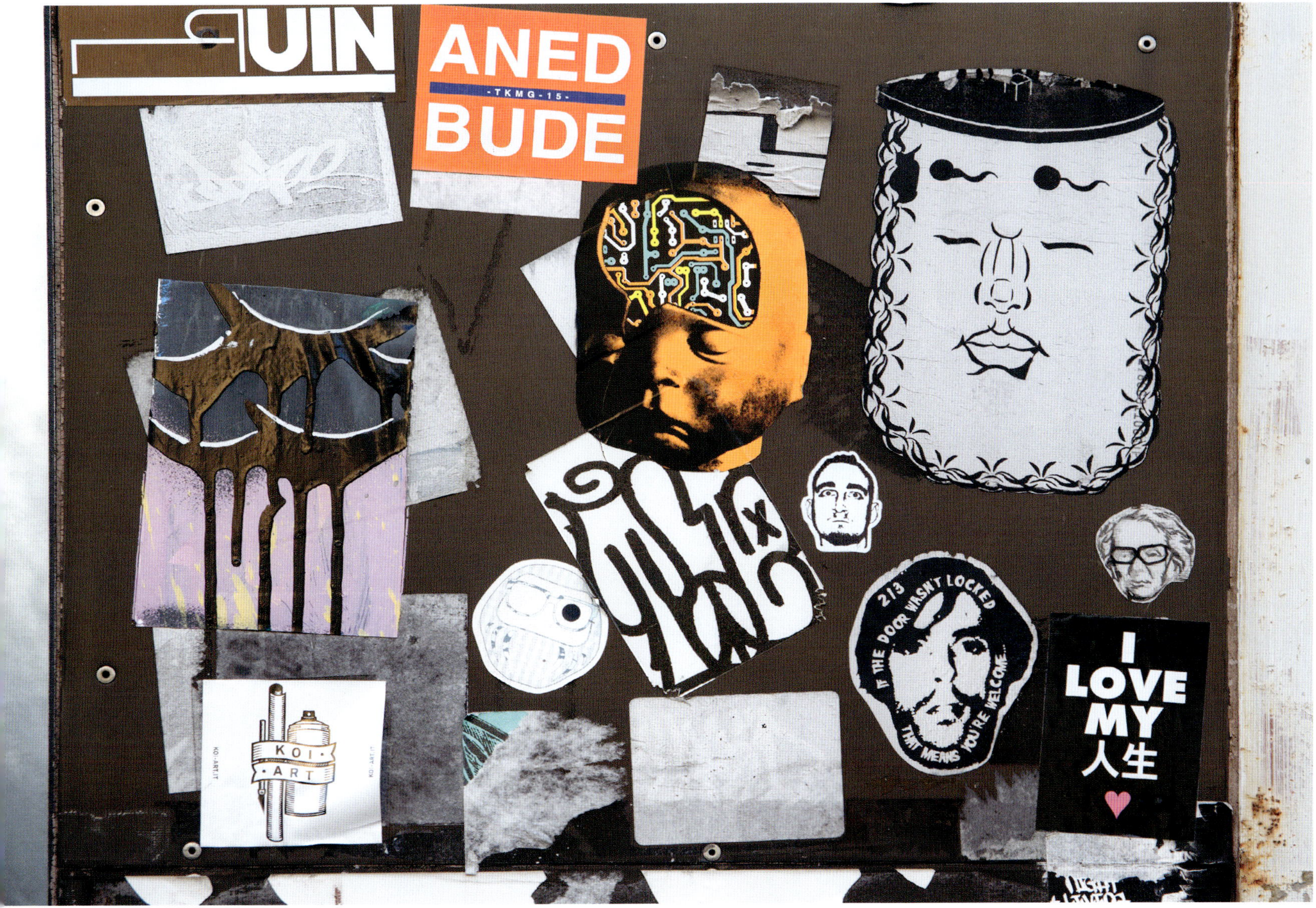

Paul Insect (orange)

Tokyo sticker bombing is the most prevalent form of urban art in Tokyo. It's quick and attracts less attention than spray cans. In a city sprawling with inhabitants it's unlikely your actions will go unnoticed. Sticker culture in Tokyo is not only the most visible method of graffiti, it is also a huge part of a collectible culture. From small companies like B-Side Label in Harajuku to massive corporations like LINE App., stickers have become the trading cards of today. Seen everywhere from tunnels, bridges, traffic signs, and lamp posts, stickers make up a large component of outdoor art and embody the brightly colored, graphic Japanese aesthetic.

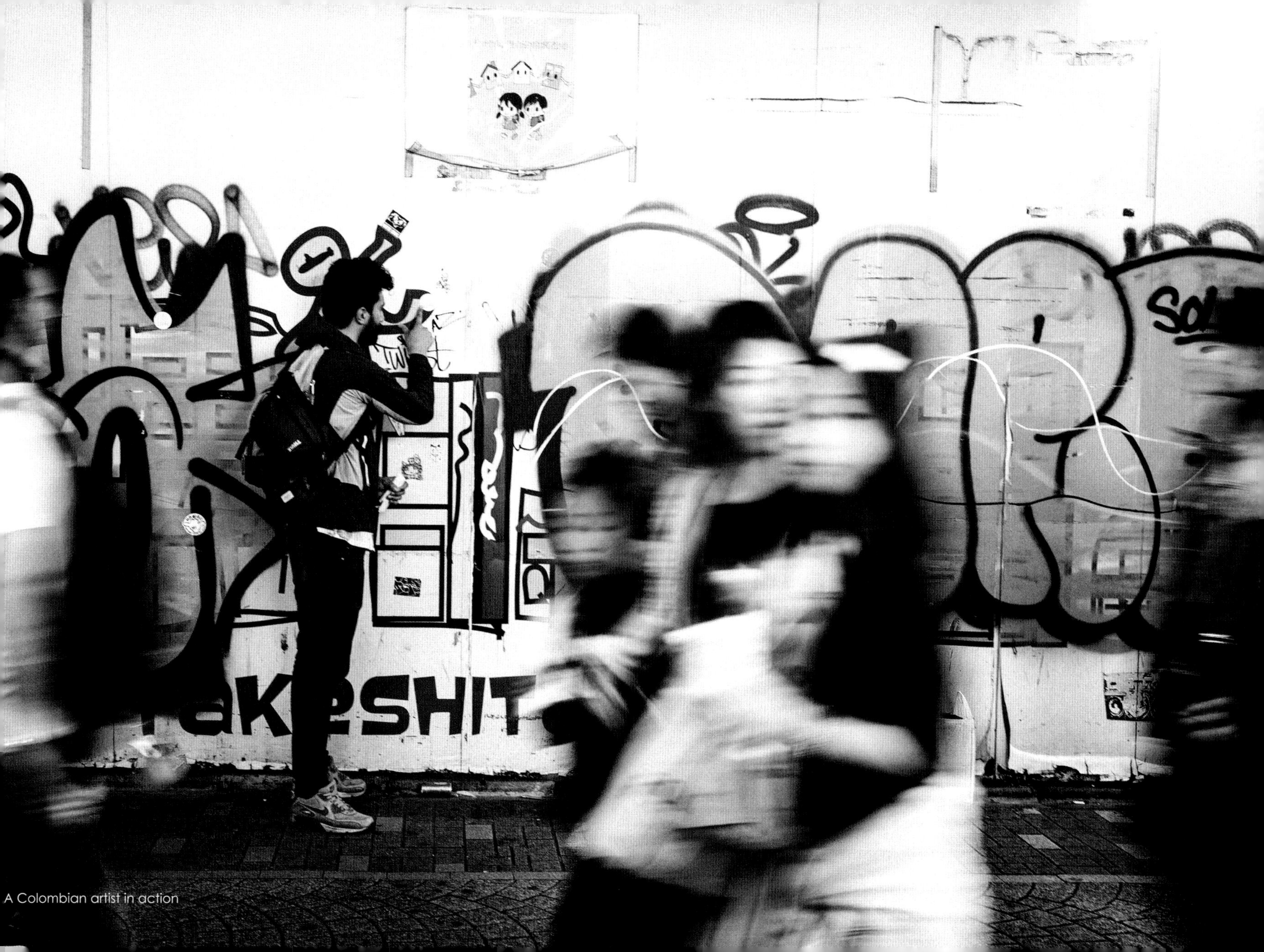

A Colombian artist in action

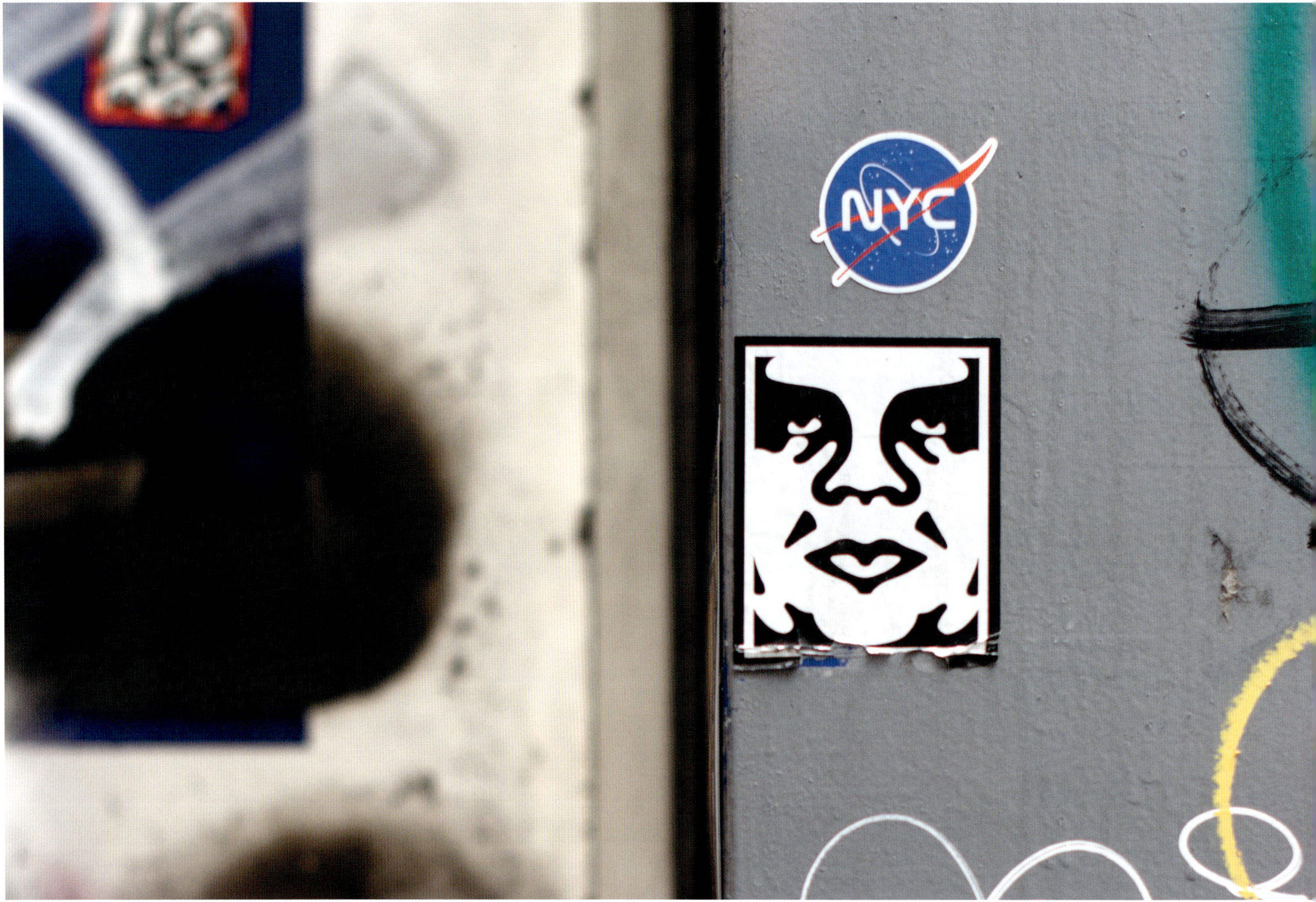

Obey

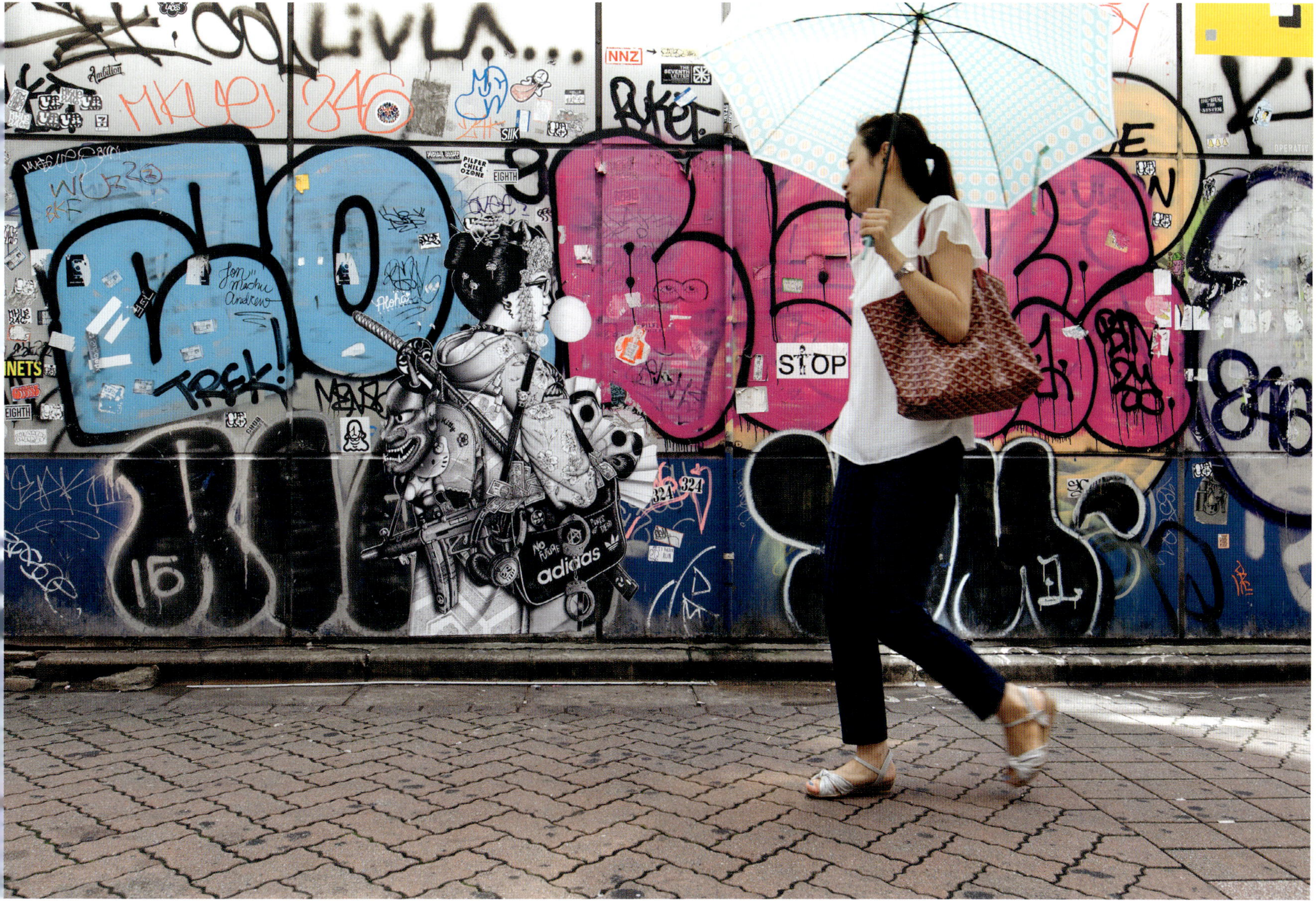
NNZ
THE SEVENTH LETTER
PILFER
CHILE
OZONE
EIGHTH
SIIK
STOP
324
adidas

Tsuchinoko

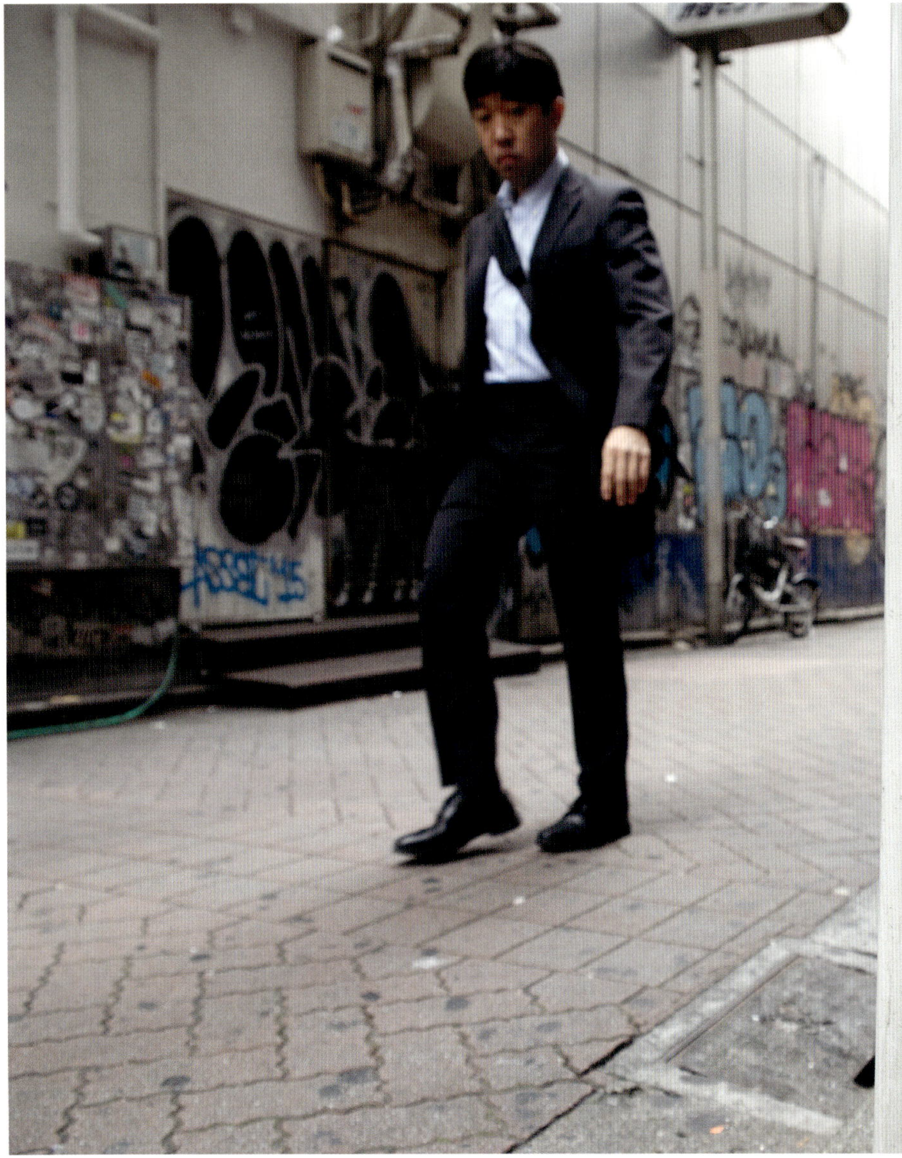

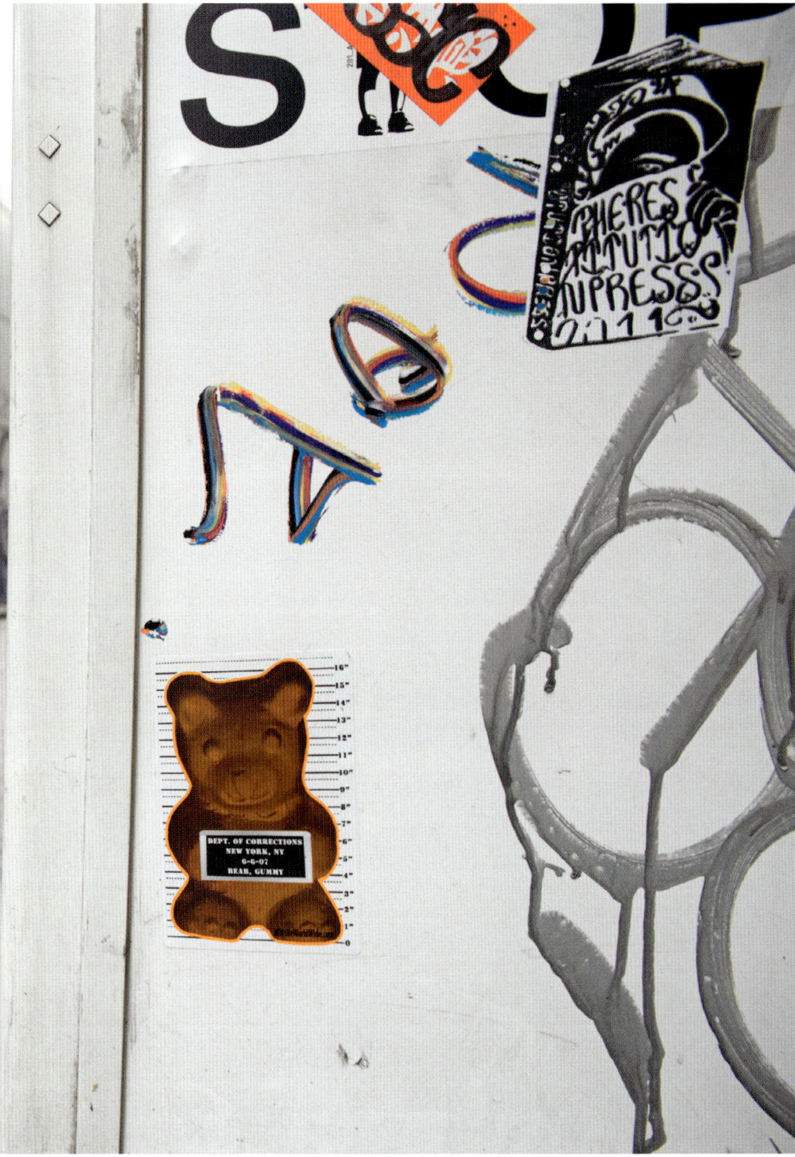

Whisbe

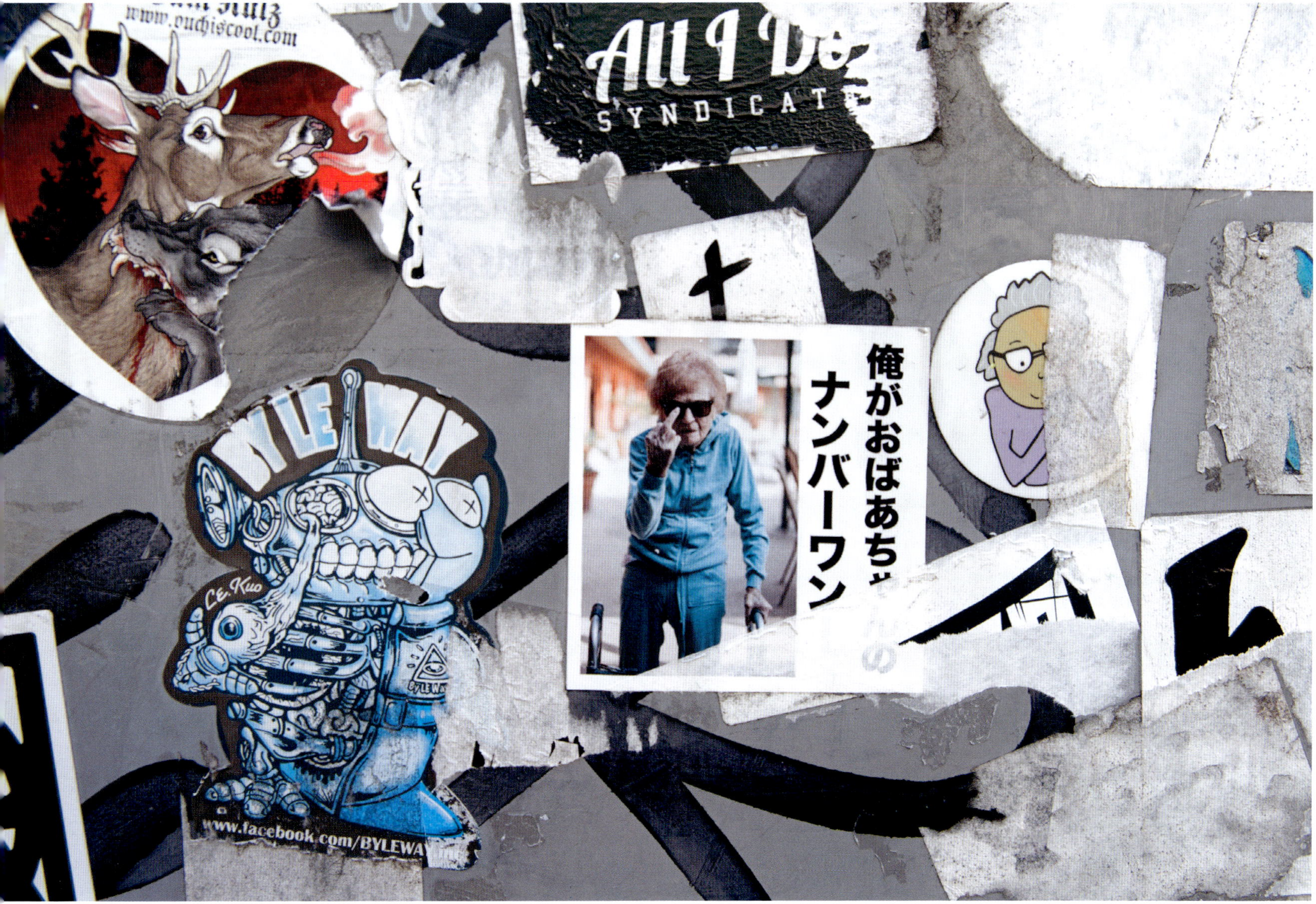

Location: Harajuku

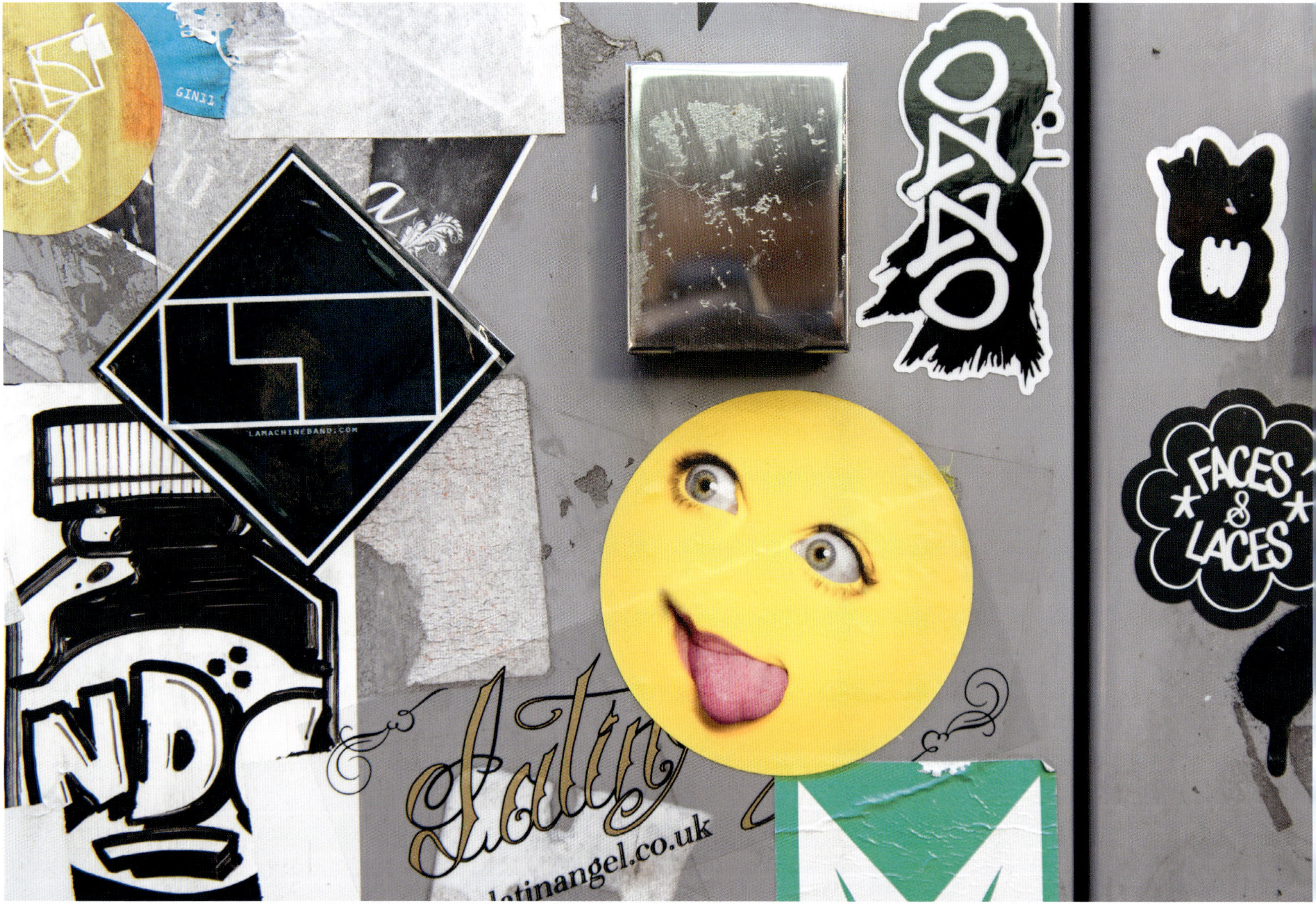

Location: Harajuku

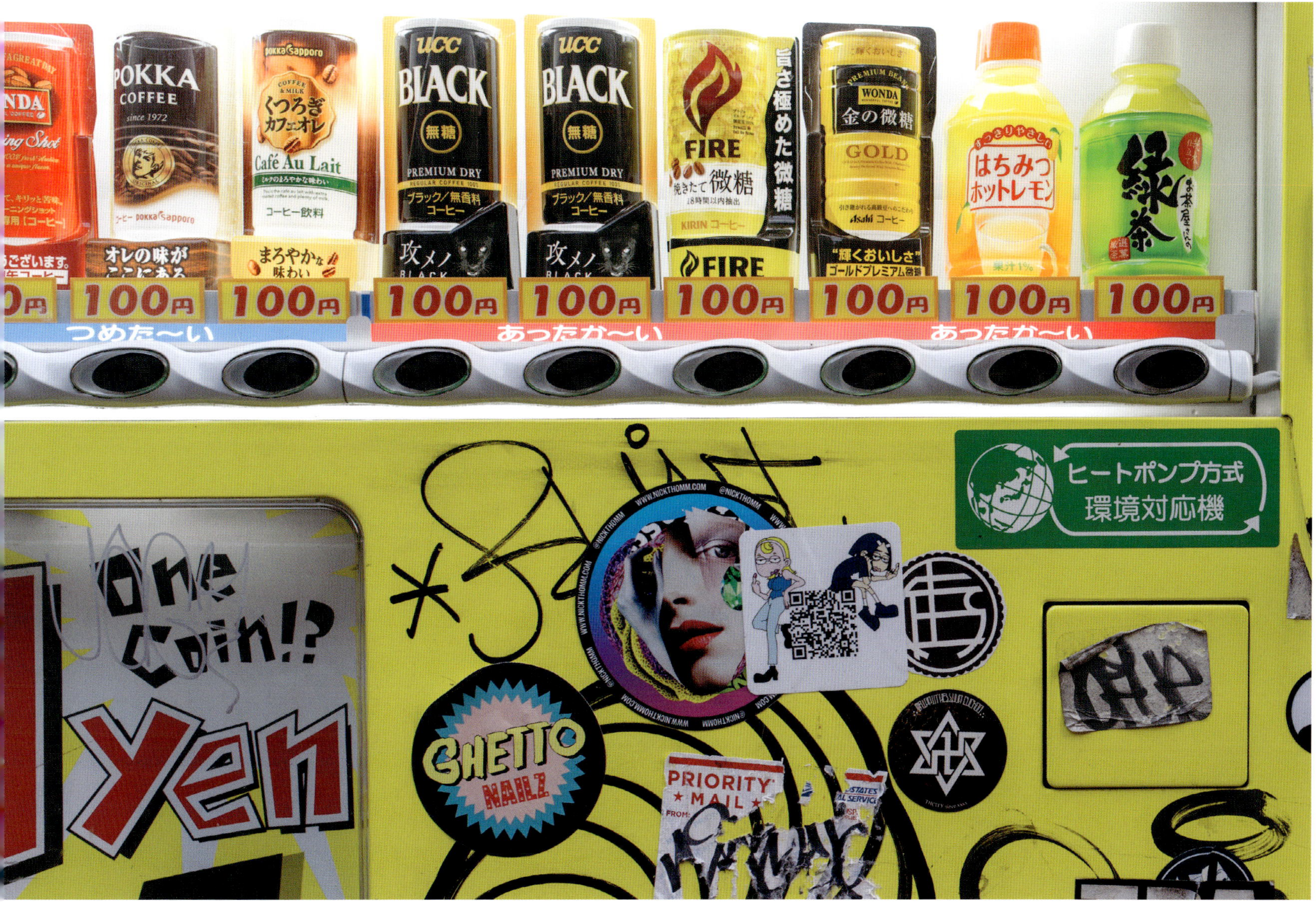

Nick Thomm amongst other stickers

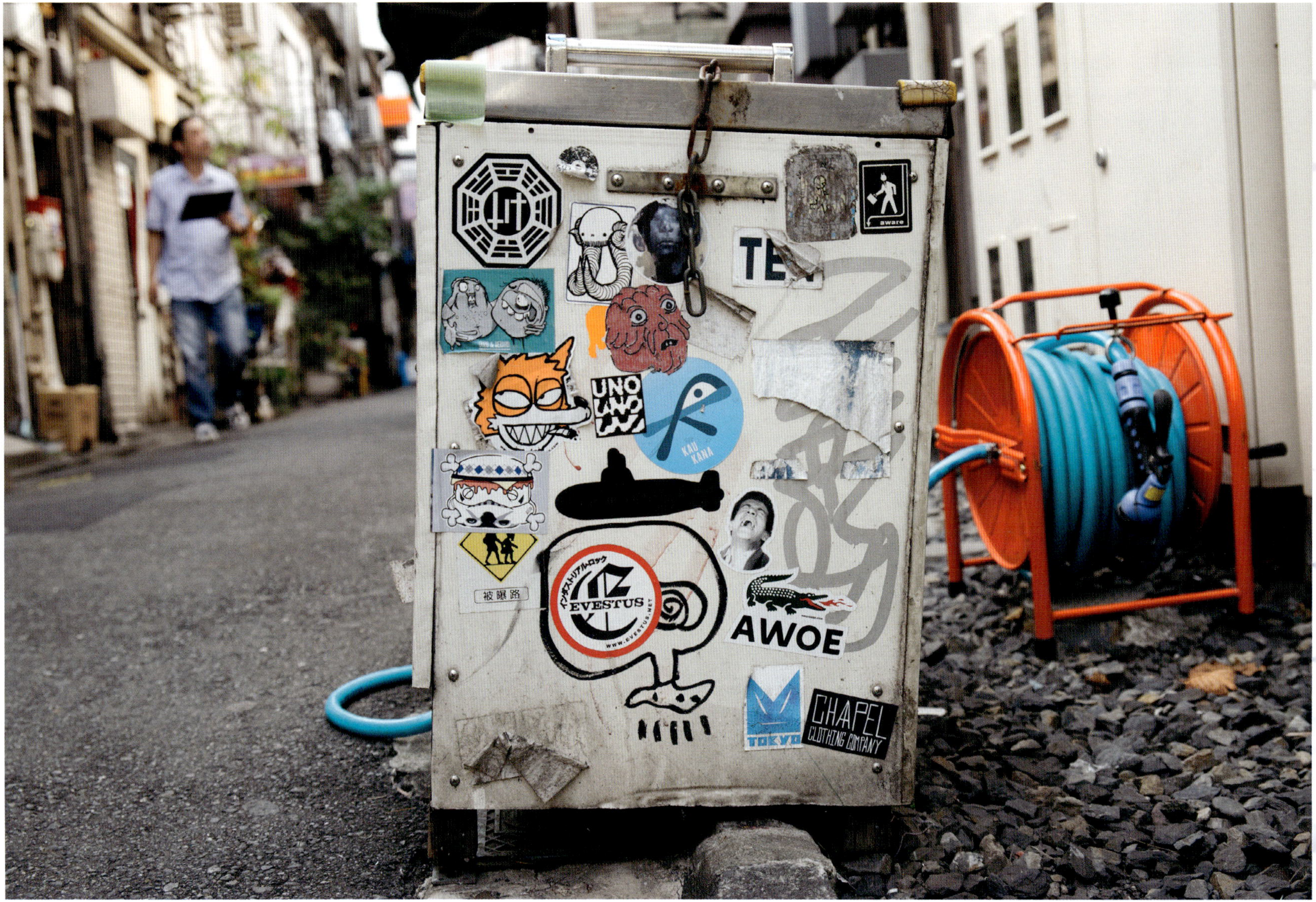

Location: Golden Gai

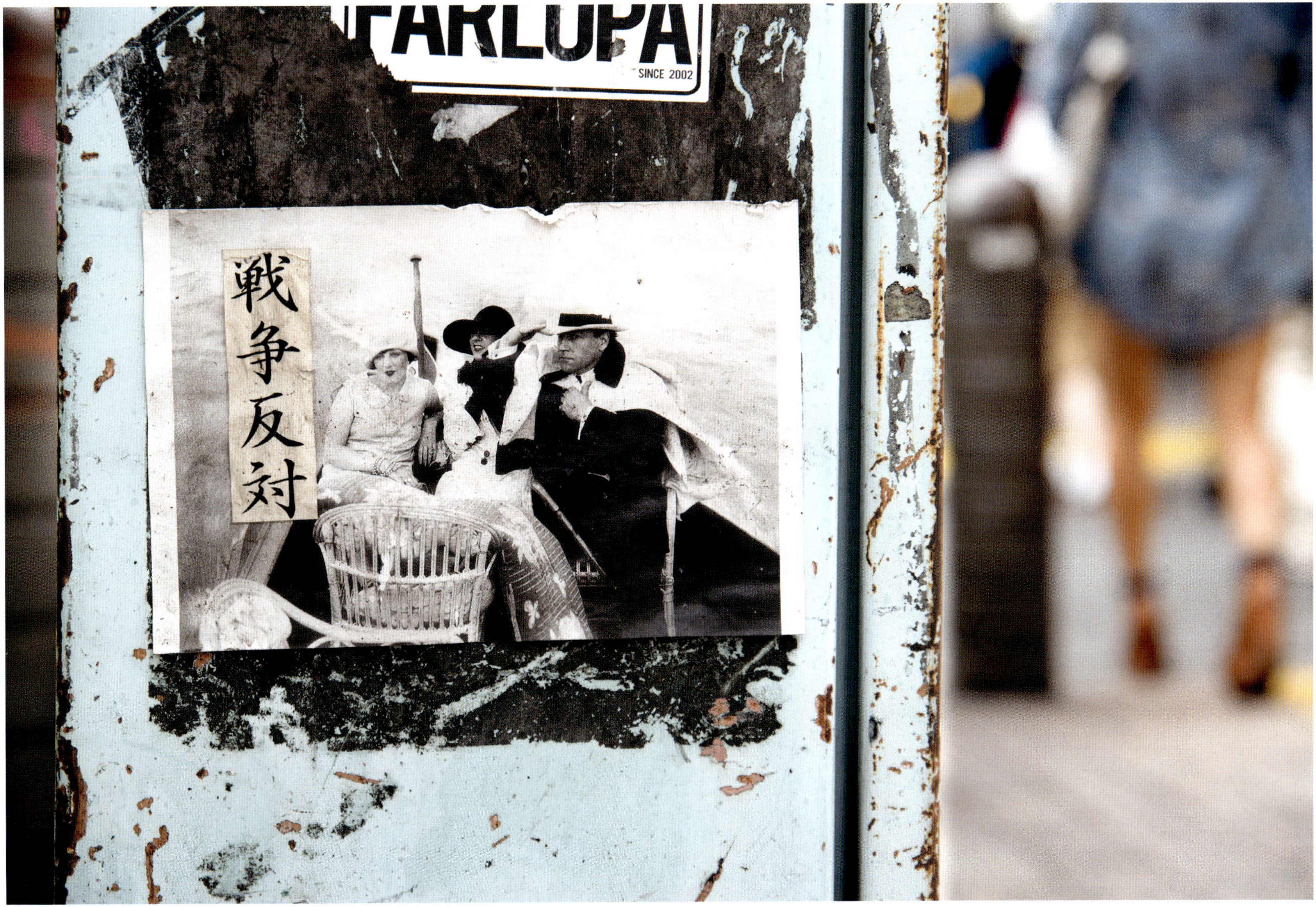

A sticker of a photo by Jacques Henri Lartigue

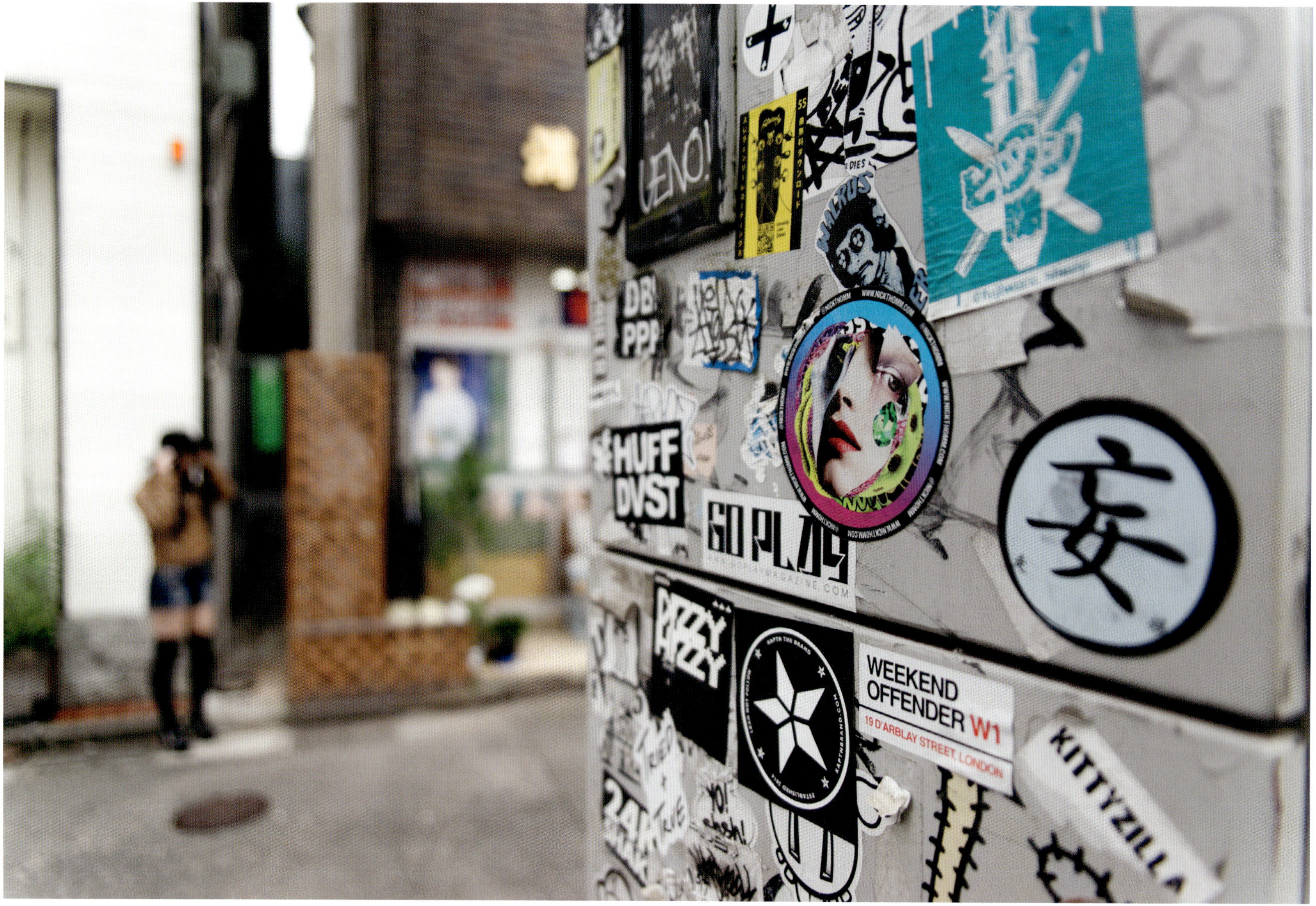
UENO!
WALRUS
DB!
PPP
HUFF
DVST
GO PLAY
GOPLAYMAGAZINE.COM
WEEKEND
OFFENDER W1
19 D'ARBLAY STREET, LONDON
KITTYZILLA

Nick Thomm

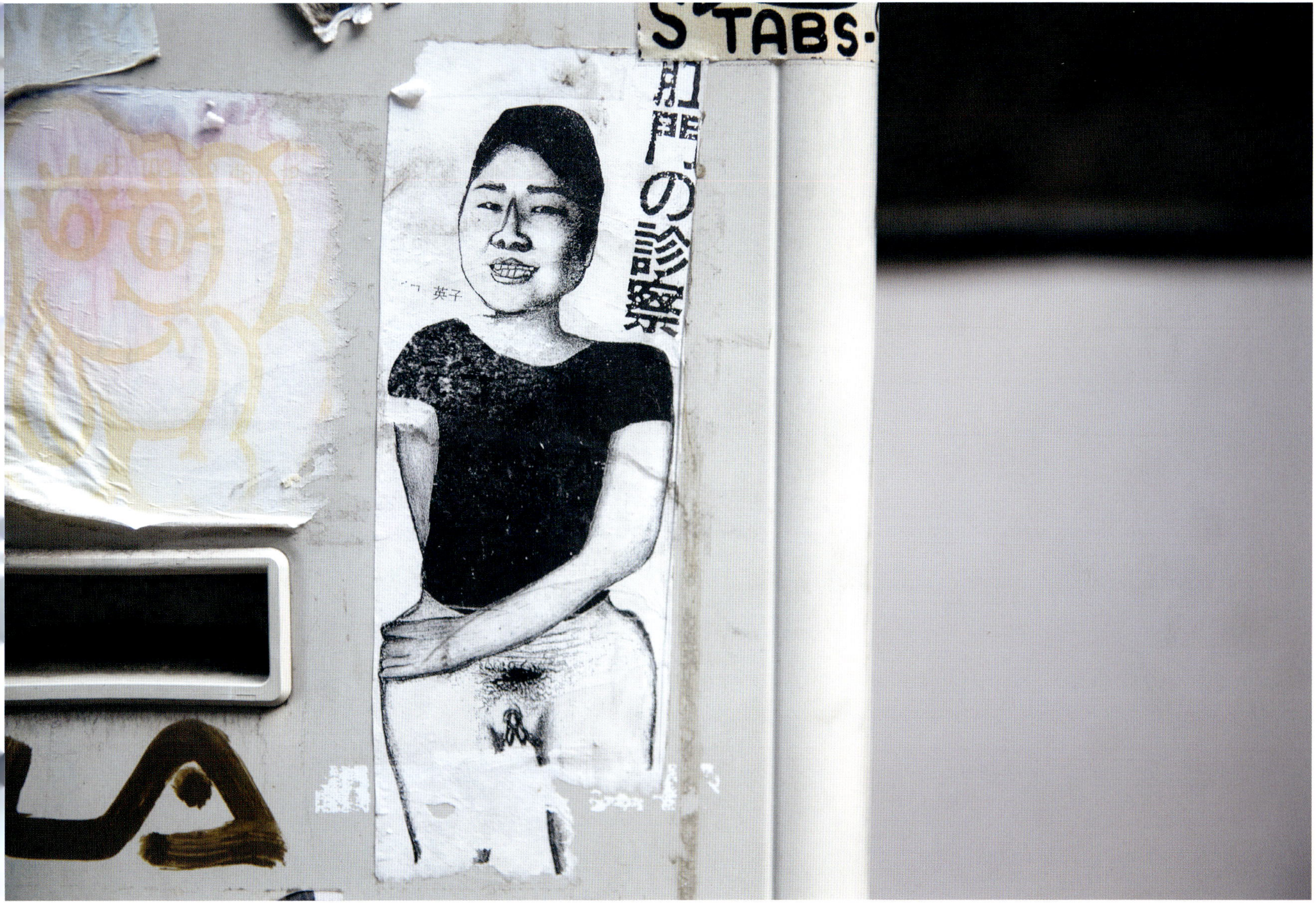

Location: Shinjuku

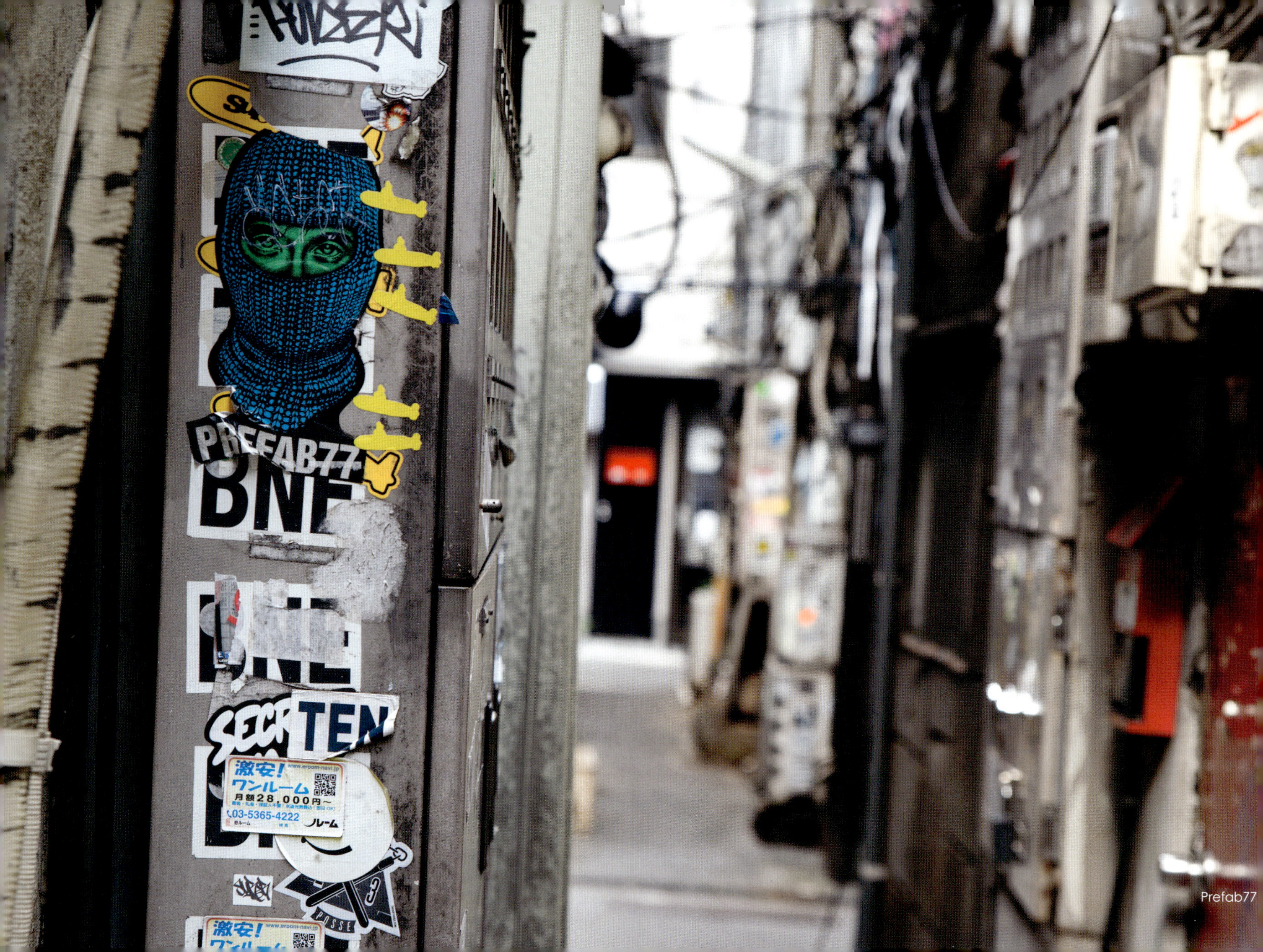

Prefab77

Stickers are most prevalent in Shibuya, Harajuku, and Golden Gai. They are stuck all over vending machines, lamp posts, billboards, electricity boxes, and the backs of street signs. International street artists view Tokyo as a capital for leaving their mark on the streets. Even in busy areas, with police presence or security cameras, artists can slap up a sticker and disappear into the crowd. Often times there is a hierarchy amongst graffiti artists or battles between individuals who cover each other's work. Sticking pieces in impossibly high or out of reach locations not only gains visibility and less likelihood of being taken down, it also garners street cred.

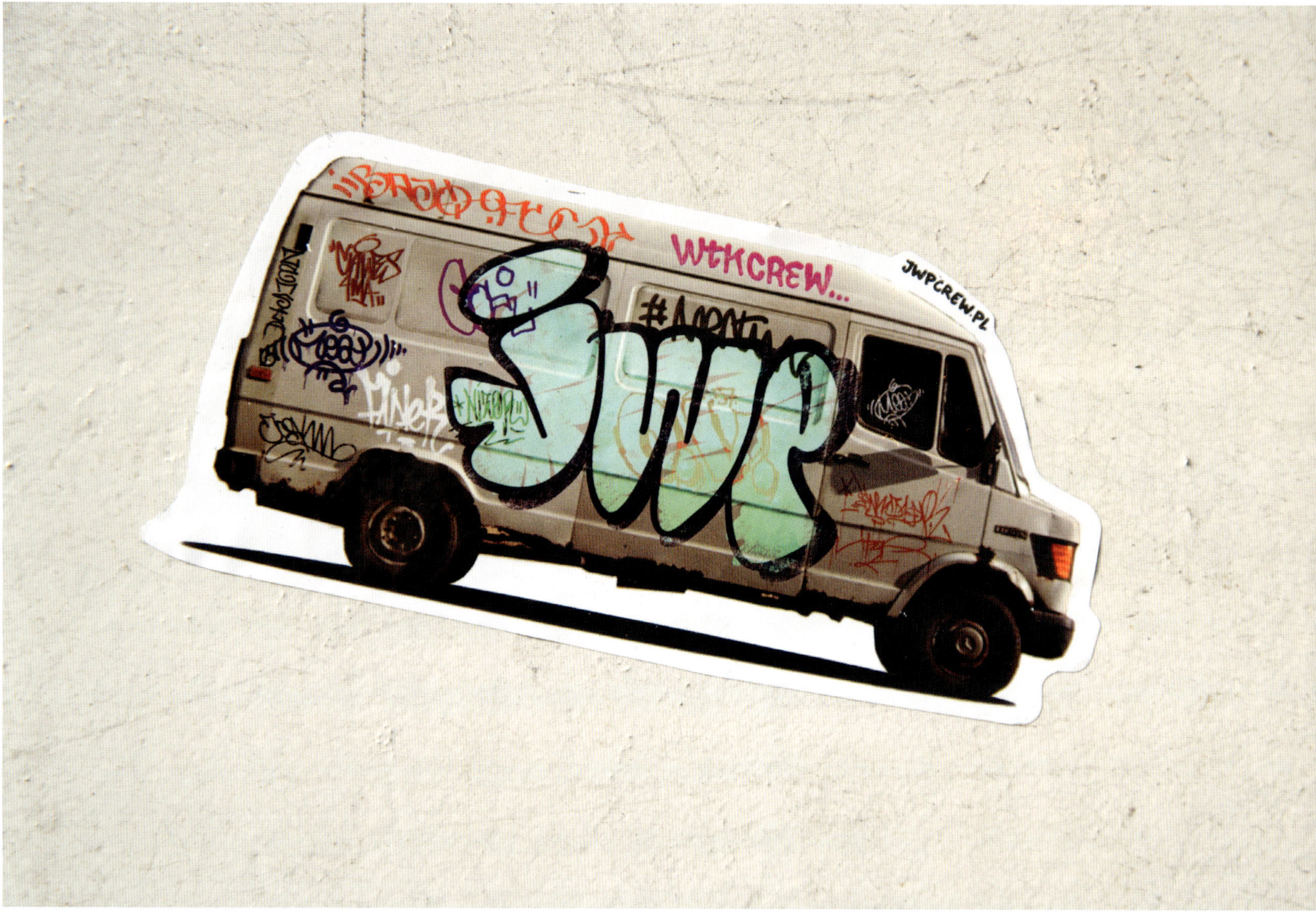

JWP Crew

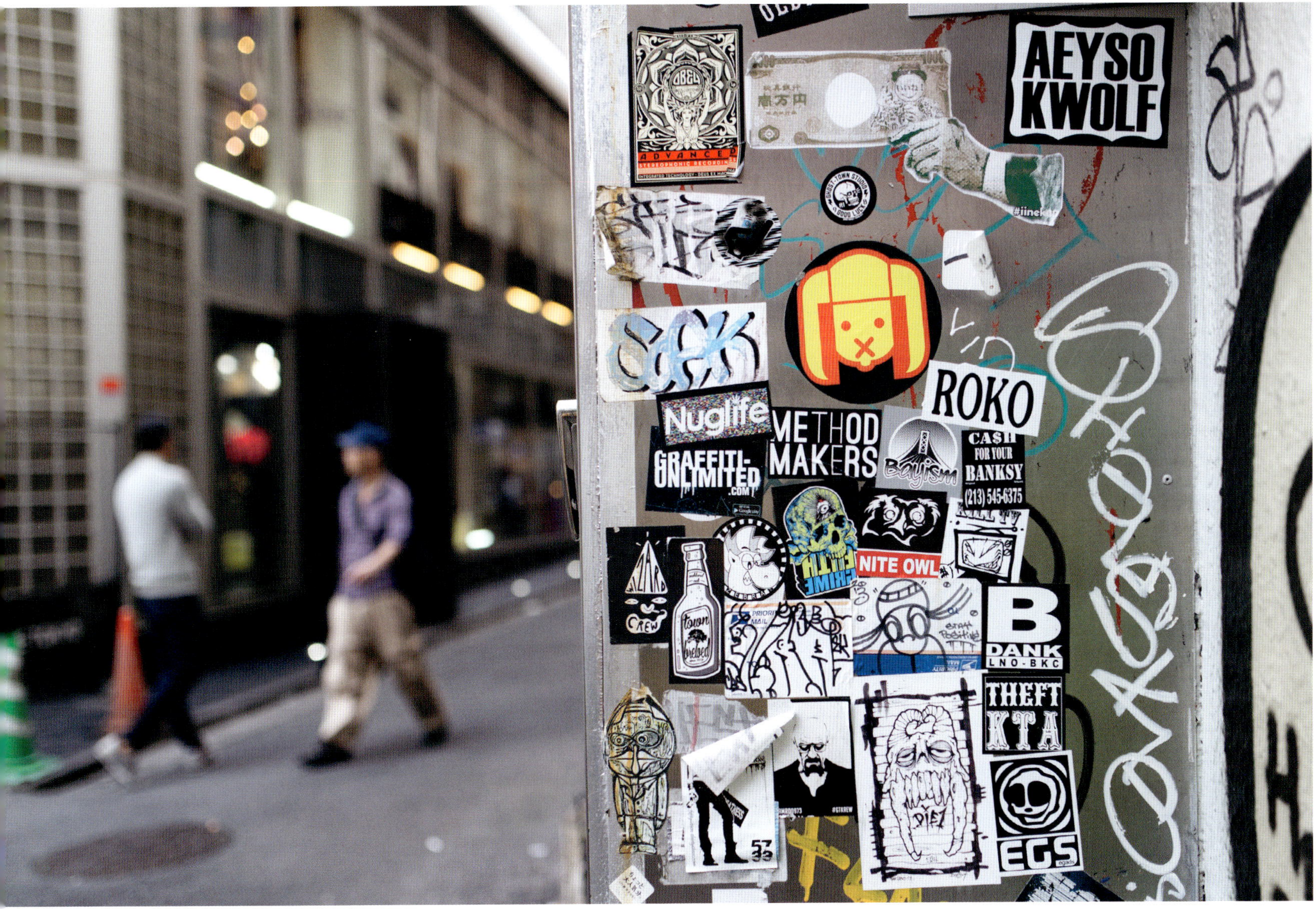

.ocation: Shibuya

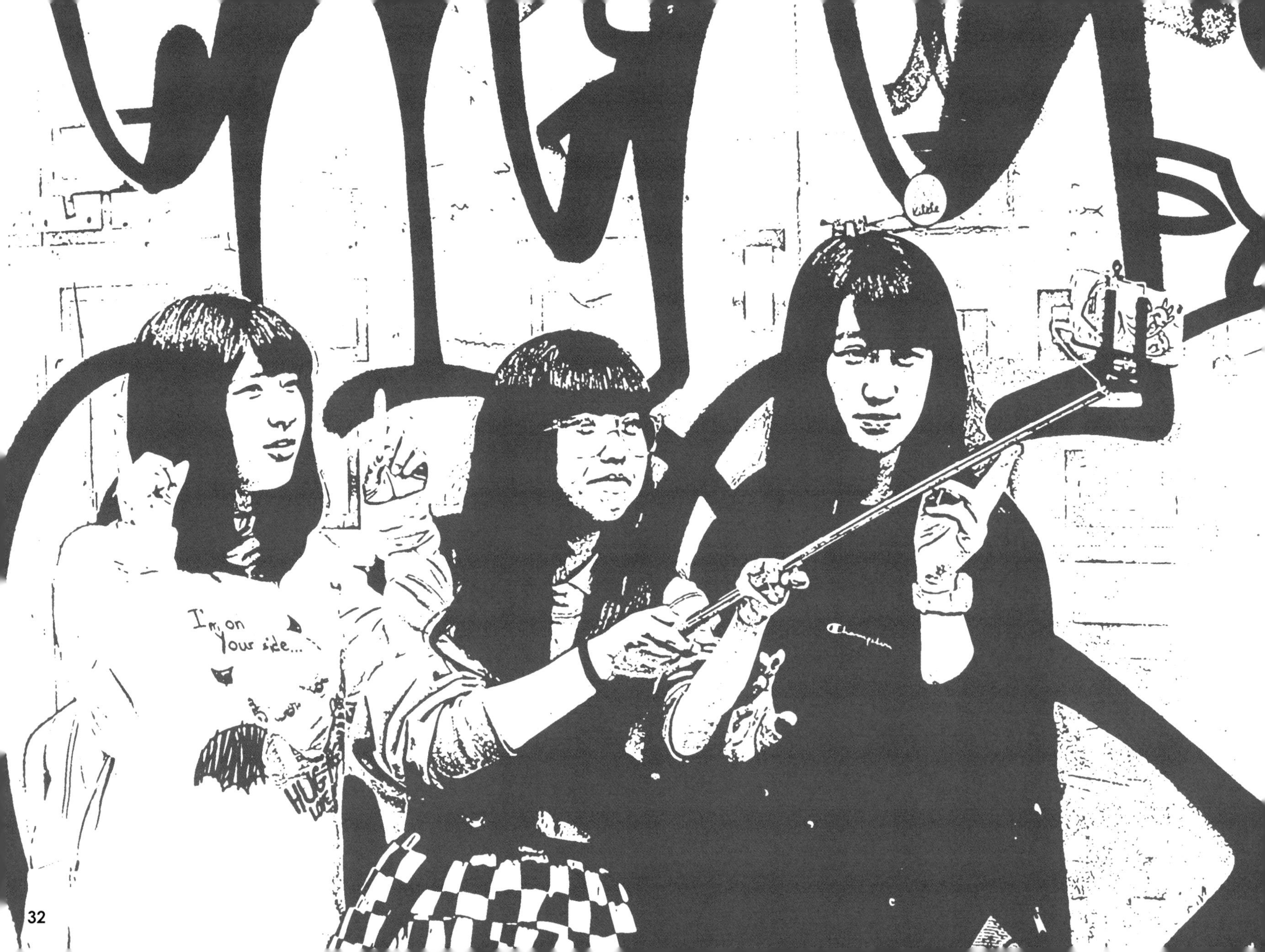
I'm on
Your side...

Uncommissioned

The city streets of Tokyo are notoriously difficult to navigate. Although public transportation is top notch, and taxis never far apart, it is not uncommon for streets to be unmarked or nameless all together. Locals seem to understand their familiar neighborhoods and the rest of the city in areas, as opposed to a grid or system of streets. This type of culture creates community and many young artists who bomb, tag, or write graffiti are just "coming up." They need to remain anonymous to the authorities and are not necessarily considering an art career but are looking for a way to buck the system and be recognized in their community as alternative. Some individuals infuse social commentary into their work, while others may simply be acting subconsciously, rejecting the rules of their community. Regardless of what's driving their immediate impulse to create, many artists' modus operandi is to work on uncommissioned pieces on illegal or out-of-the-way walls late at night or early in the morning, intentionally unnoticed.

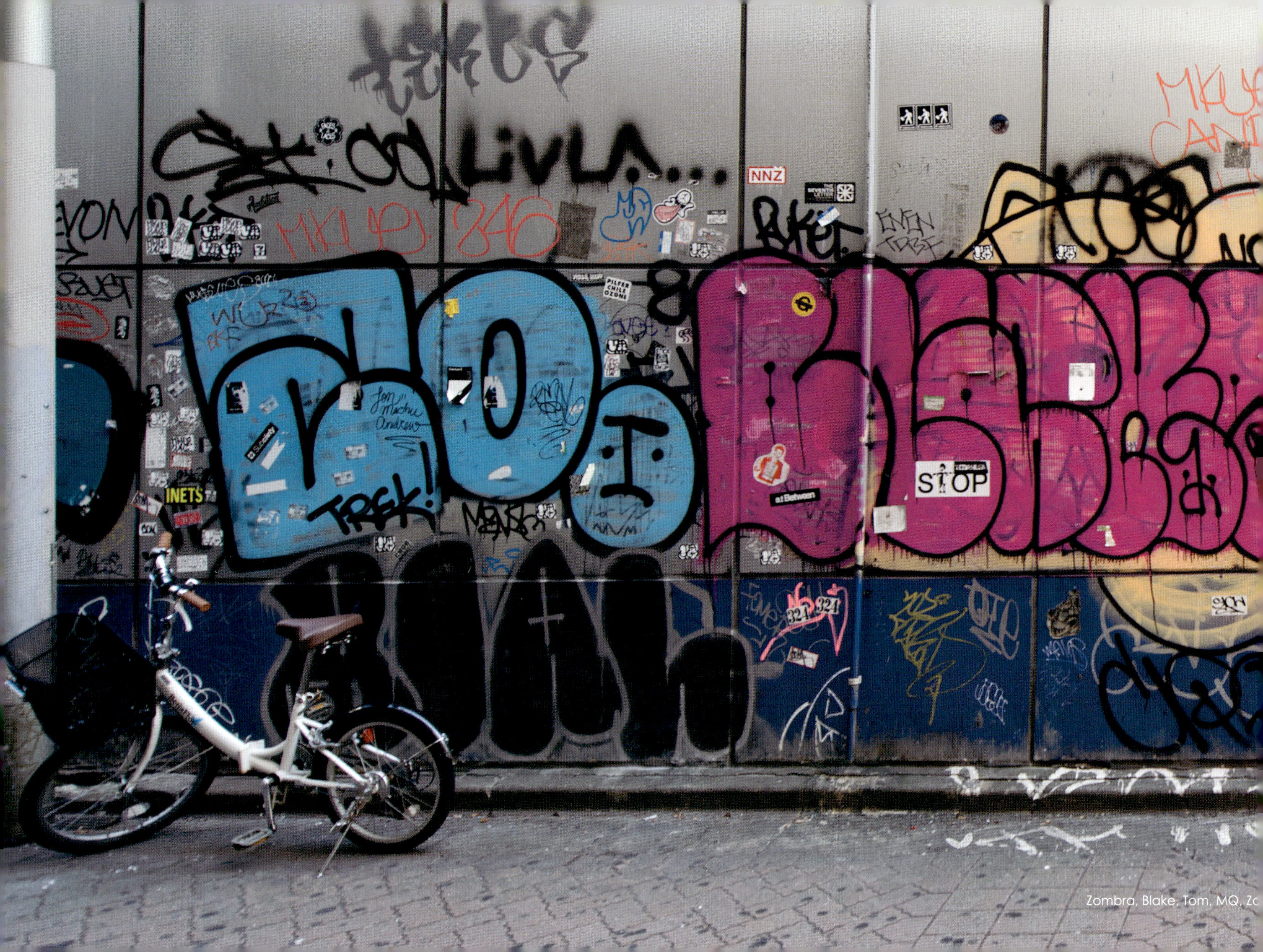

Zombra, Blake, Tom, MQ, Zc

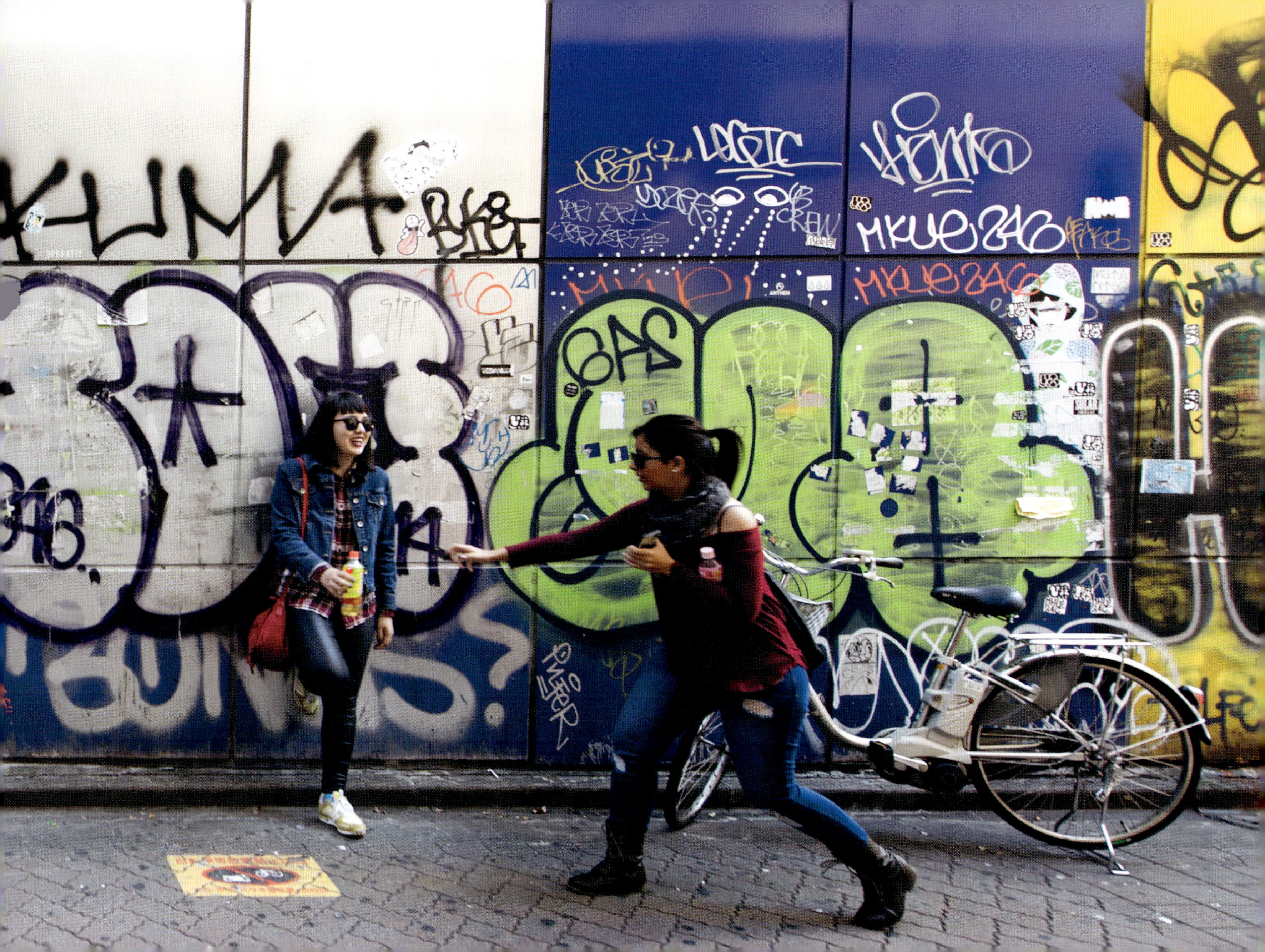

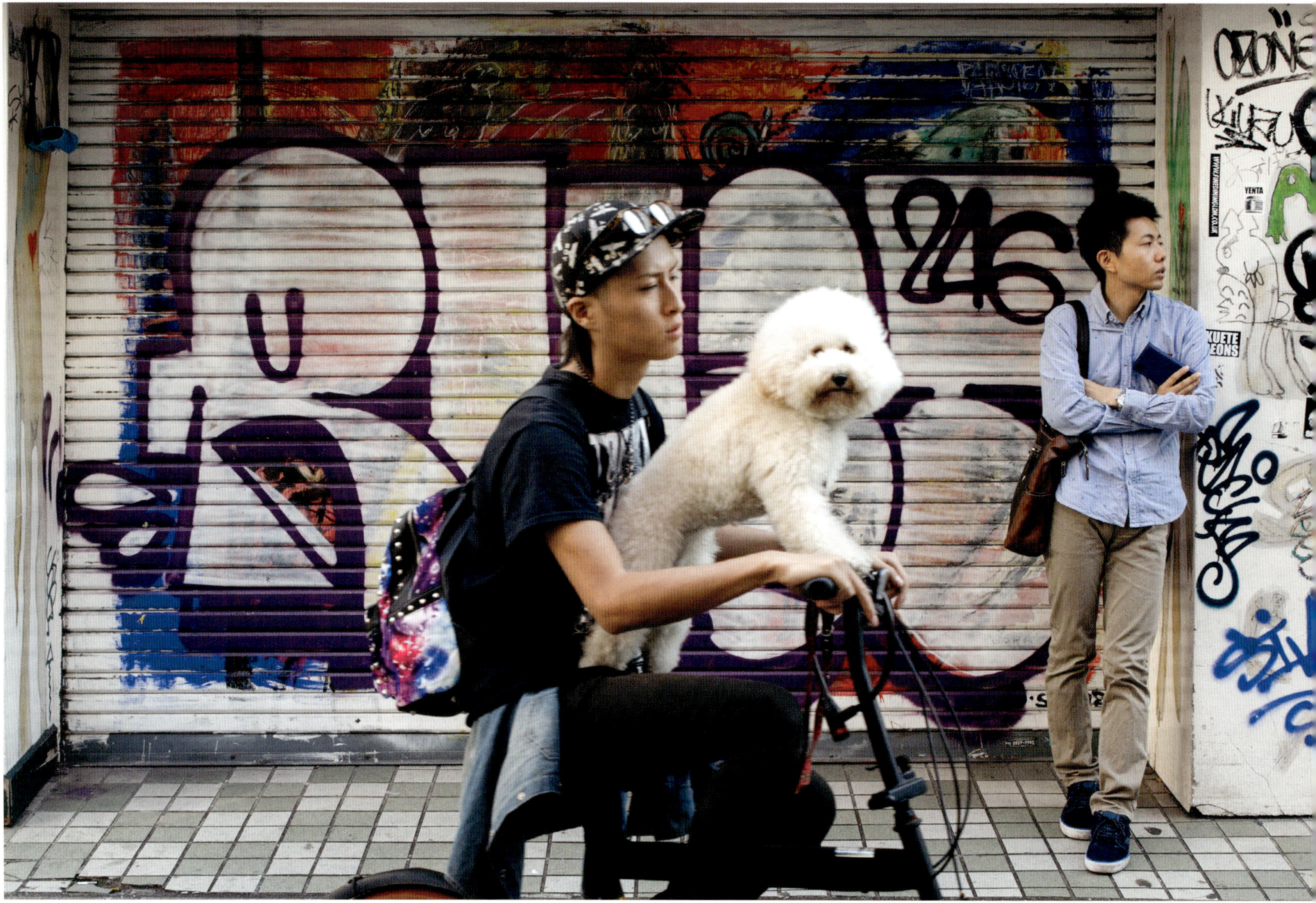

Rust

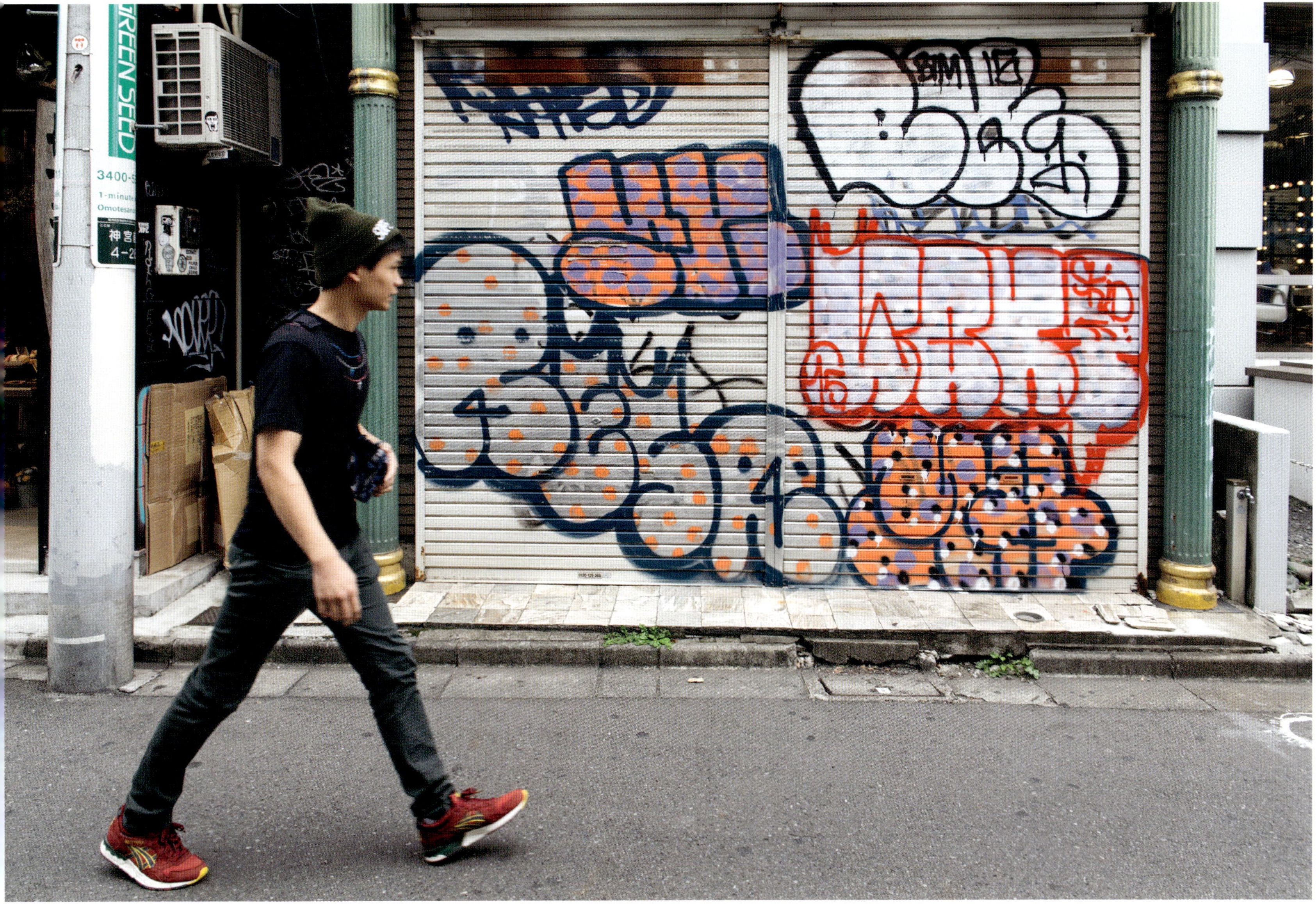

Want, Blake, MQ, Resq, YK Box

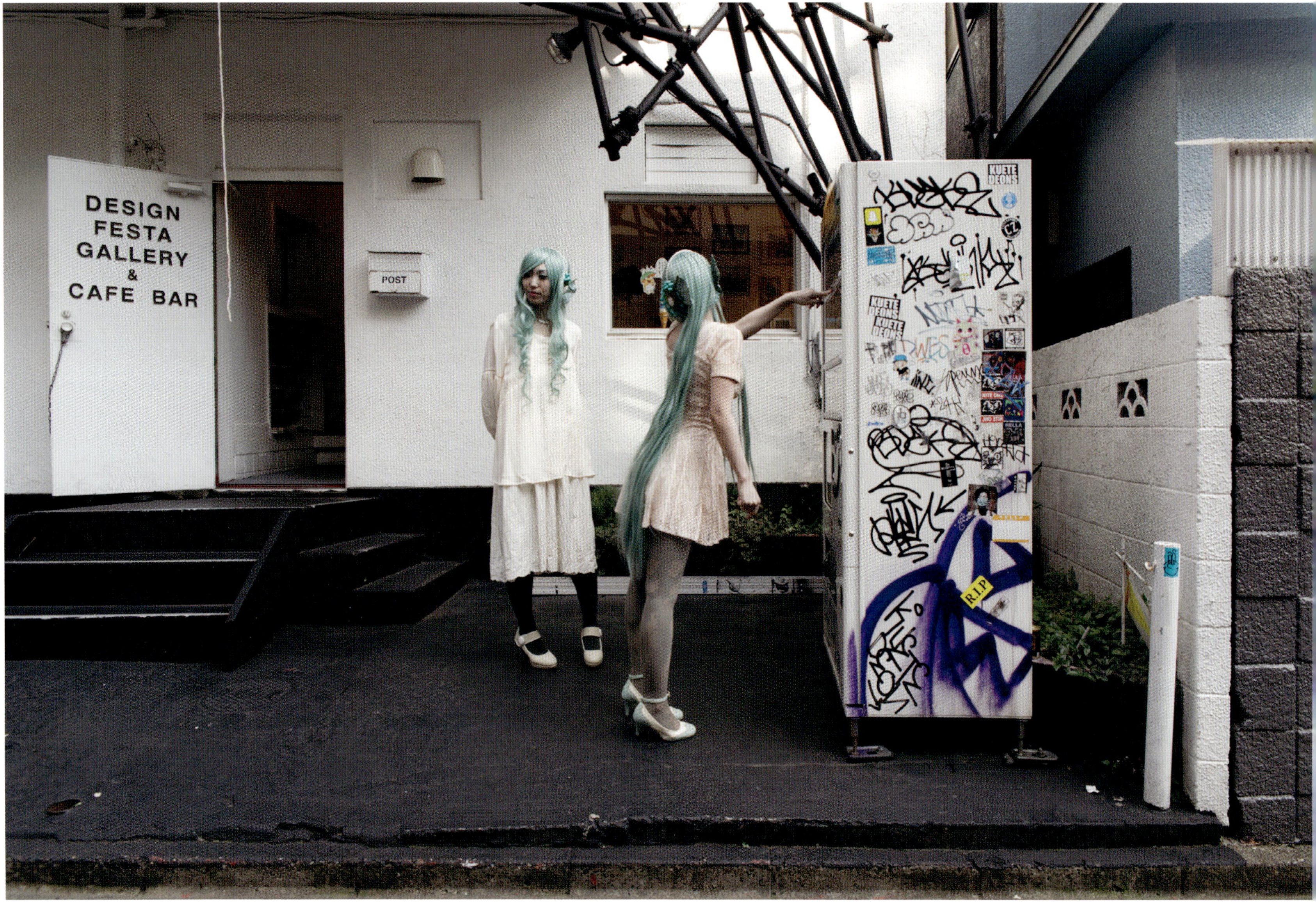

Crasty

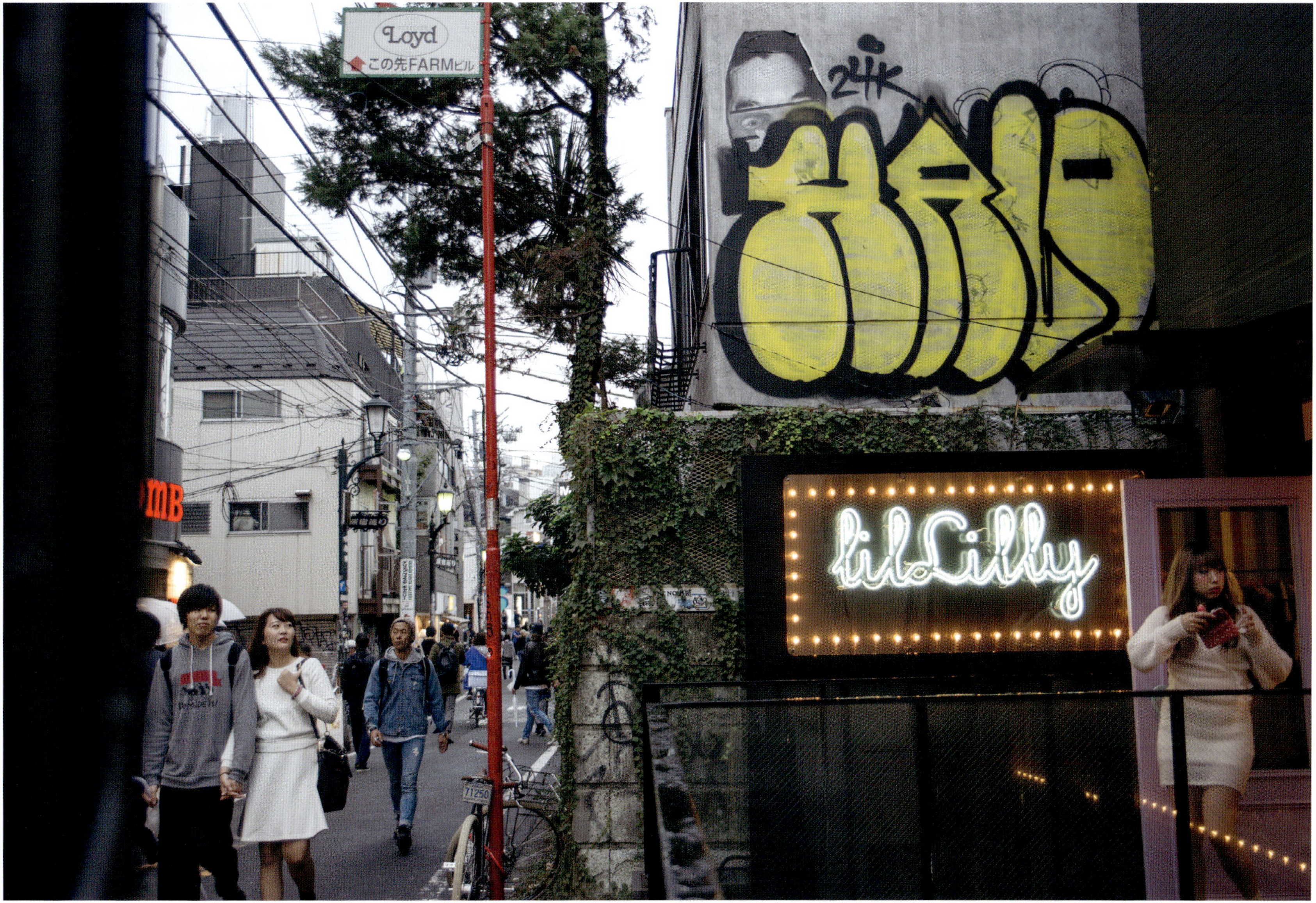

Halo

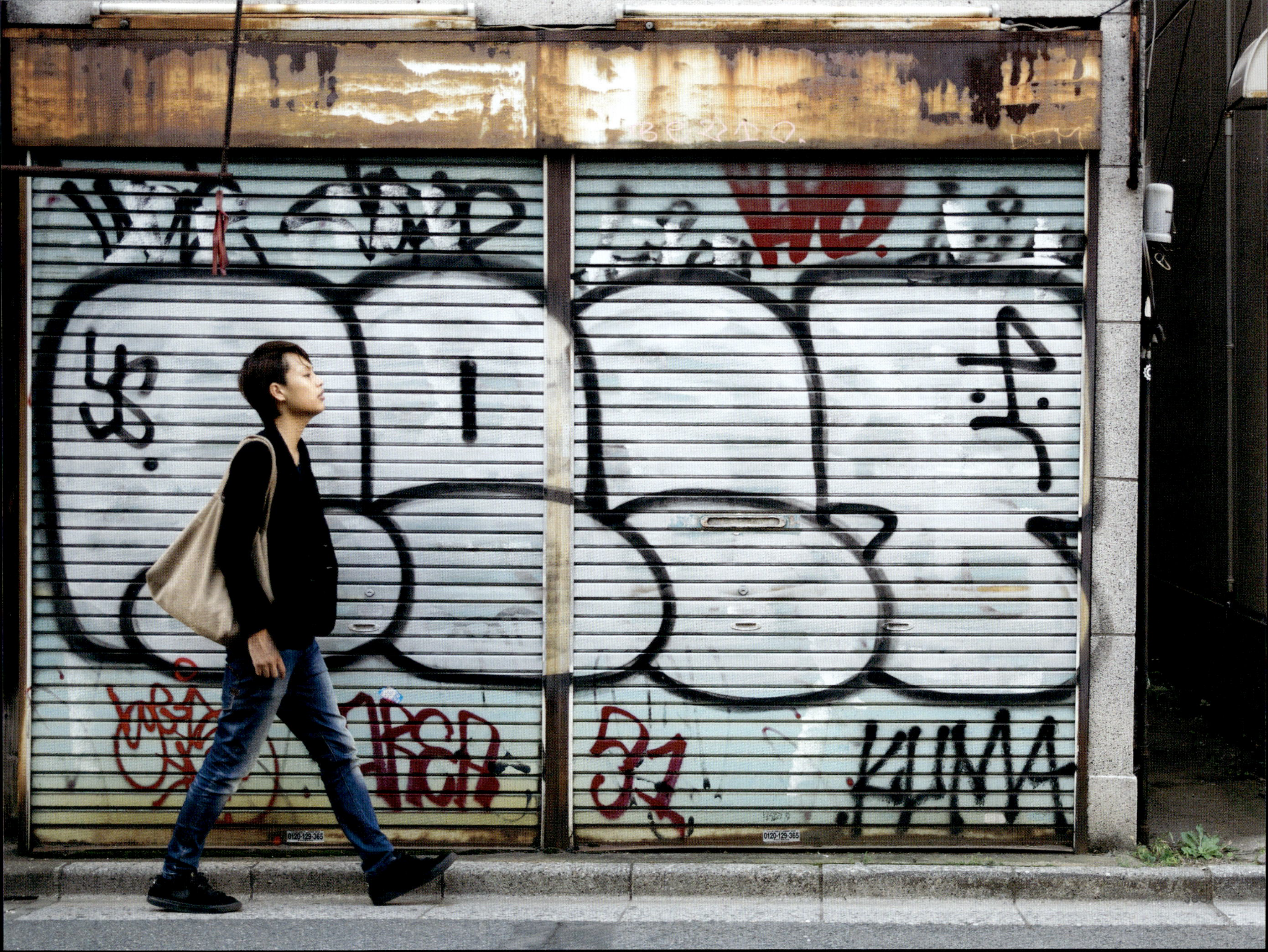
KUMA
0120-129-365
0120-129-365

In slightly quieter neighborhoods like Shimakitazawa, Asakusa, and Kita-Senju, the spider's web of streets, Izakaya-style eateries, thrift stores, covered passageways, and pop-up shops tend to be smaller and privately run. After the businesses close their shutters for the night, a display of hand-painted murals line the streets. These pieces often feature traditional Japanese landscapes and comedic figures rendered in bright colors or in a style reminiscent of Hokusai's wood cuts and classical scenes on sliding paper walls. Bonsai trees, cranes, pagoda-style rooftops, and a wide variety of sea creatures decorate the alleys at dusk, adorning unsightly garages with visions of the past. Illegal throw ups and tags are also popular on shutters.

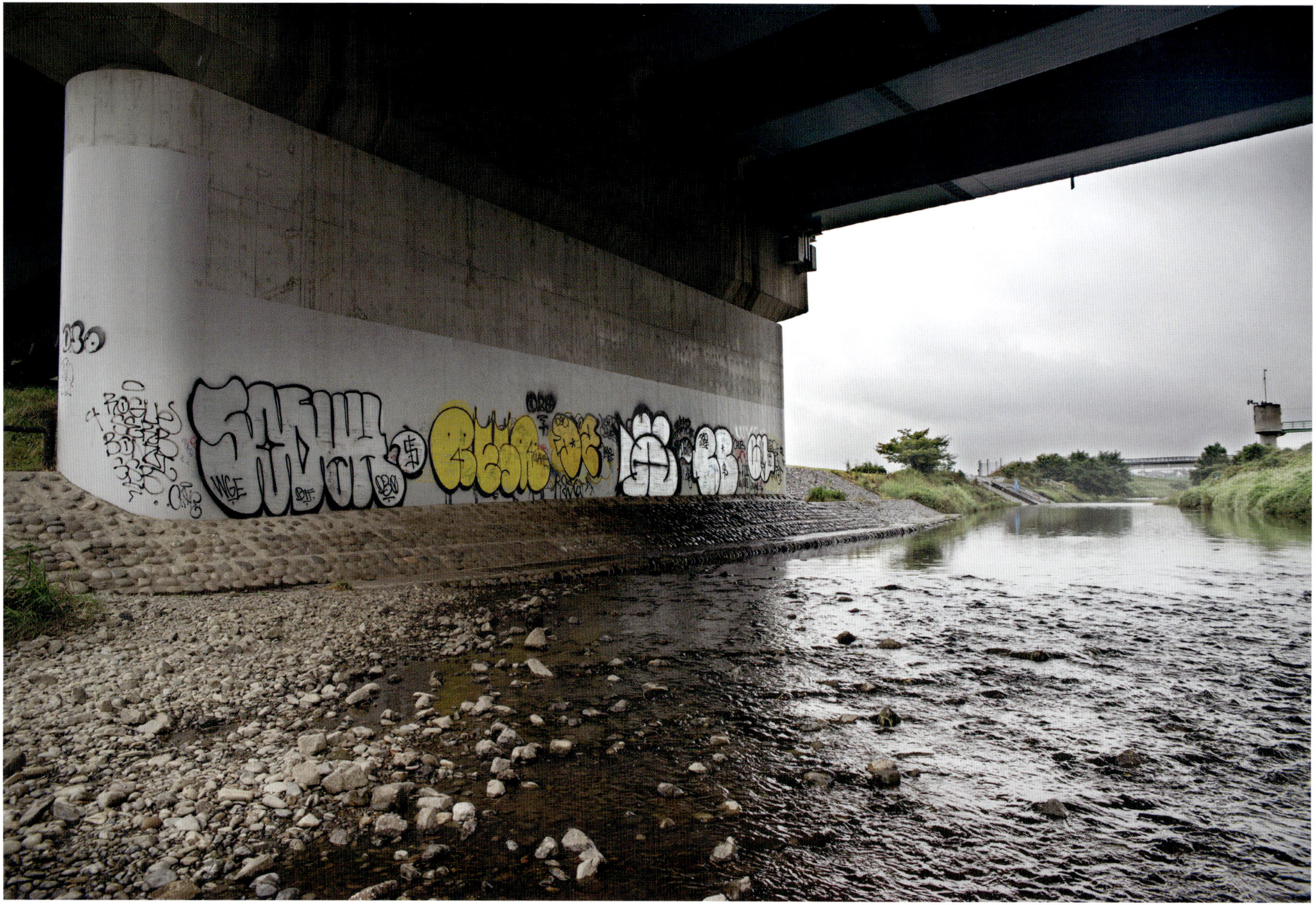

Location: Tama Riverbanks

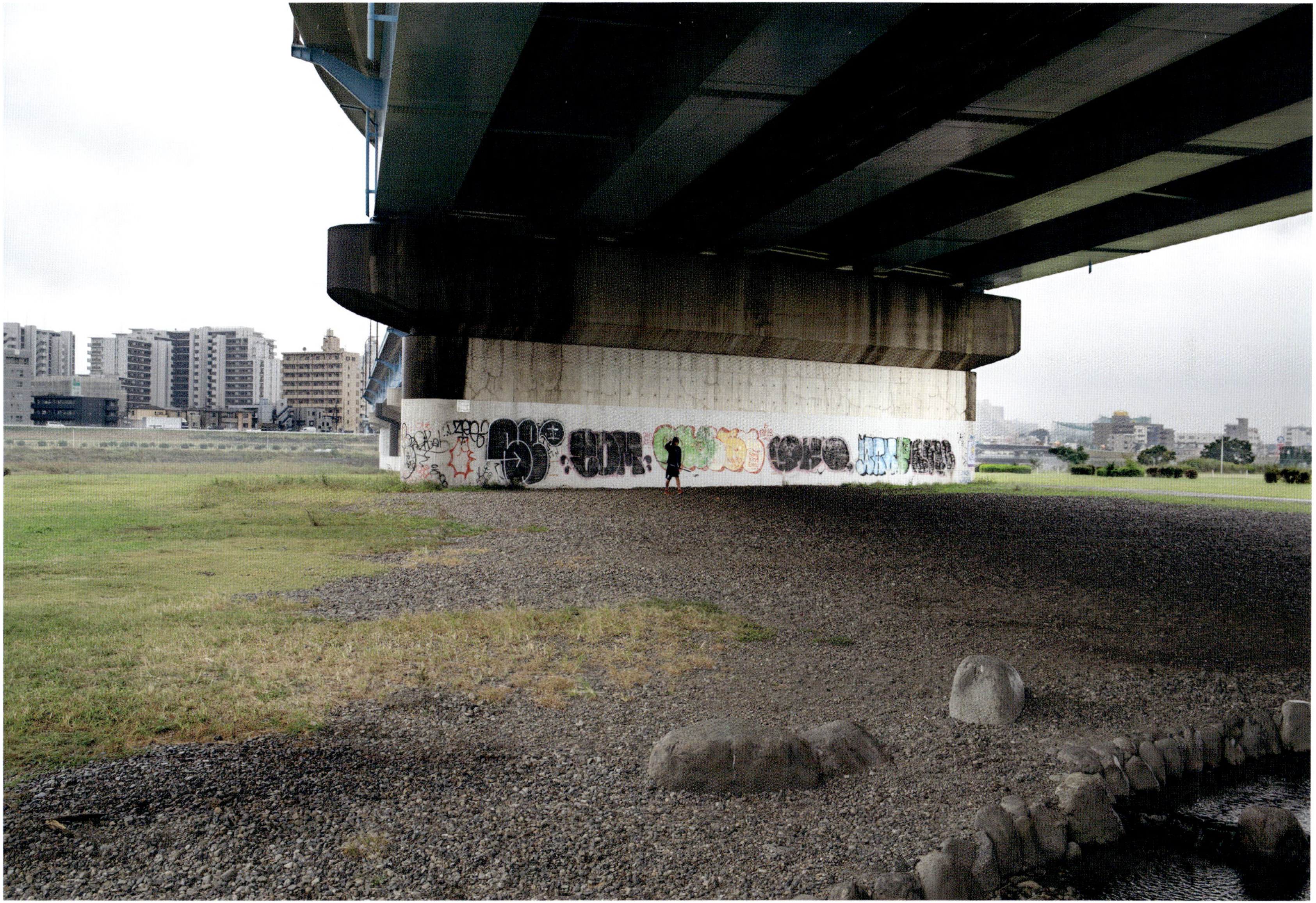

Location: Tama Riverbanks

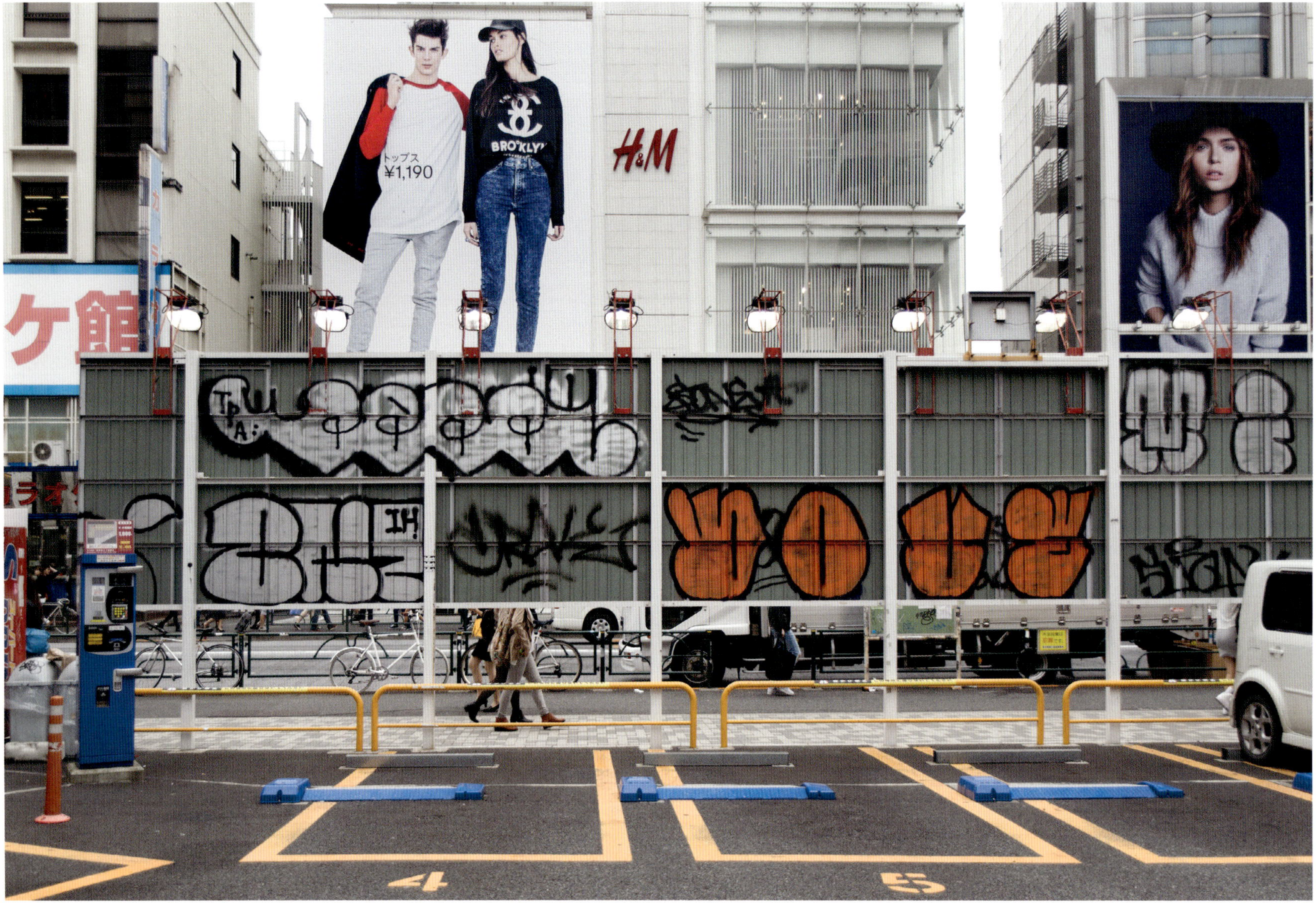

Teck, BNZ, Mint

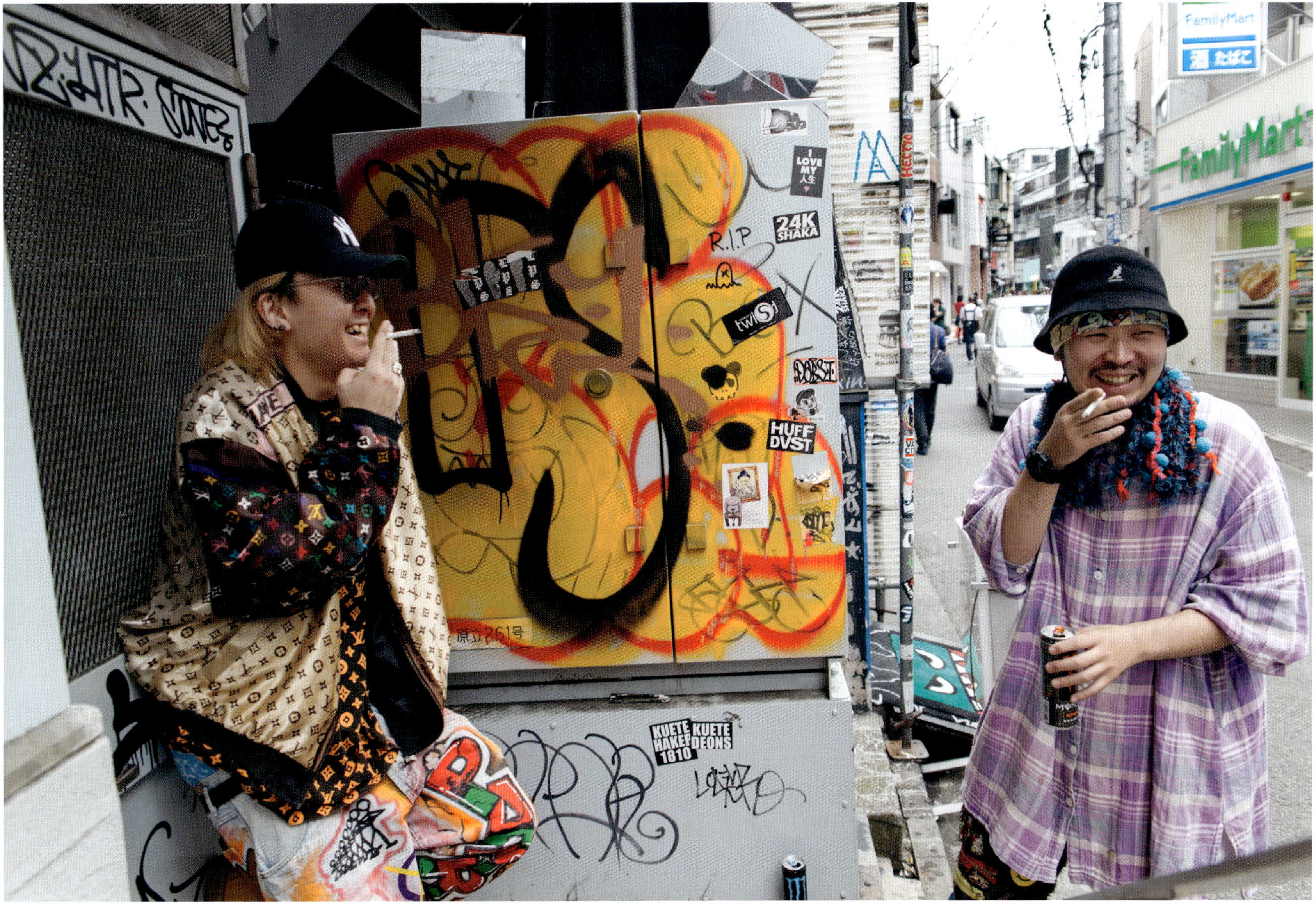
FamilyMart
酒 たばこ
I LOVE MY 人生
R.I.P
24K SHAKA
HUFF DVST
KUETE HAKEF 1810
KUETE DEONS

Blake, LPS

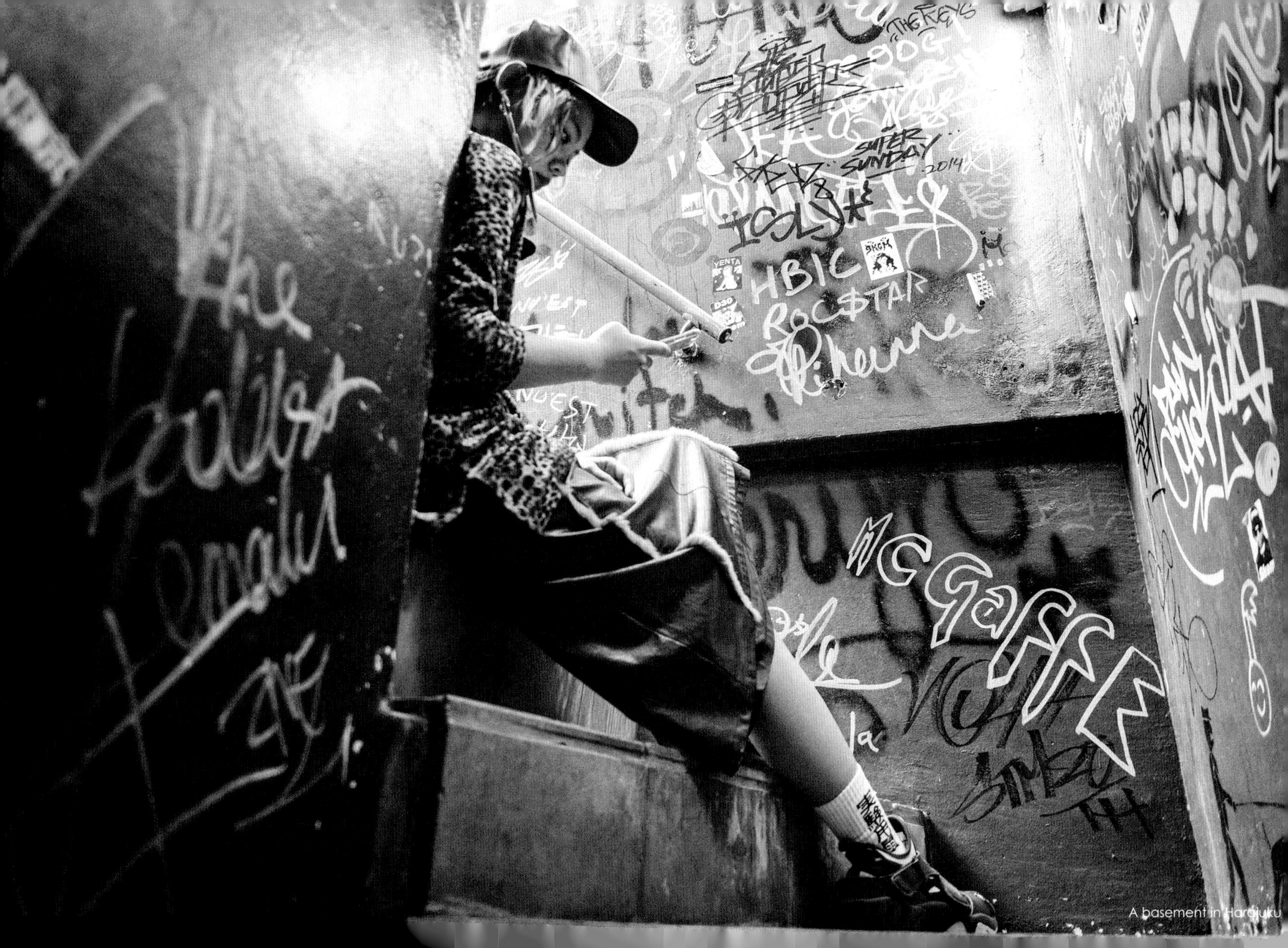

A basement in Harajuku

In Tokyo, quick tags and old school style fonts are the most popular spray-painted graffiti. Stenciling is less common and legal walls are often temporary or difficult to gain permission to access. Crossing the rivers as you enter Tokyo on the train, you see tags or names of crews and bigger spray pieces on the concrete dams below. Styles similar to pieces found on New York subway cars and car yards of the 1980s are common. These areas are far away from neighborhoods and largely go unpoliced, making it safer to work for longer periods of time. Once you are in the center of the city, smaller tags and the use of paint markers are easier to find on vending machines, electrical boxes, and metal shutters. Although the herds of people in a busy street are distracting, antivandalism is still strictly enforced and bigger tags or murals are not as easy to find. Even though artists tend to prefer highly visible spots, in Tokyo, they are prepared to make do with indoor locations when the opportunity arises.

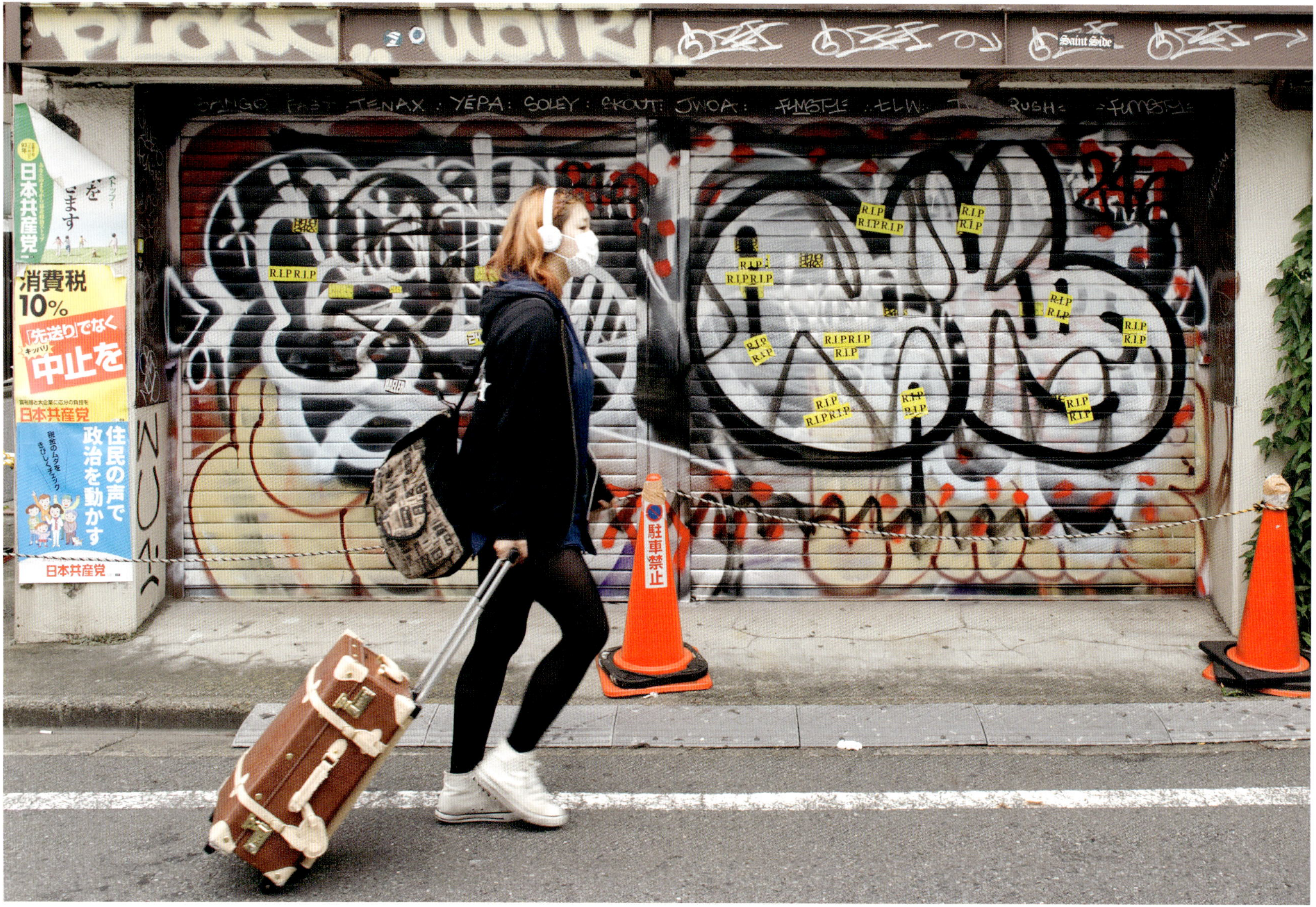
日本共産党
消費税
10%
「先送り」でなく
キッパリ
中止を
日本共産党
住民の声で
政治を動かす
日本共産党
駐車禁止
R.I.P

Ater, Box

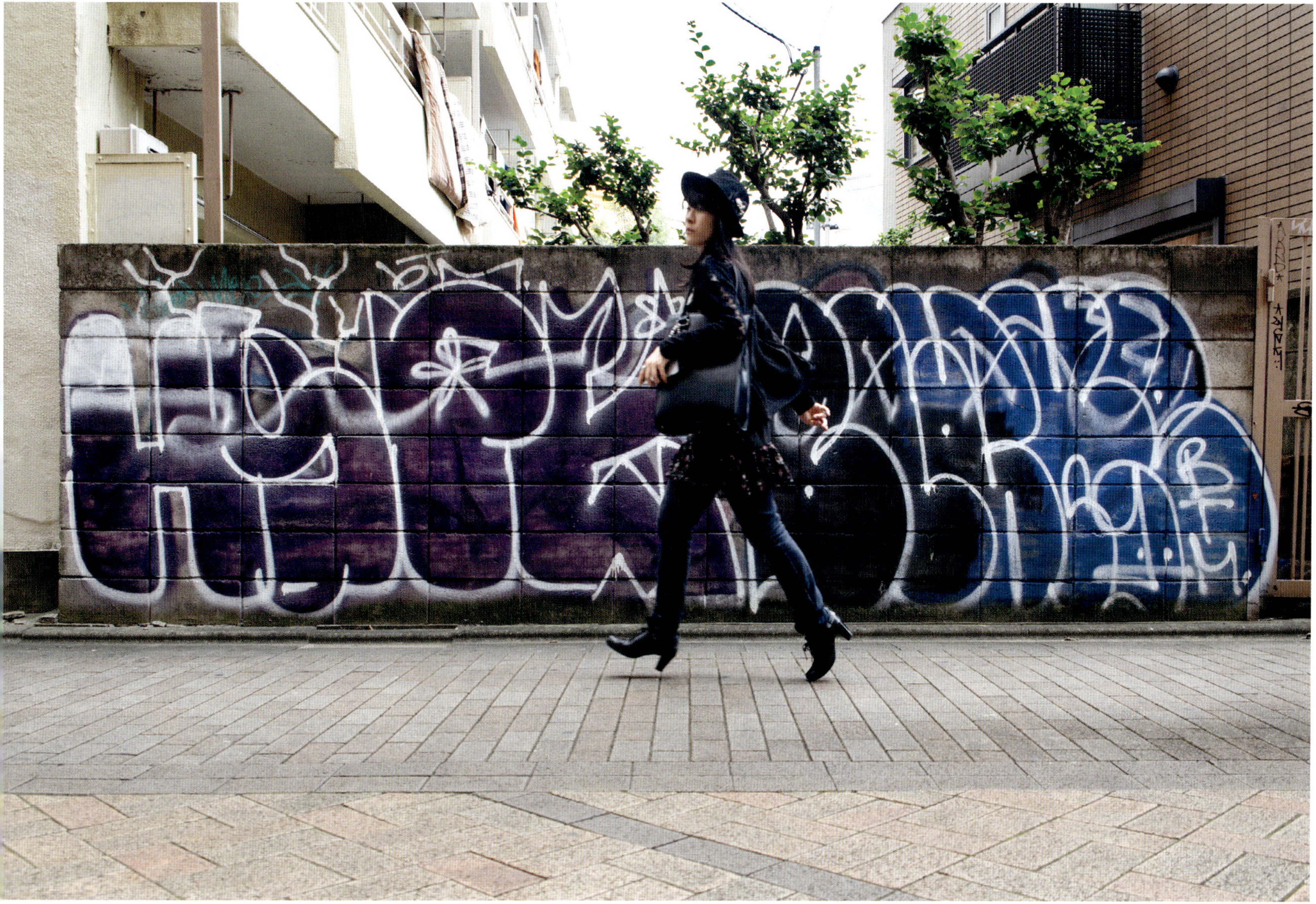

Hype and Blake

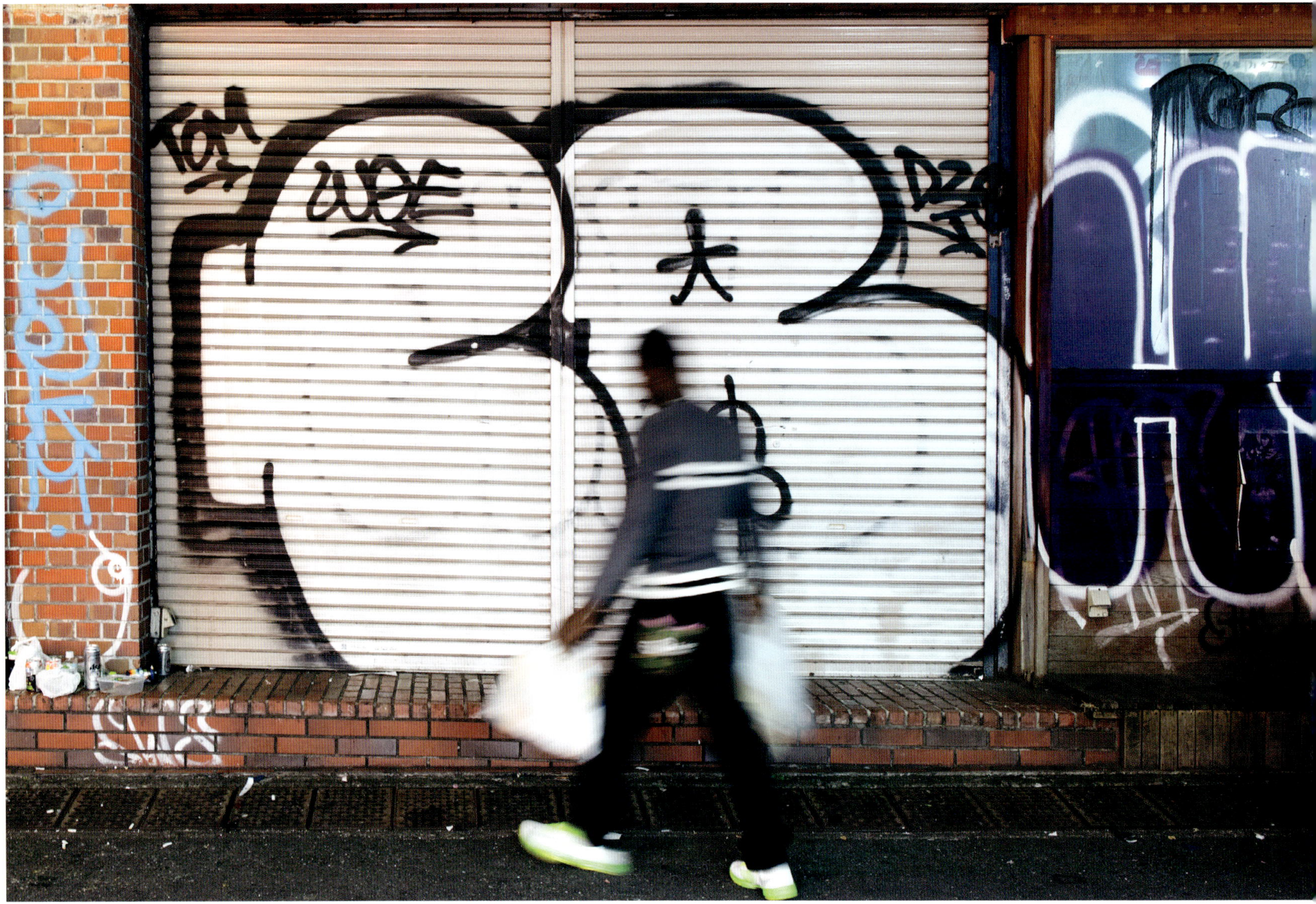

Location: Harajuku

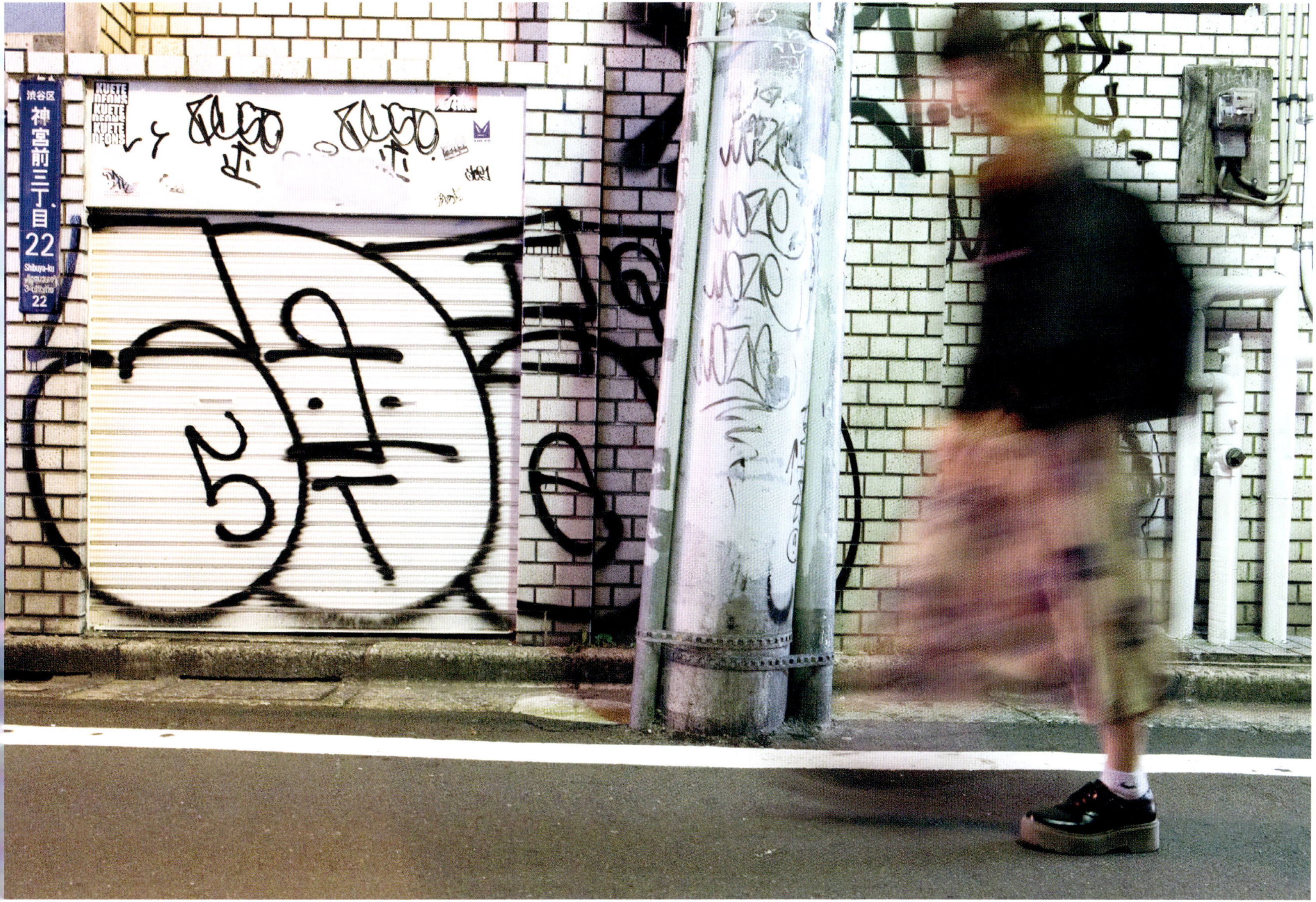

Tofu

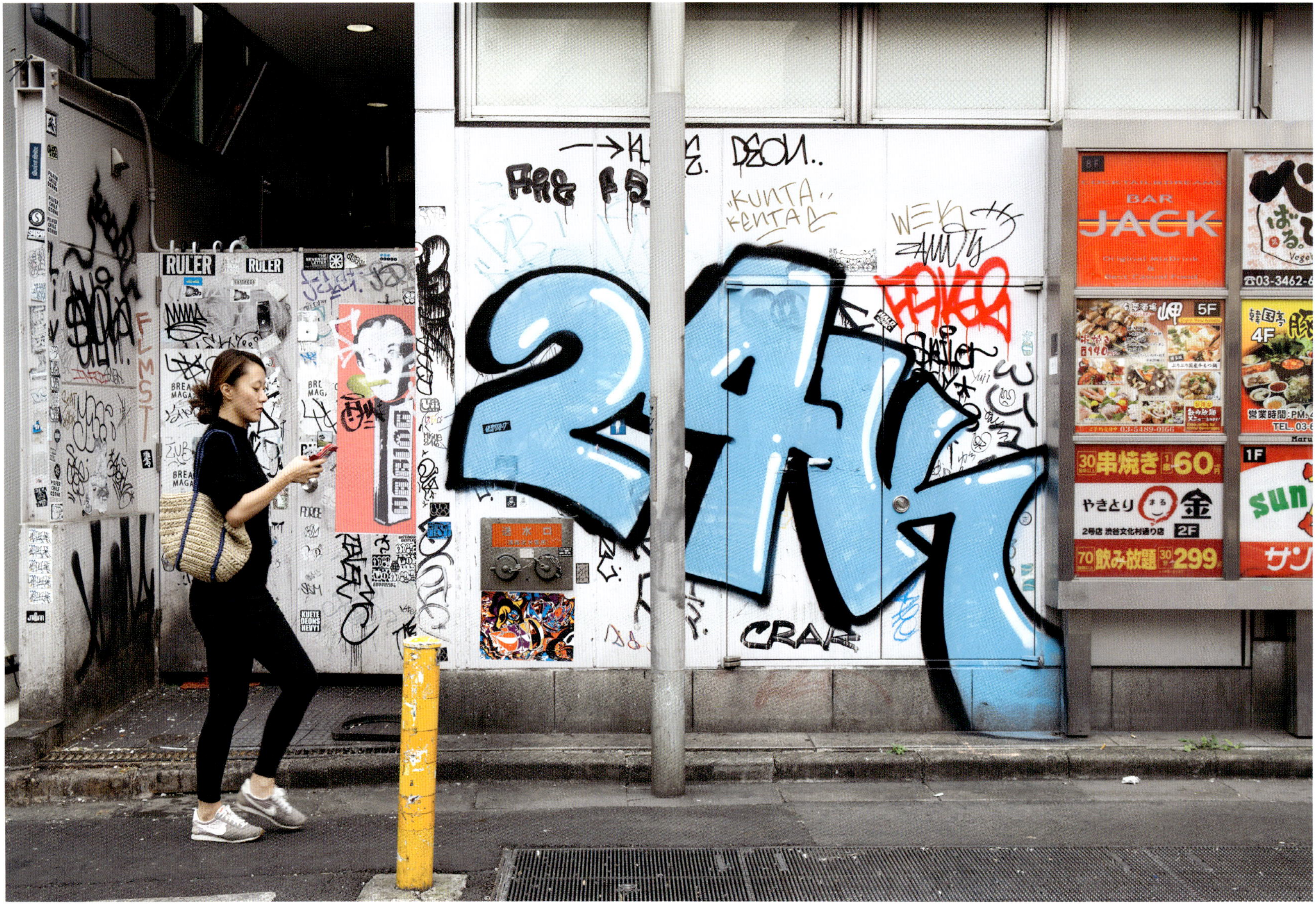

24Killaz

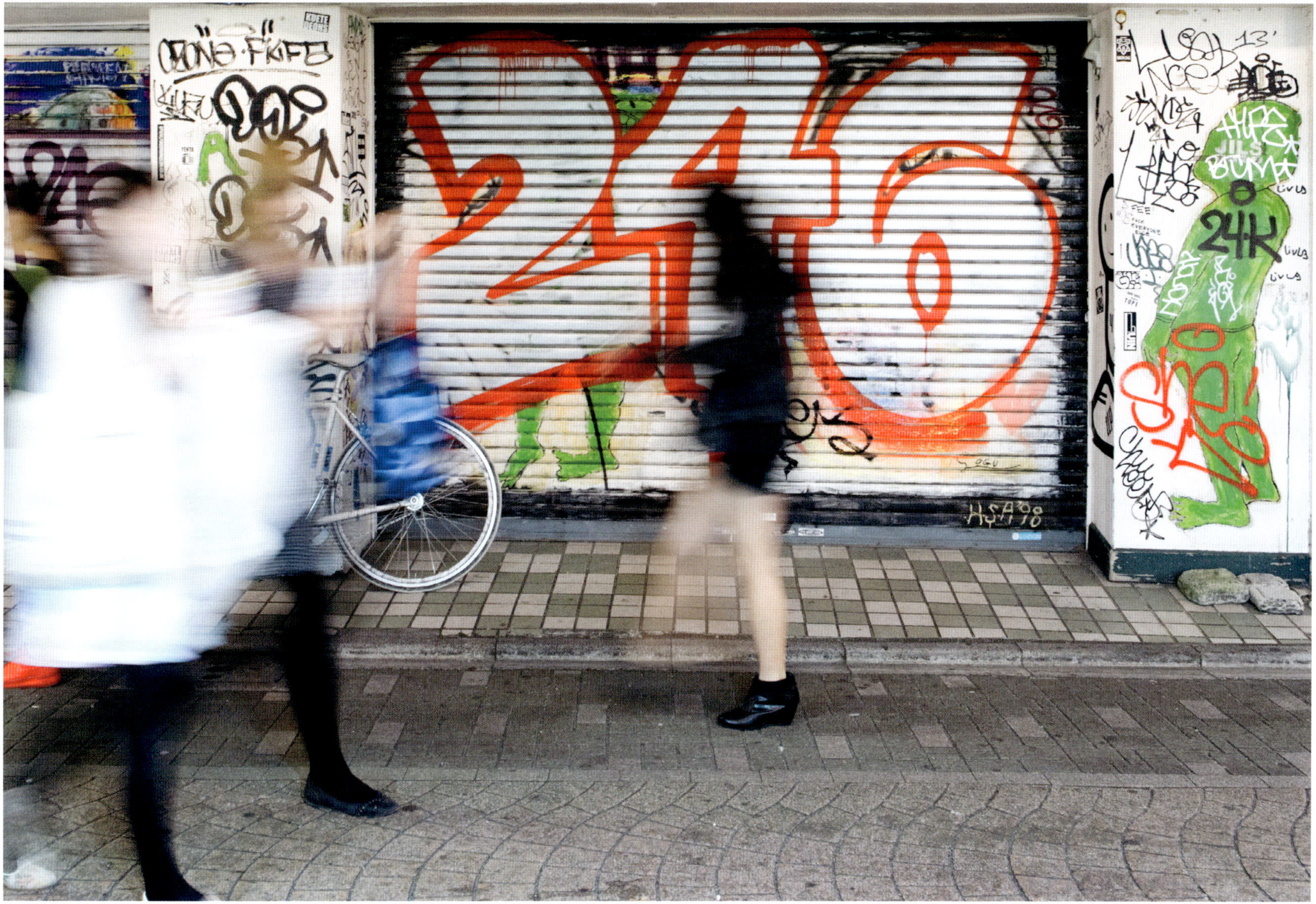

Team 246

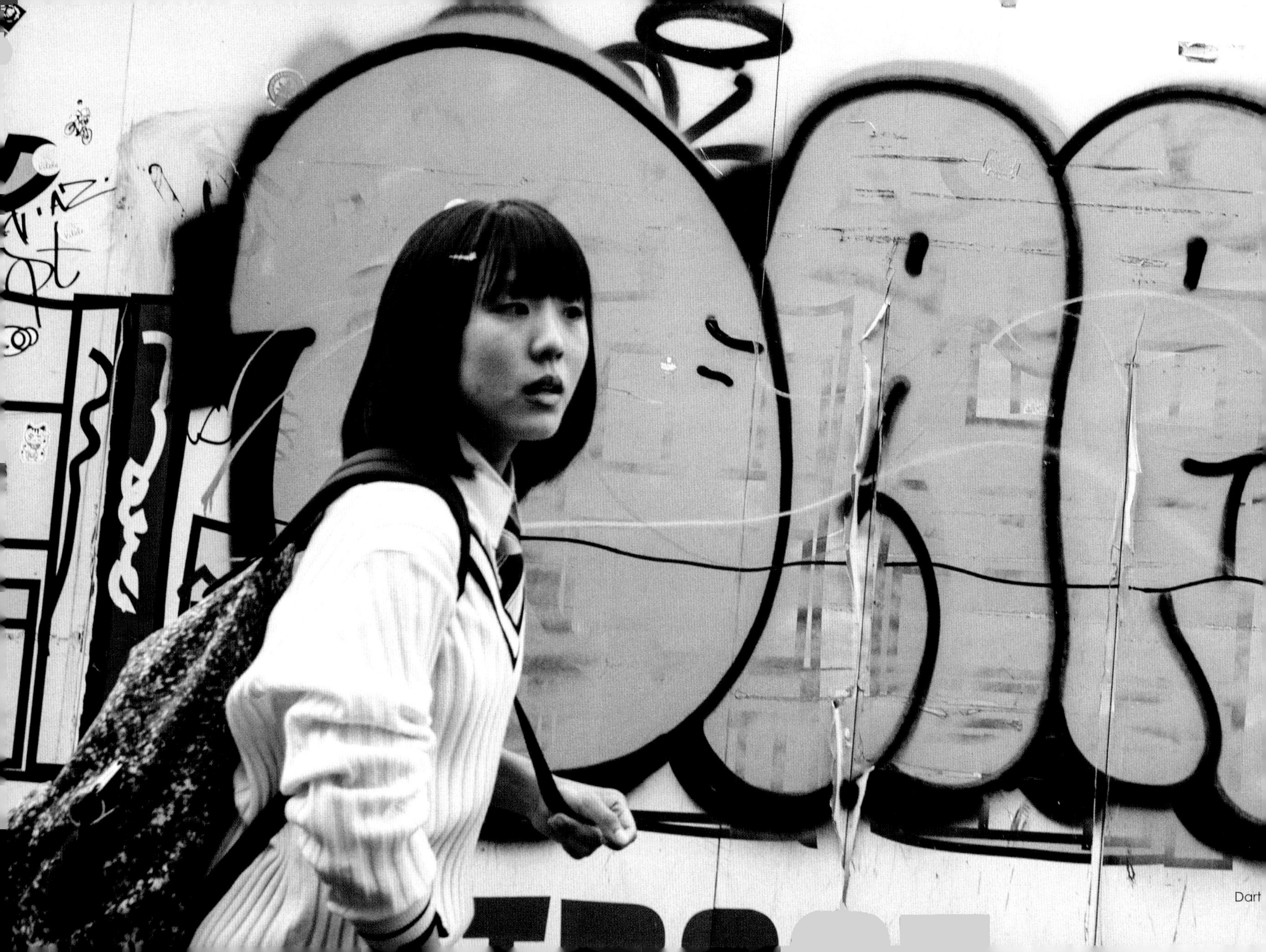

Dart

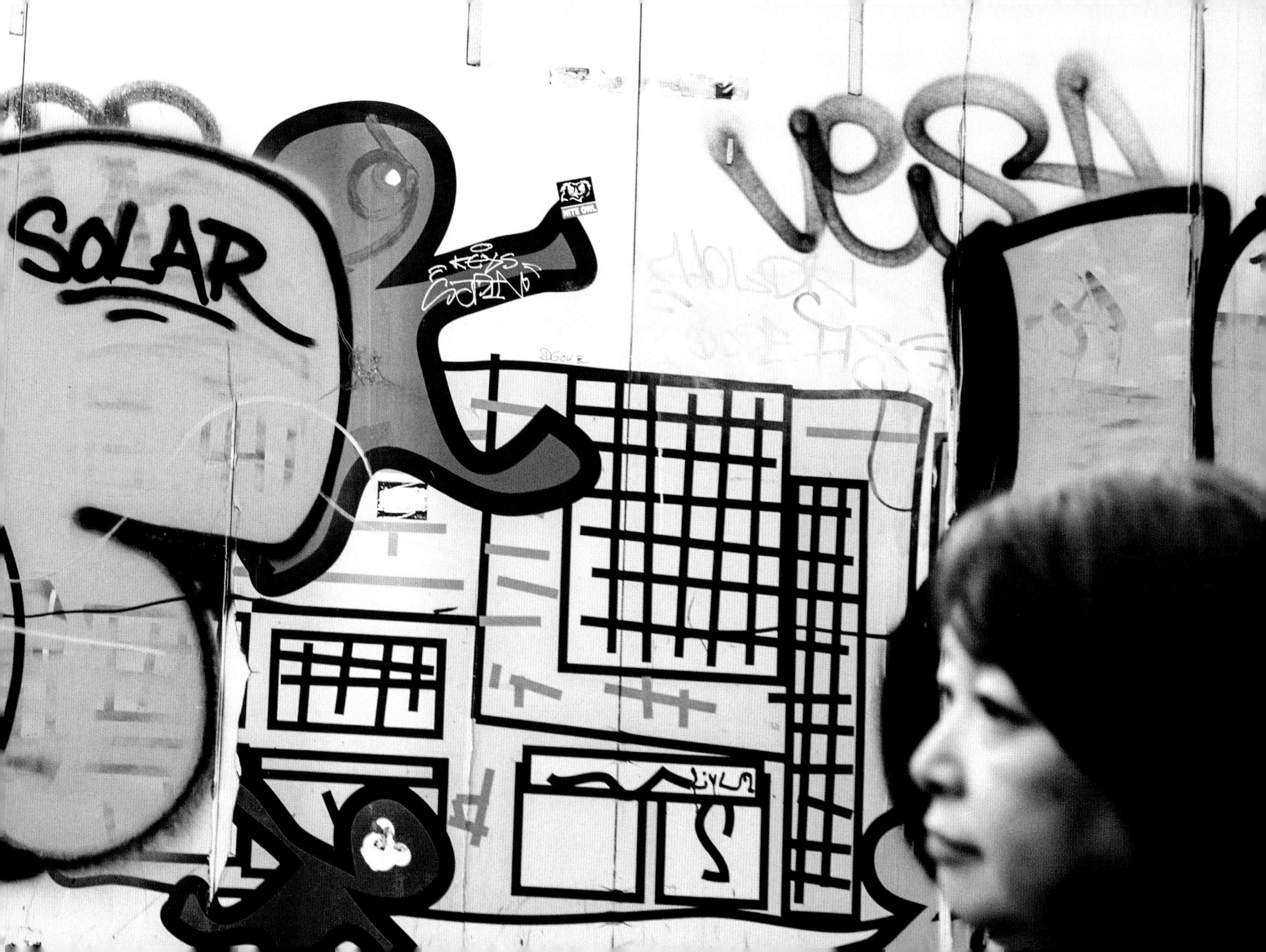
SOLAR
NITE OWL

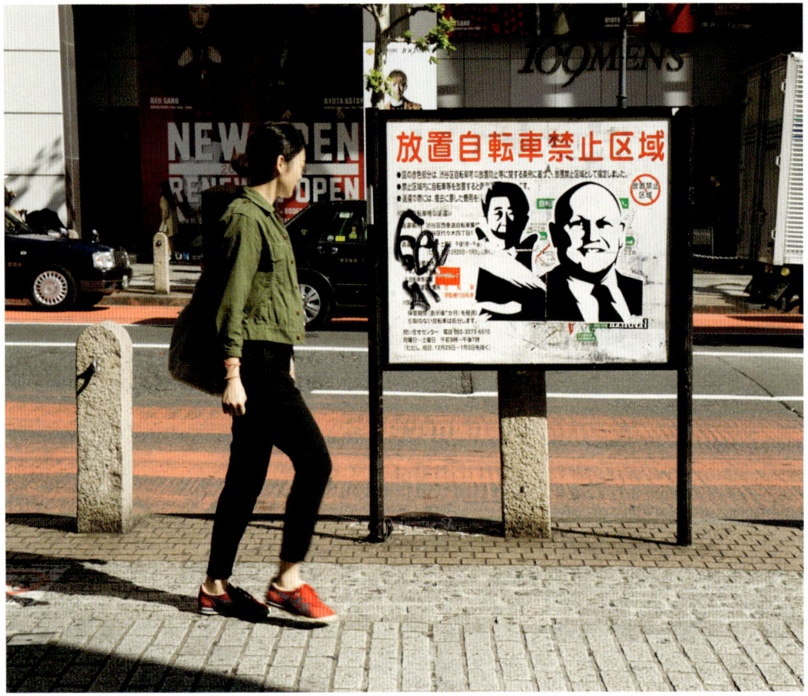

281_AntiNuke

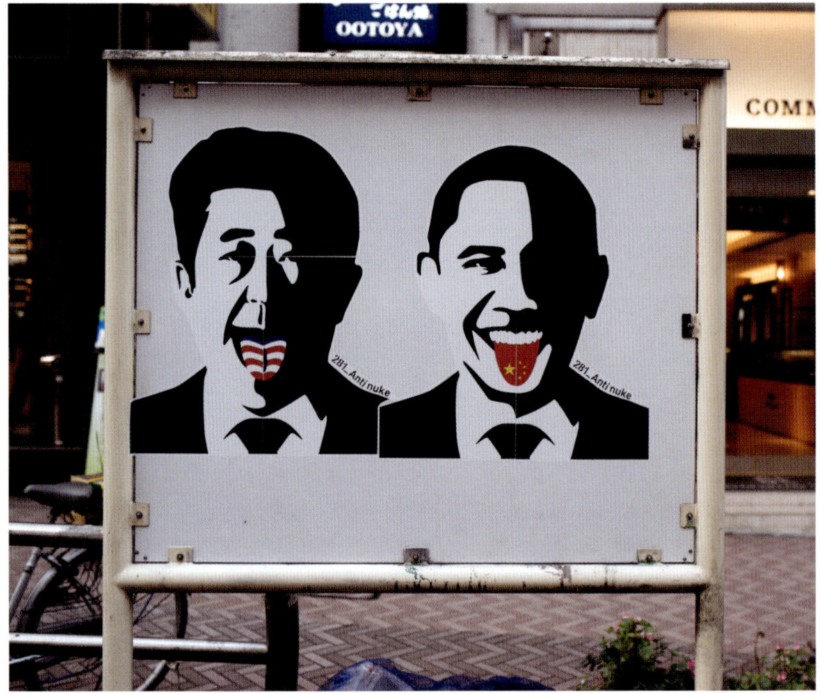

281_AntiNuke

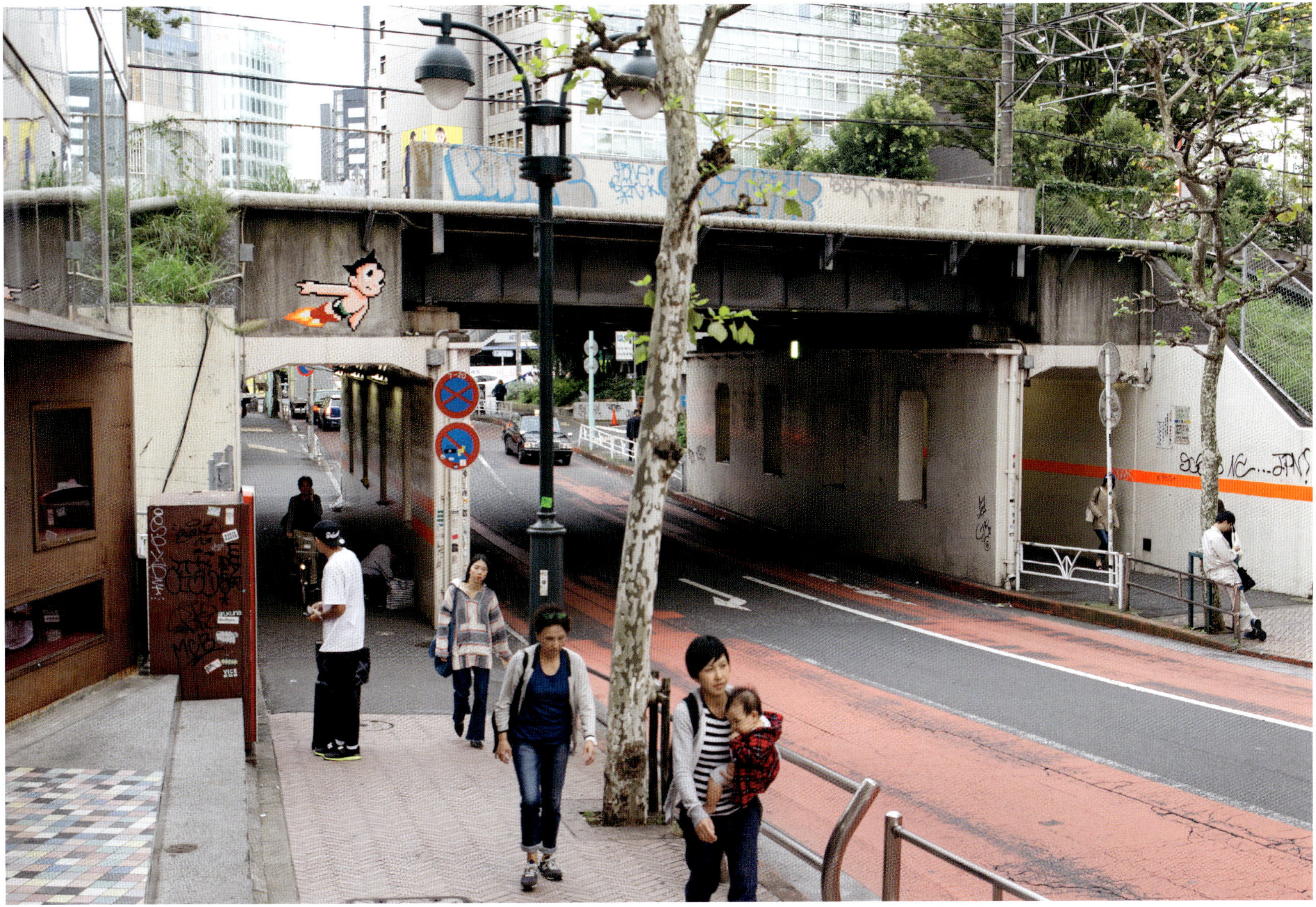

Space Invader

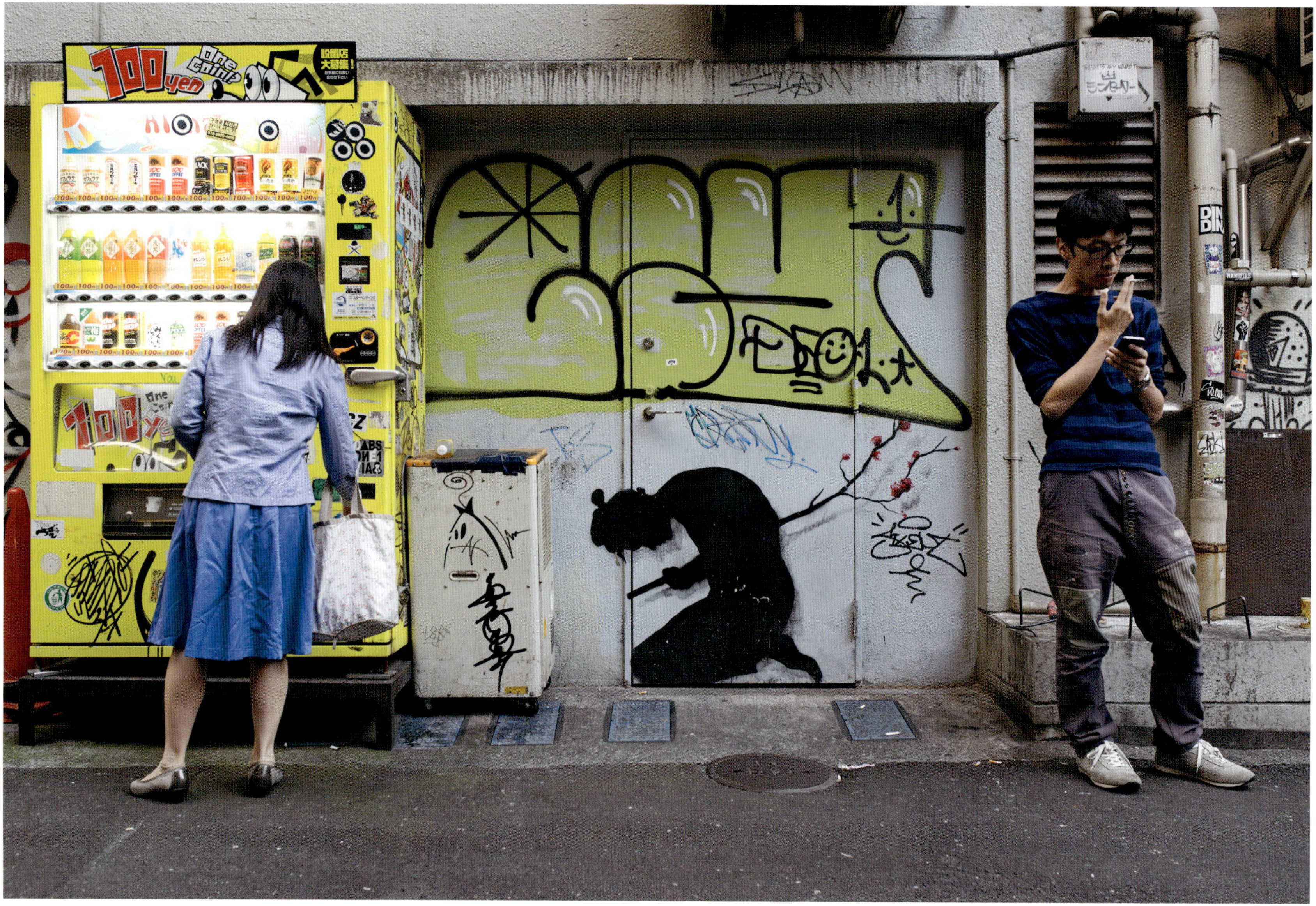

Pejac

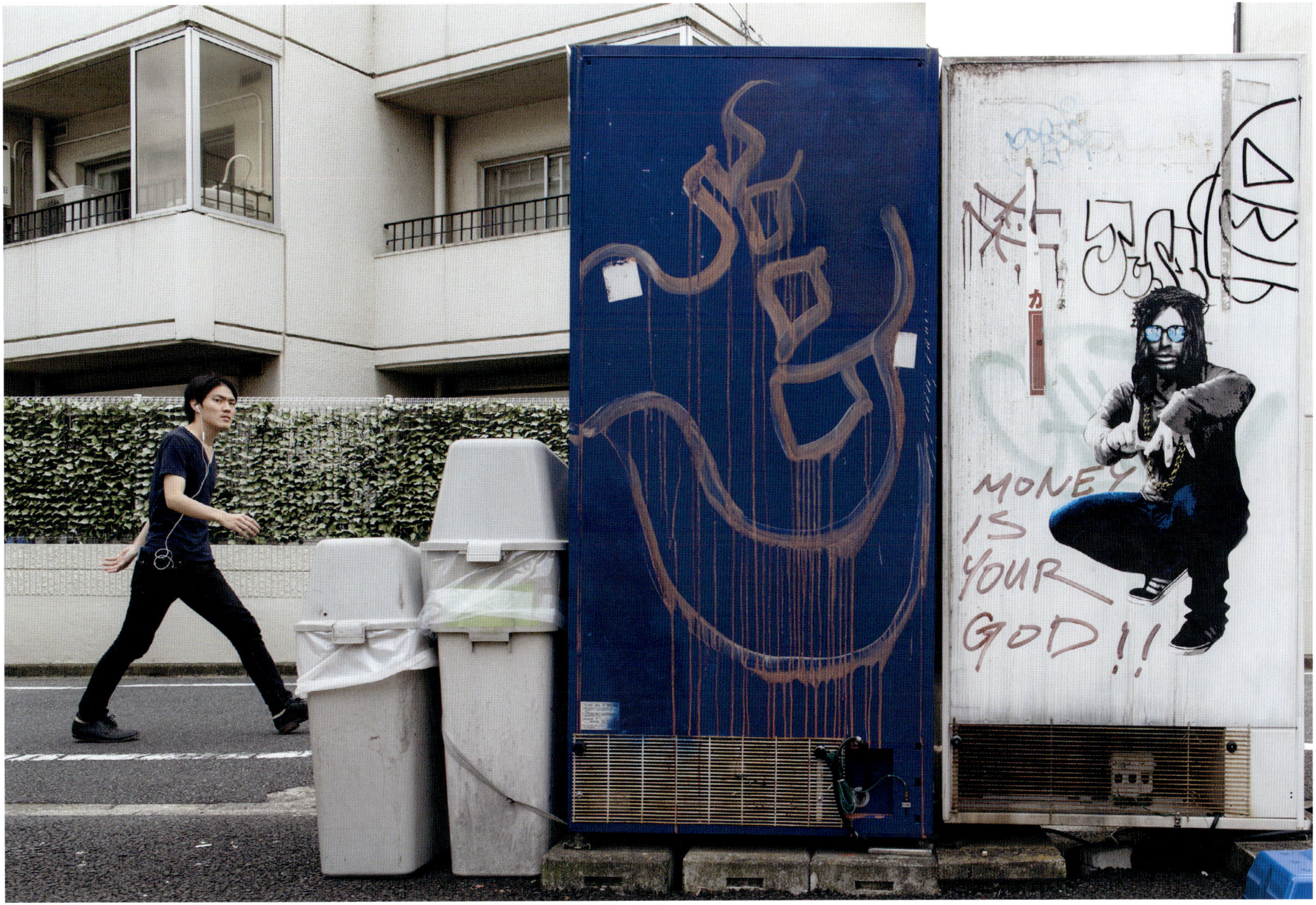

VOID

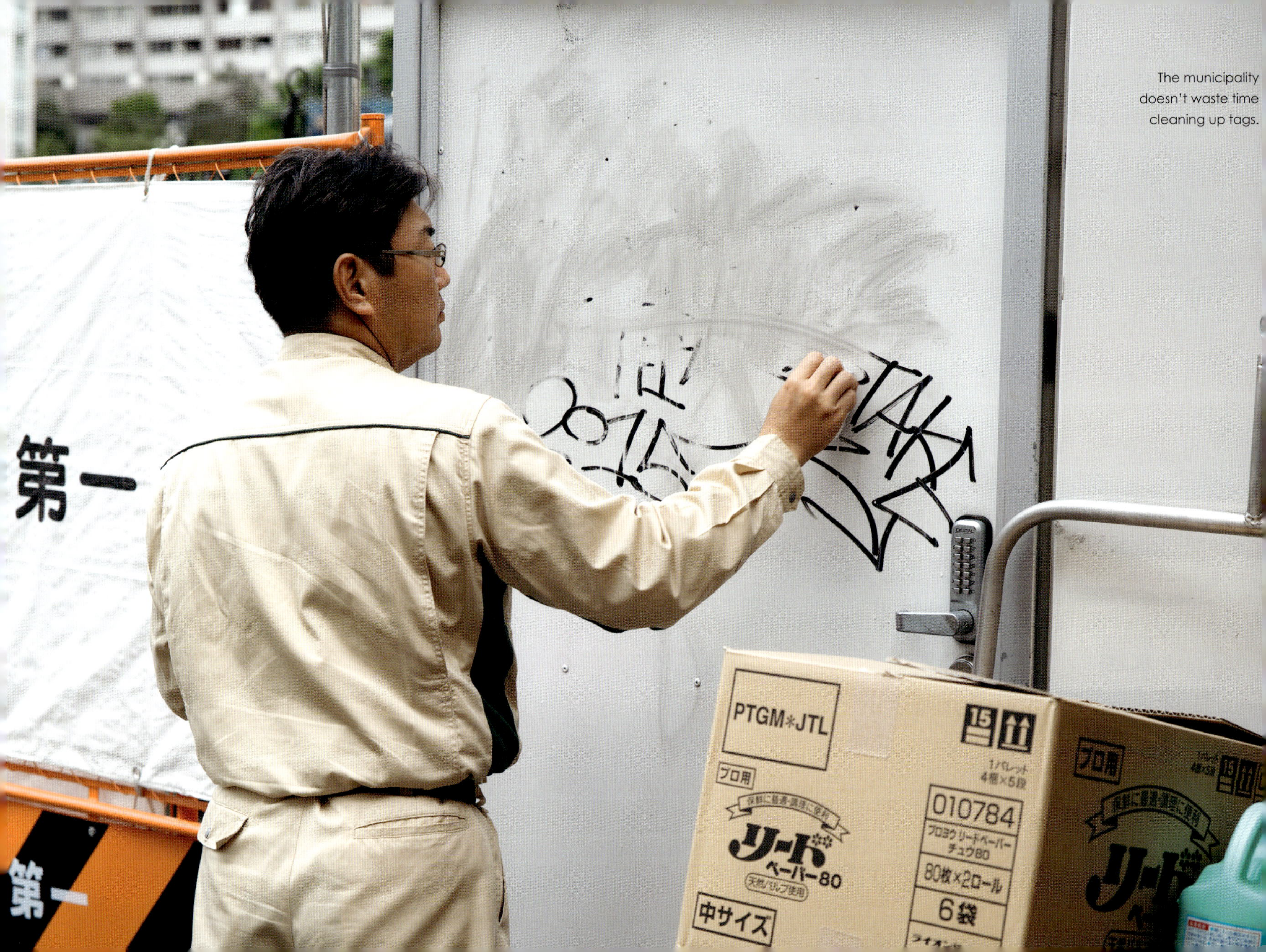

The municipality doesn't waste time cleaning up tags.

As in New York, Paris, or London, street art continues to be about being seen. In Tokyo, the presence of street art varies by area, depending on its visibility to the public and the sub-cultures popular in the area. Artists from all over the world visit Tokyo to leave their mark and overlap with other international artists in the vibrant hubs of the city. Tokyo is often rated as one of the cleanest cities to visit, from its unparalleled methods of disposing of rubbish to its automated toilets and high-speed bullet trains. Visiting artists may find that a majority of surfaces in the city are graffiti resistant which also adds to the localization of street art. Plasticized, tiled, and painted finishes limit the ability to leave permanent work and force artists to rely more on stickers and tags.

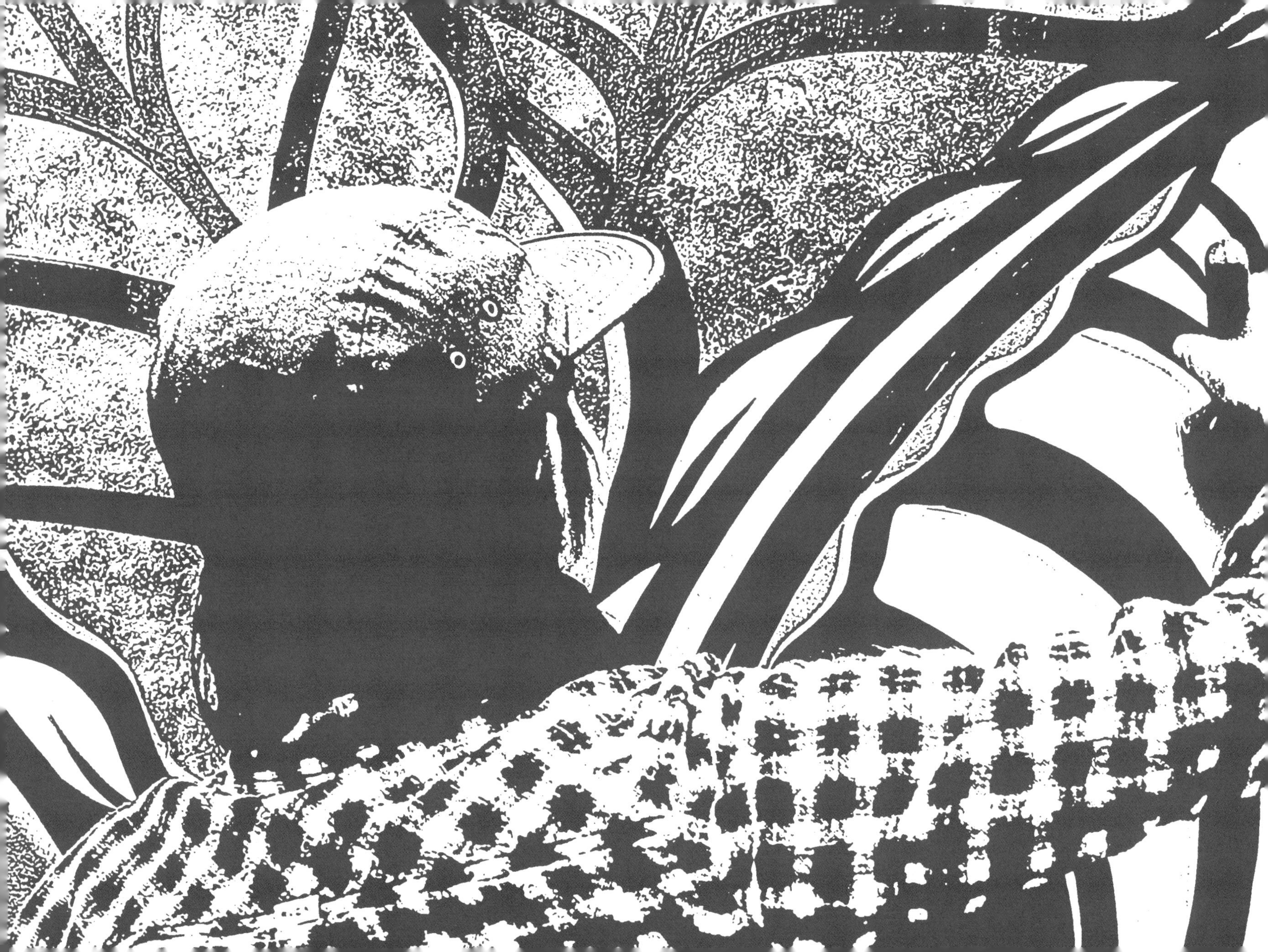

Behind the Scenes

The bustling capital city of Tokyo seems to never stop. There are many common stereotypes about exhausted salary men, coy women, endless karaoke, and delicacies of every description. But behind the scenes, Tokyo offers a converse experience. Many equate the culture to a maze of contradiction and often customs and procedures can seem illogical or archaic. Upon investigation, however, a rich and symbolic ancestry supports this lively place. Women, men, young people, expats, and all walks of life exist in harmony, challenged by unique and intriguing new endeavors daily. More than merely keeping up with the rest of the world, Tokyo sets its own pace, maintaining a balance between progress and appreciation, reverence and rebellion.

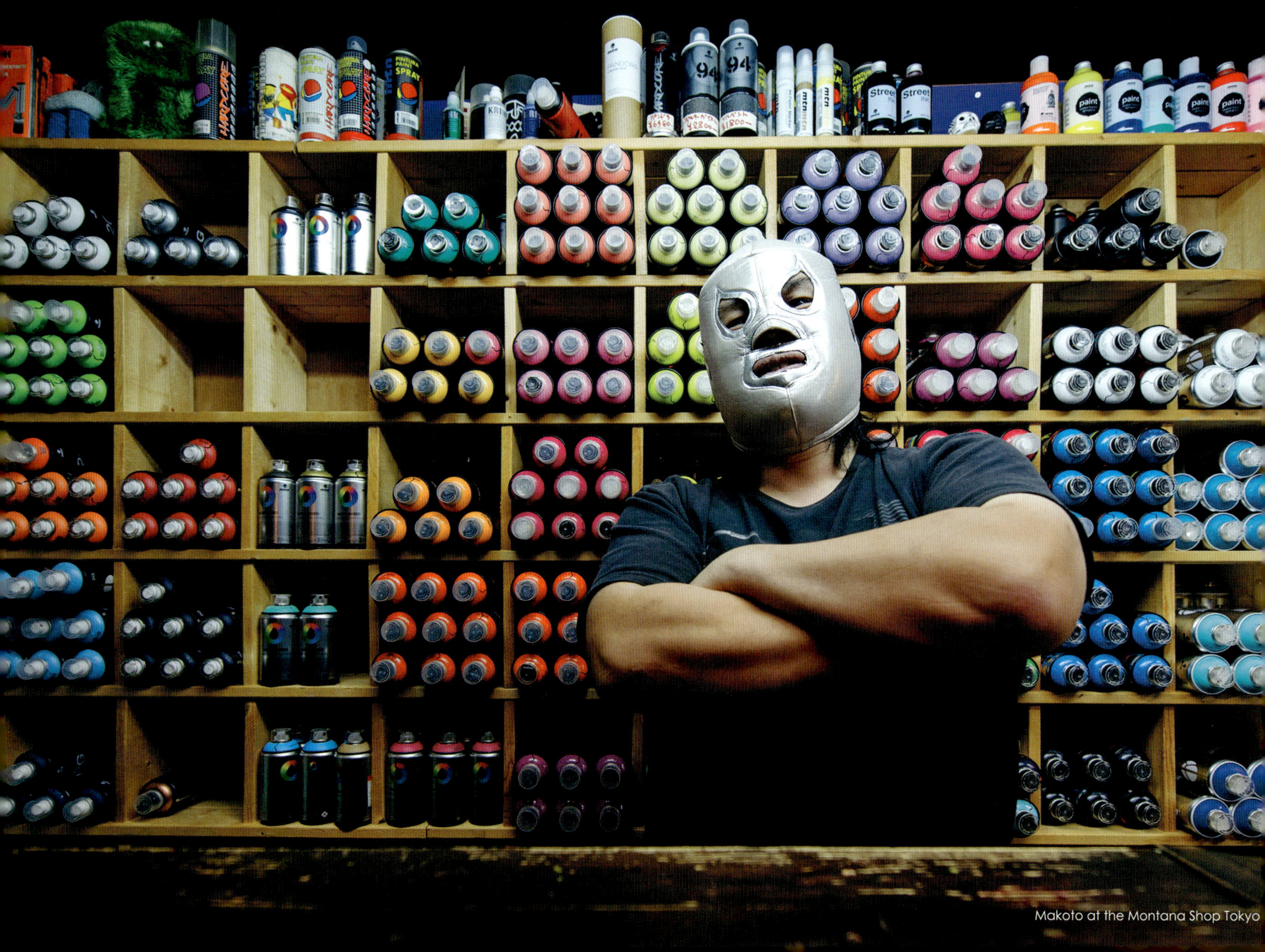

Makoto at the Montana Shop Tokyo

The Greater Tokyo Area is the most populous metropolitan area in the world, home to more than thirty-five million inhabitants. It is unique in its merging of cultures, histories, technologies, and international enterprise. With a massive pedestrian population, one can encounter thousands of individuals a day walking, cycling, or packing into busy train cars. Uniformed office workers and school children in brightly colored hats, young girls in doll-like costumes, and women in traditional kimono all make up the landscape. Millions of inhabitants stare at their feet going up escalators and scroll through their mobile devices in cafes, seeming to breathe like a singular organism. Amidst the lights and sounds of the streets, artists are pausing in the surge of activity to disrupt, engage, and inspire, yet, they are hampered by the masses of pedestrians and stringent laws. Pulling out a spray can on the streets of Tokyo would in many instances attract instant unwanted attention, hence the market for aerosol is extremely niche and mainly caters to bombers and commissioned artists.

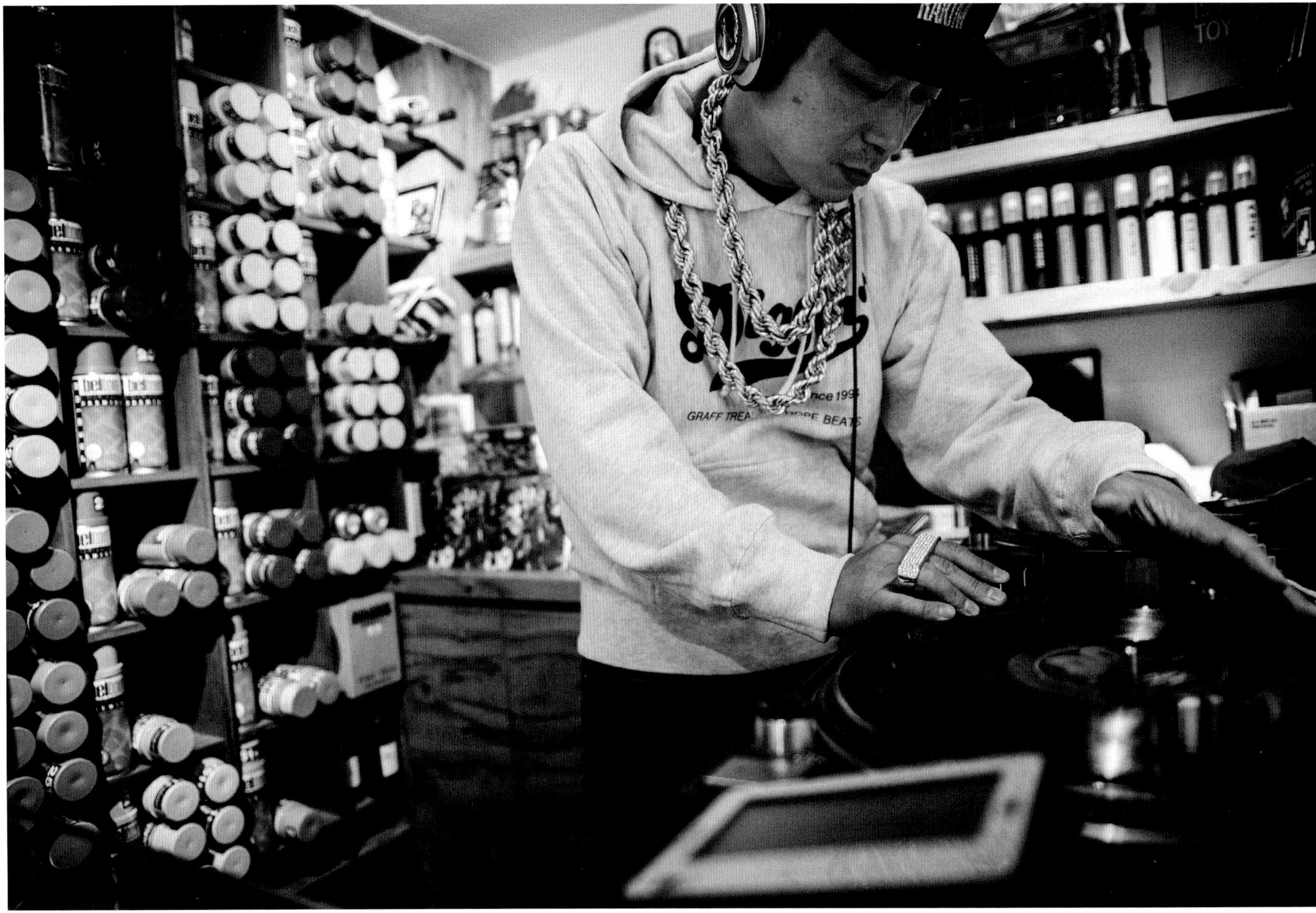

DJ Viblam in Harajuku

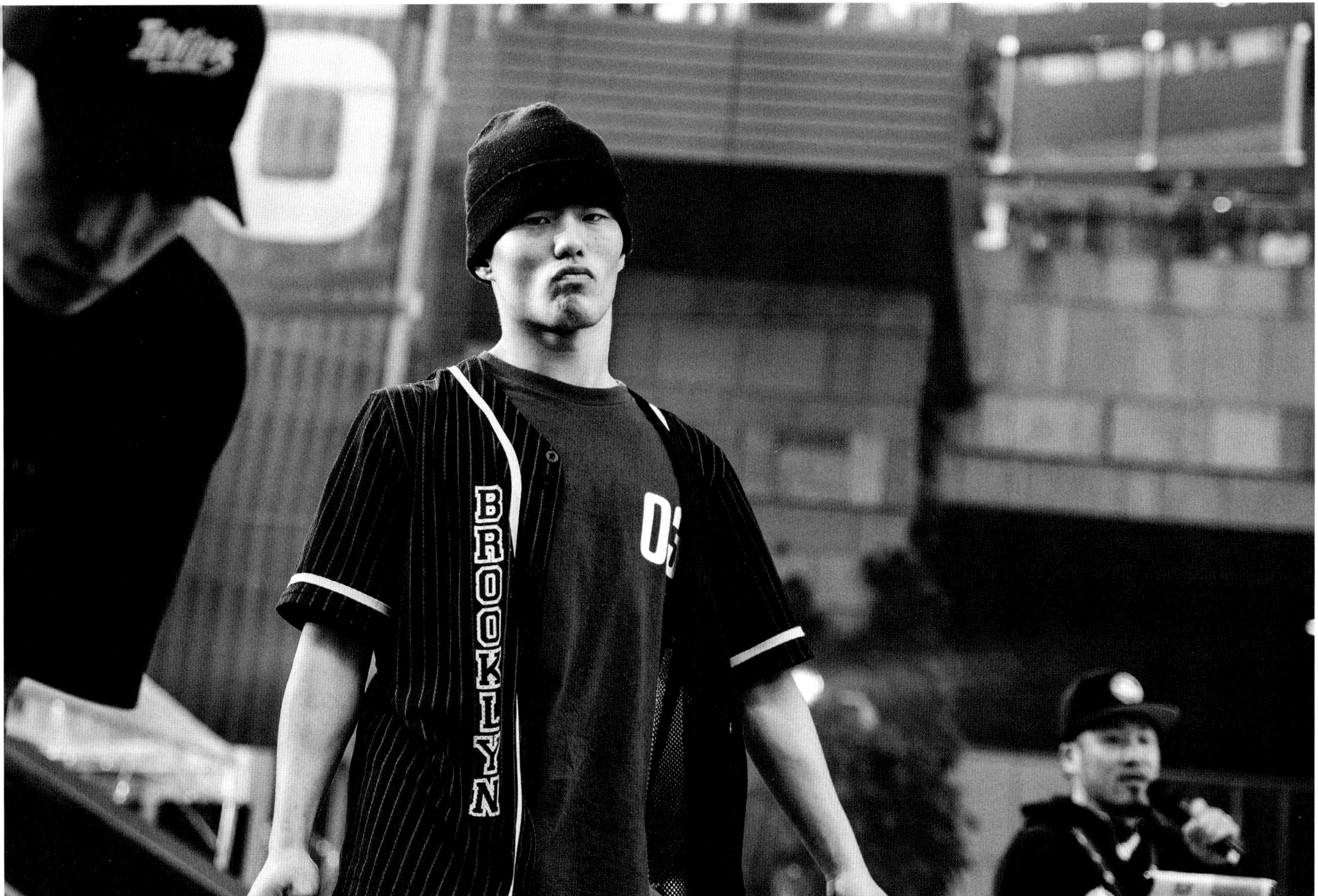

Break dancing in Roppongi Hills

In some areas of Tokyo there are shops that market British punk, west coast skater lifestyle, Parisian haute couture, or hip-hop sub-cultures. Although it can appear to be irreverent trending, these appropriations from the West continuously assimilate back into contemporary Japanese youth culture, creating something that is uniquely their own. While Japan's tanned surfer boys also don shaggy hair, canvas shoes, and board shorts, in this nation of more than 6,800 islands, they also carry a lineage of fishermen, pearl divers, and of course surfers. Similarly, the street art, graffiti culture that took root in New York and London has now begun to seamlessly weave itself into its own Japanese aesthetic. Upon first glance, Tokyo could appear to be a buzz of indistinguishable signs and noise, but behind the scenes there is a rumbling of evolution and experimentation specific to the monster that is Tokyo.

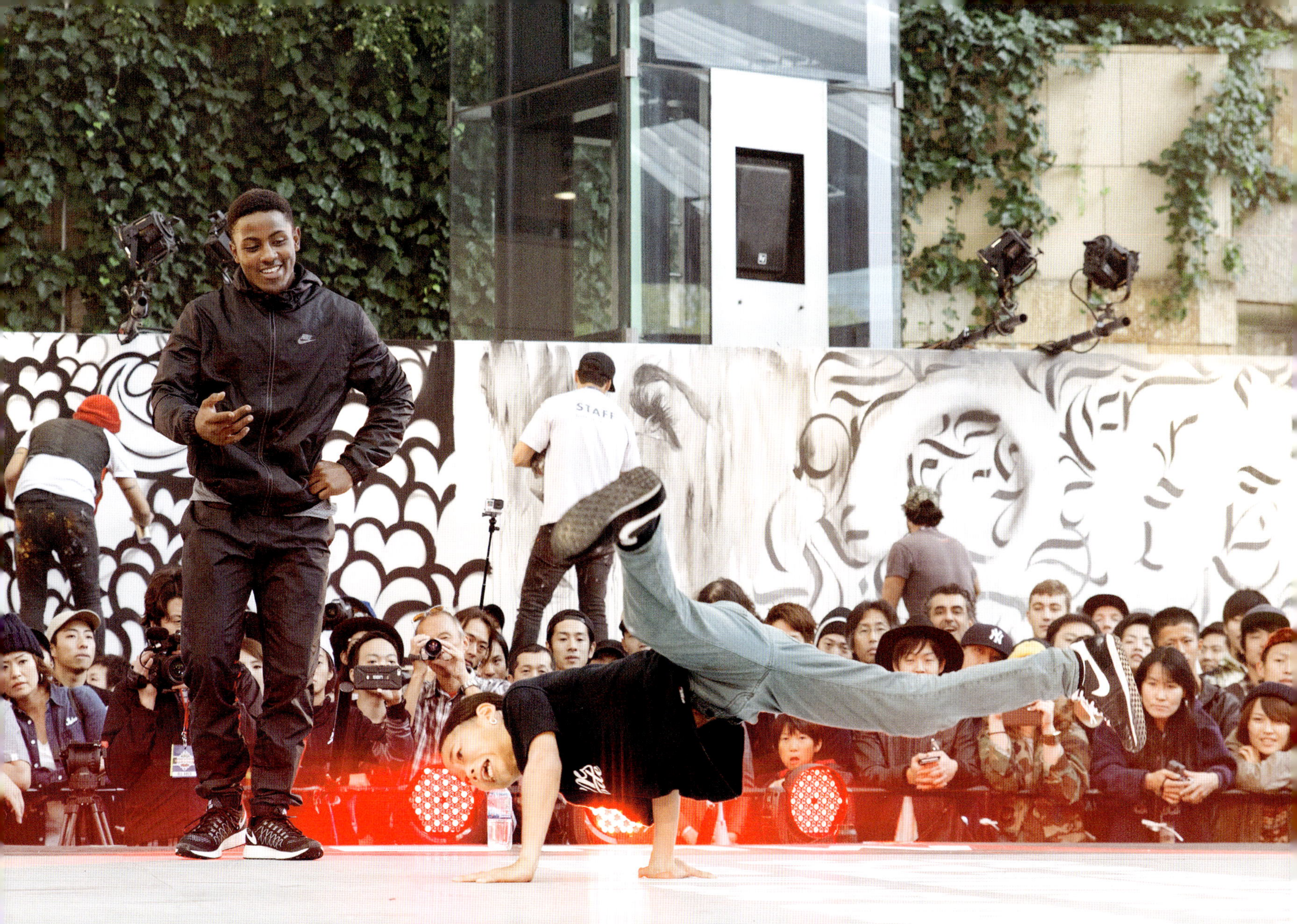

Break dancing in Roppongi Hills

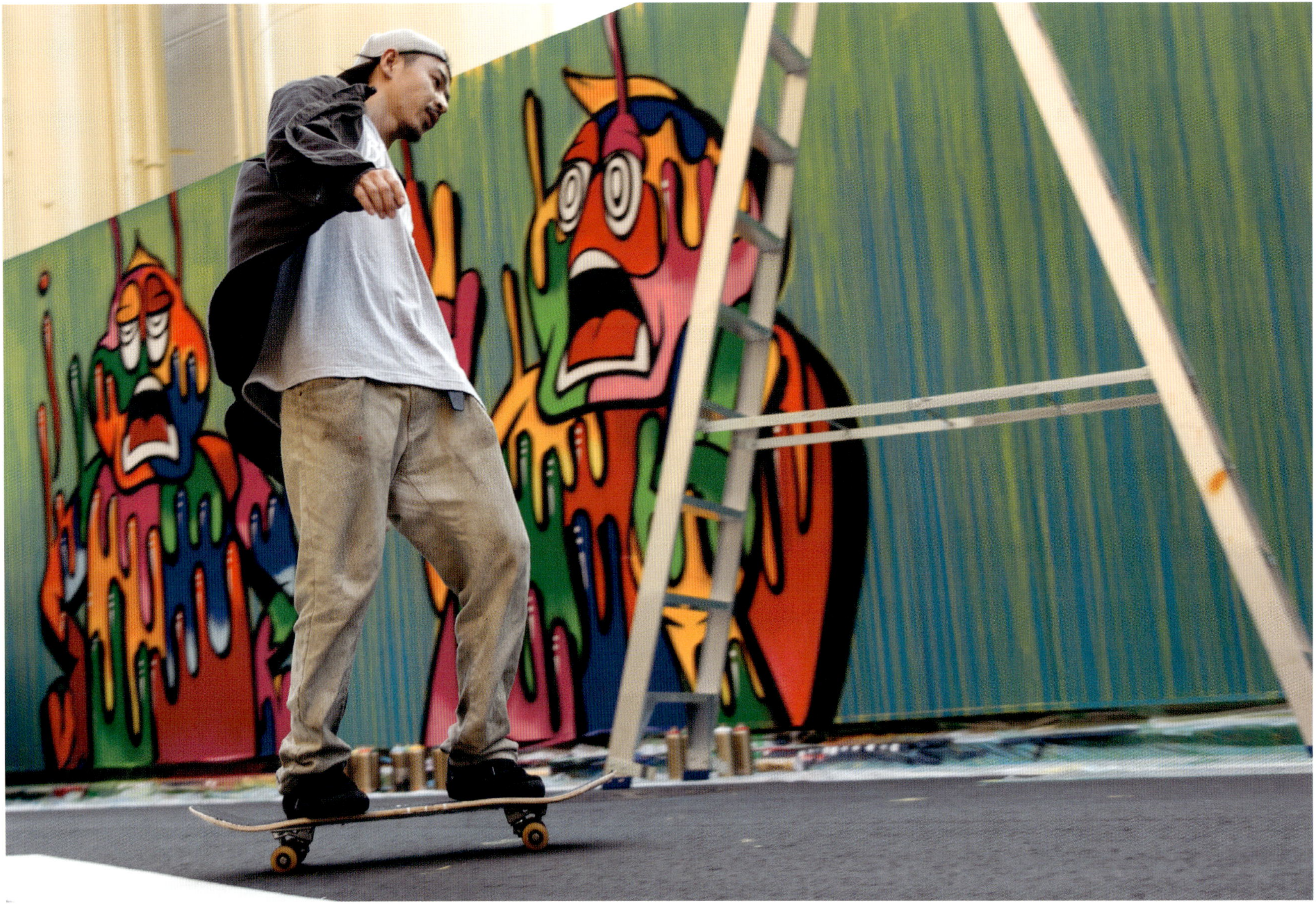

Artwork: Jay Shogo

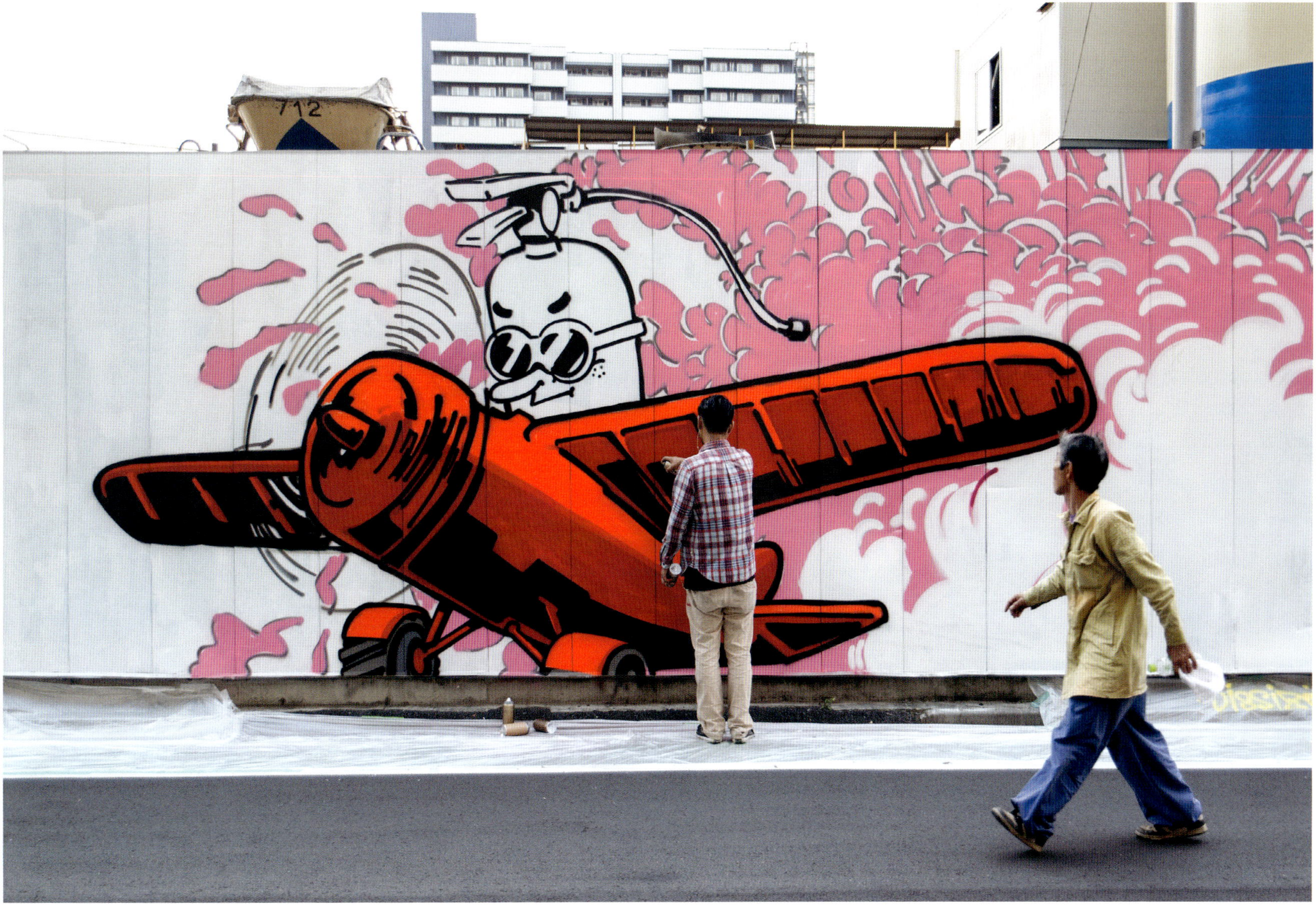

Cook1

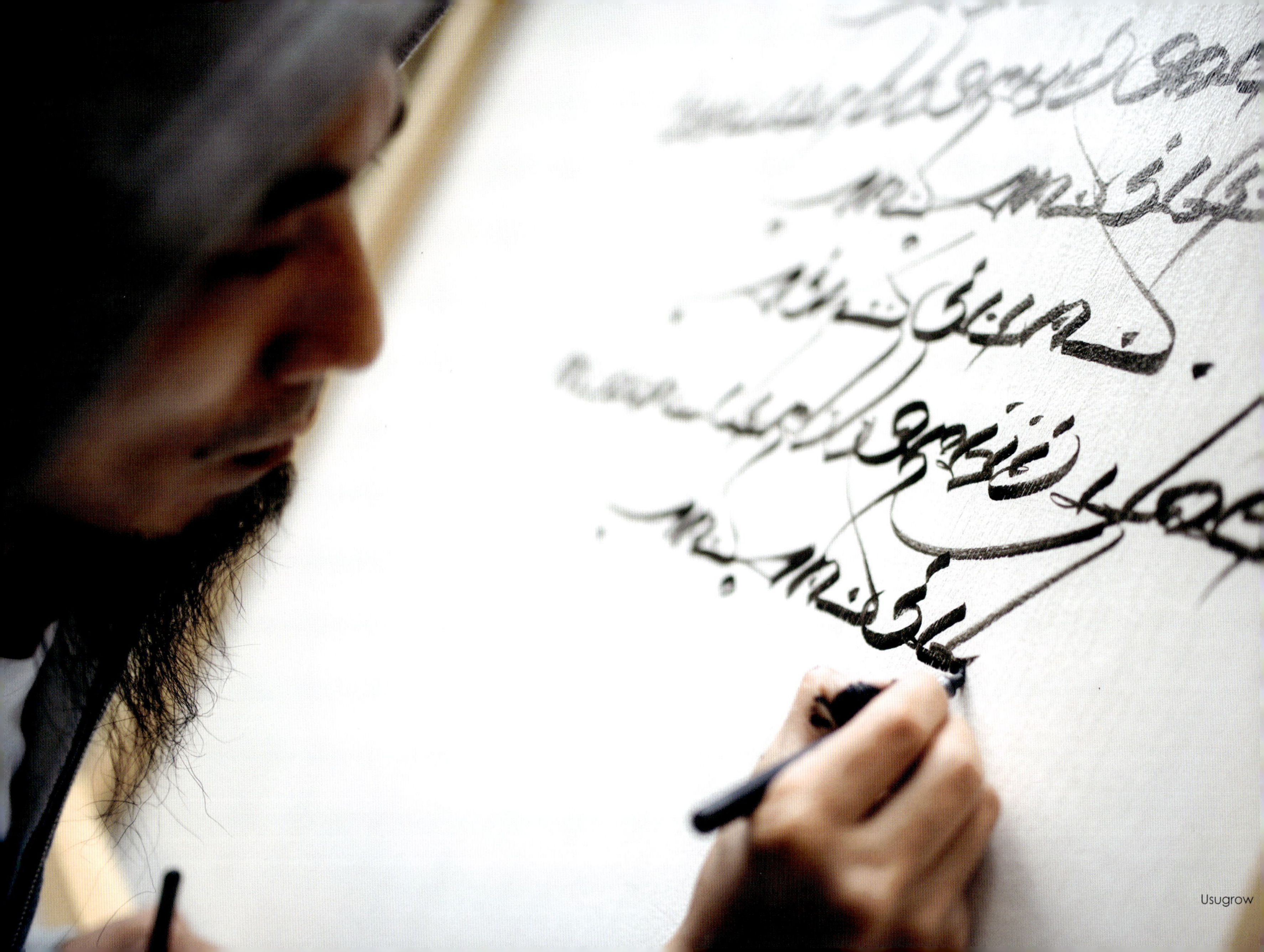

Usugrow

Japan's rich history is present underneath the new surface of Tokyo. There are three written alphabets widely used in Japan, the first of which derives most of its characters from Chinese. The precision, skill, and practice it takes to write any of these characters has imparted a deeply influential principle of balance. Even though much of Japan's modern design draws influences from western advertising, international standards of high fashion, and industry, there the delicate balance of Japanese composition and style is still present. Elements found in nature, like the principle of *Wabi-sabi*, the beauty of imperfections, can be seen in the silks of obi belts and the mural and urban scene. Similarly images of demons and dragons still haunt the backdrops of contemporary street art.

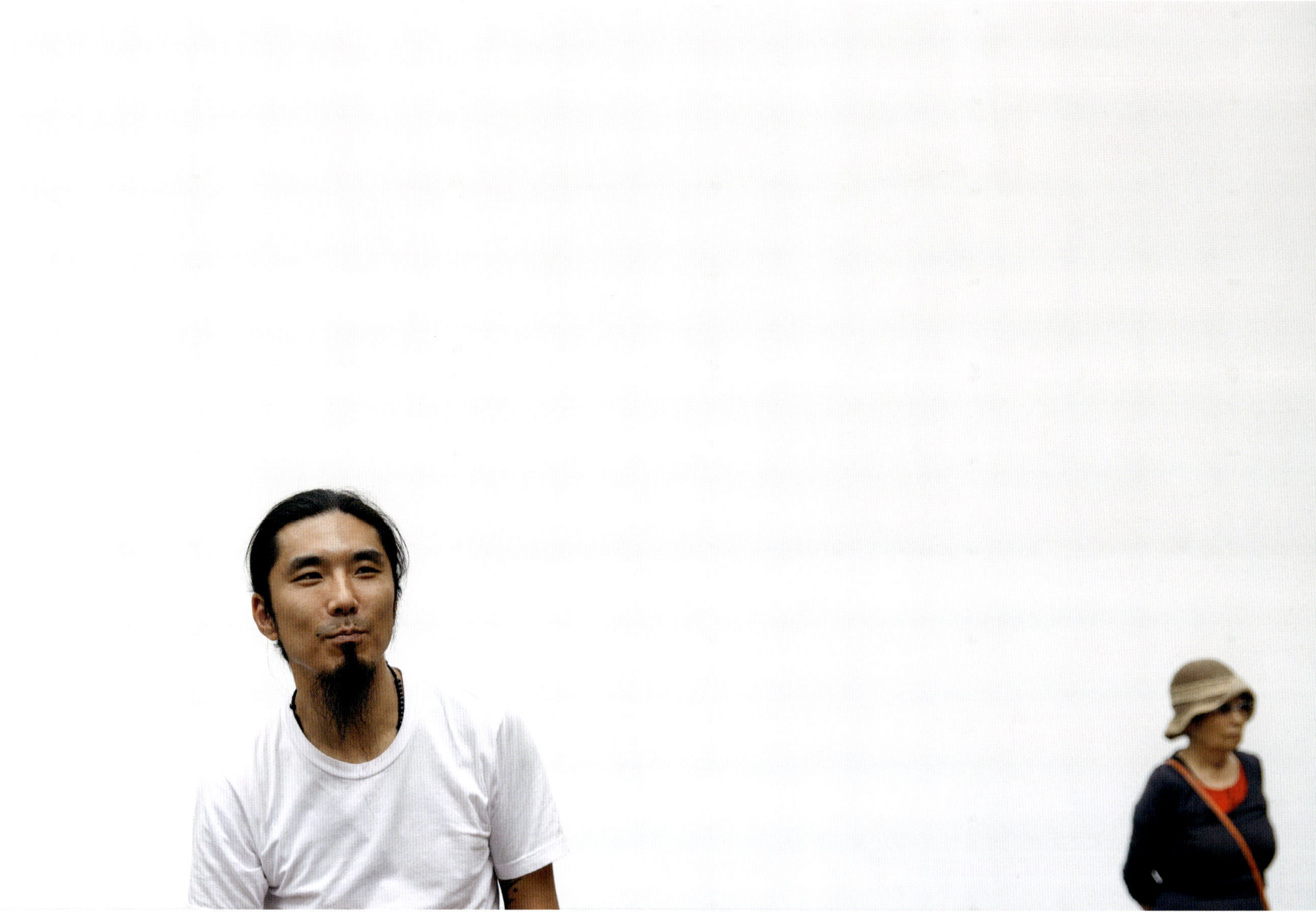

Usugrow

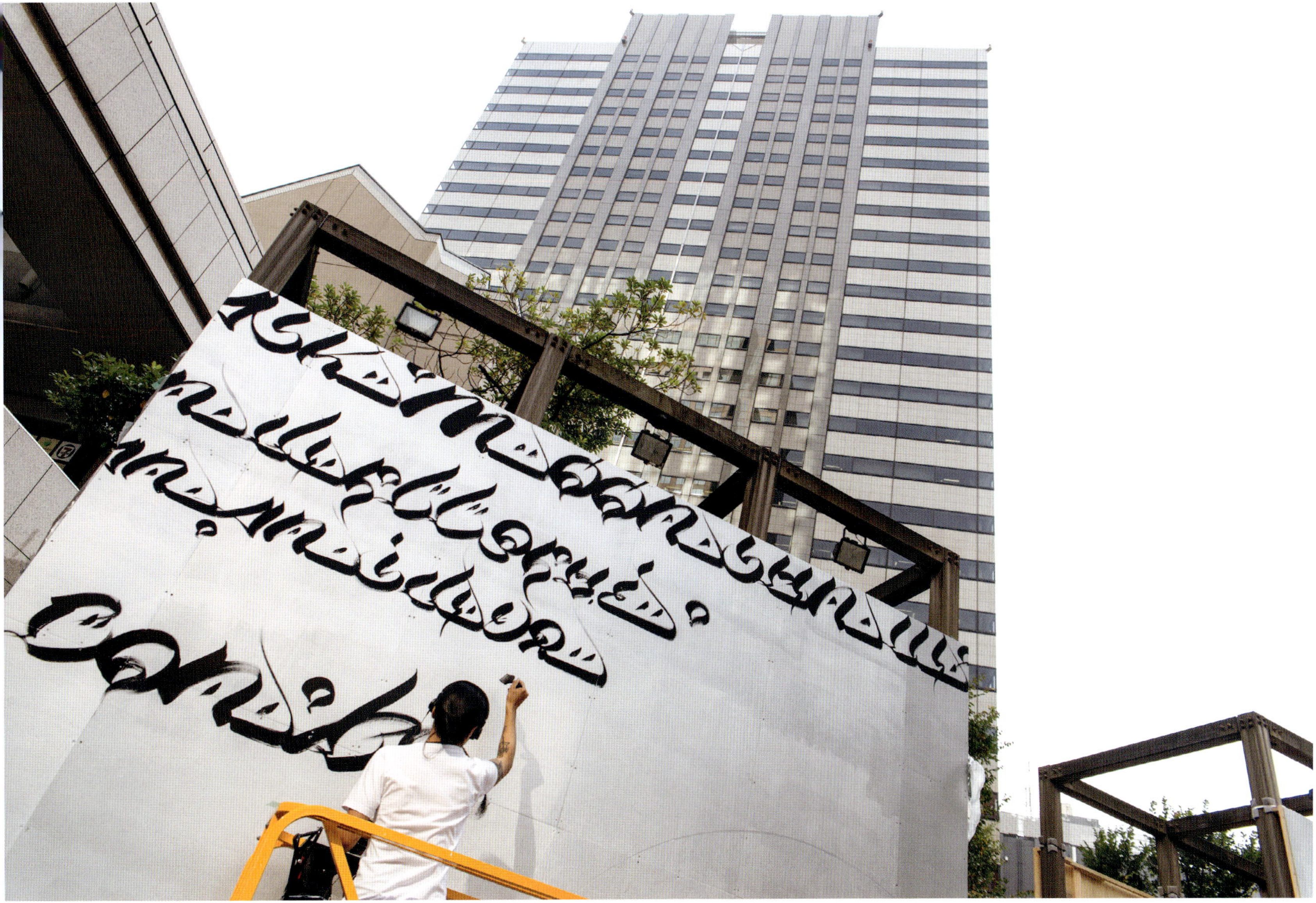

Usugrow

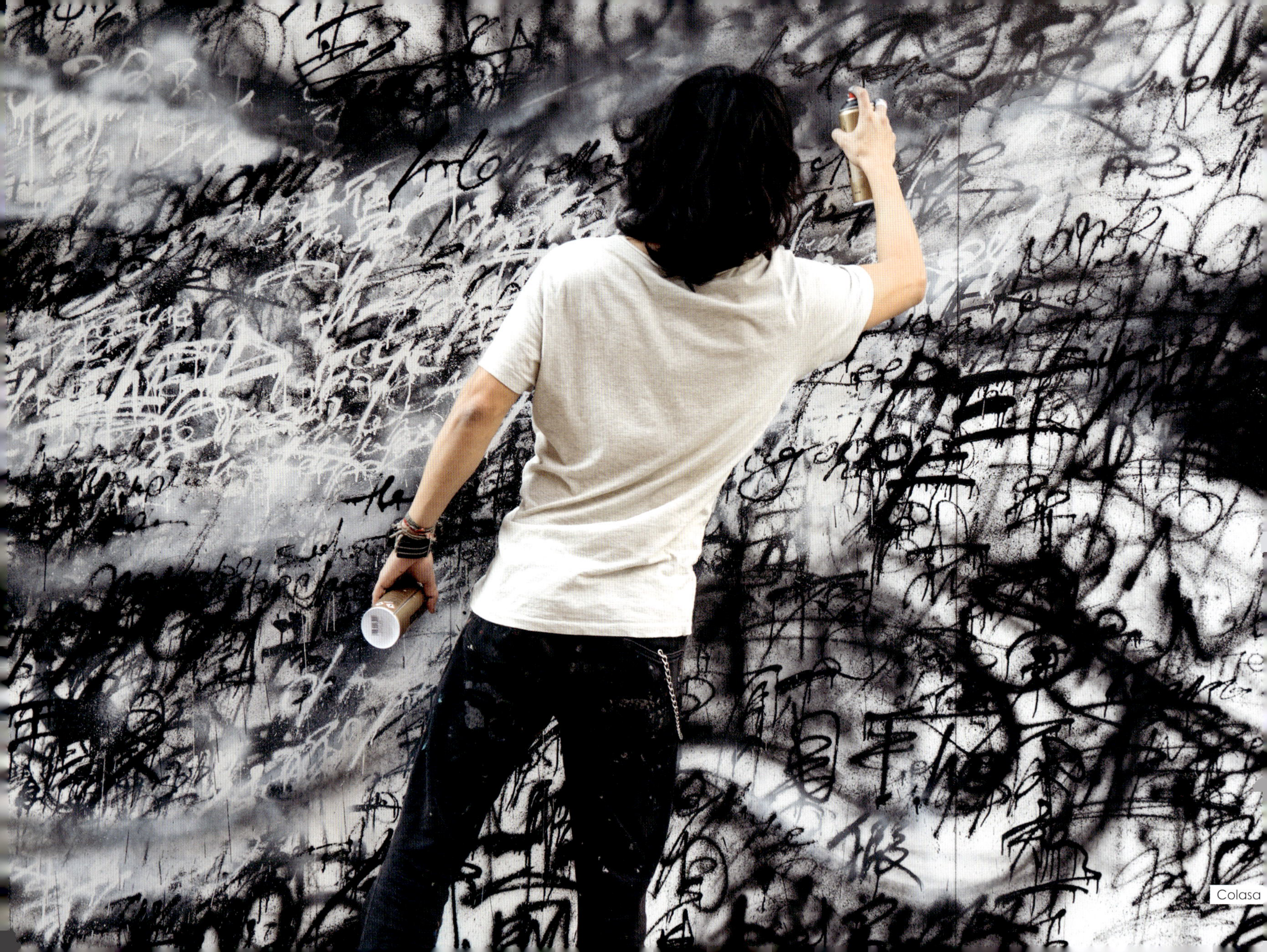

Colasa

The young people of Tokyo and the new generation of urban artists are a fascinating representation of an incredible city. They are shaped by modest ideals, progressive sexuality, traditional design aesthetic, beauty, and high fashion from all over the world. For many young men, the prescribed path seems to be to work constantly and spend what free hours are remaining drinking heavily, playing in arcades, hiring simulated experience services, or viewing anime. The new generation struggles to find appropriate methods of rebellion and some choose art and the street art lifestyle as an outlet. Japanese women explore their identities in other extreme ways, some trying to alter their appearance toward a perfect ideal of beauty, using false eyelashes, colored contacts, eyelid creasing tape, facial exercise toys, posture-correcting harnesses, teeth implants, and of course an entire vocabulary of cute poses and camera-friendly faces. Even to creatives from neighboring continents and similarly rooted cultures, some Japanese practices seem bizarre. But at first glance this seems like freedom and this looks like individuality. Although young people everywhere work to maintain respect, equality, and happiness, adolescents in Tokyo are trudging a road centuries old. This generation is undertaking a new journey crowded with its own conflicting ideals.

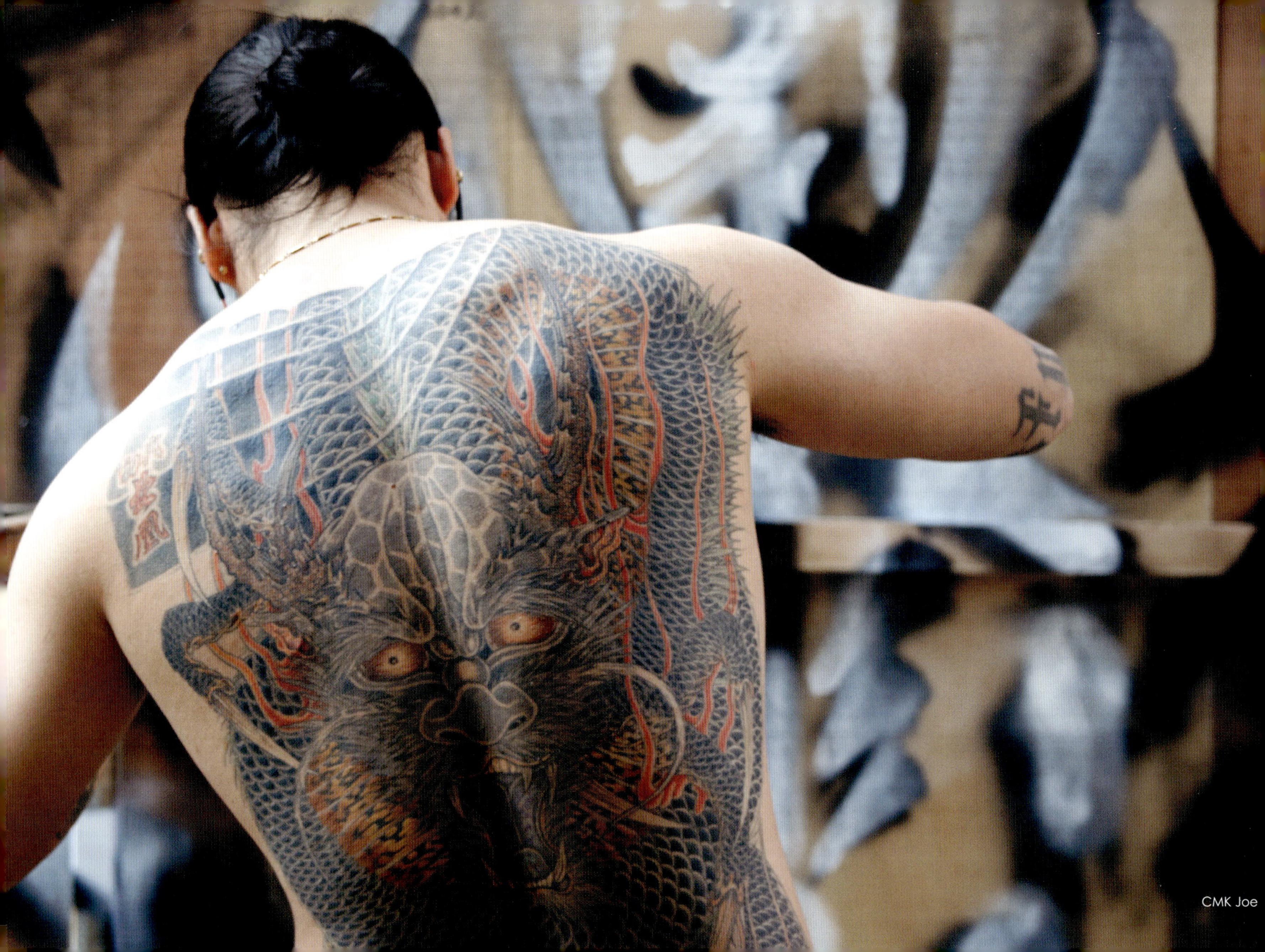

CMK Joe

Modern day Japan retains a sense of respectful, self-surveillance. The crime rate in Japan is one of the lowest in the world, though the exact reason is unclear. A communal ethics code amongst Japanese people is undeniably founded in honesty, integrity, and peaceful behavior. However, the "peace" on the streets may also be accredited to organized crime syndicates known as Yakuza. These groups are recognized by the government, and often maintain balance and city-wide relief in the busy metropolis. Some of these mafia-like organizations are known for protecting small businesses, offering relief after natural disasters, and forbidding the trafficking of drugs, while others are heavily involved with drugs and prostitution. Theft, vandalism, and small crimes are not simply frowned upon in Japan, they are also treated seriously by the police and individuals are shamed and expected to repent. Because of this many street artists are deterred from working illegally, publicly, or on a large scale in Japan.

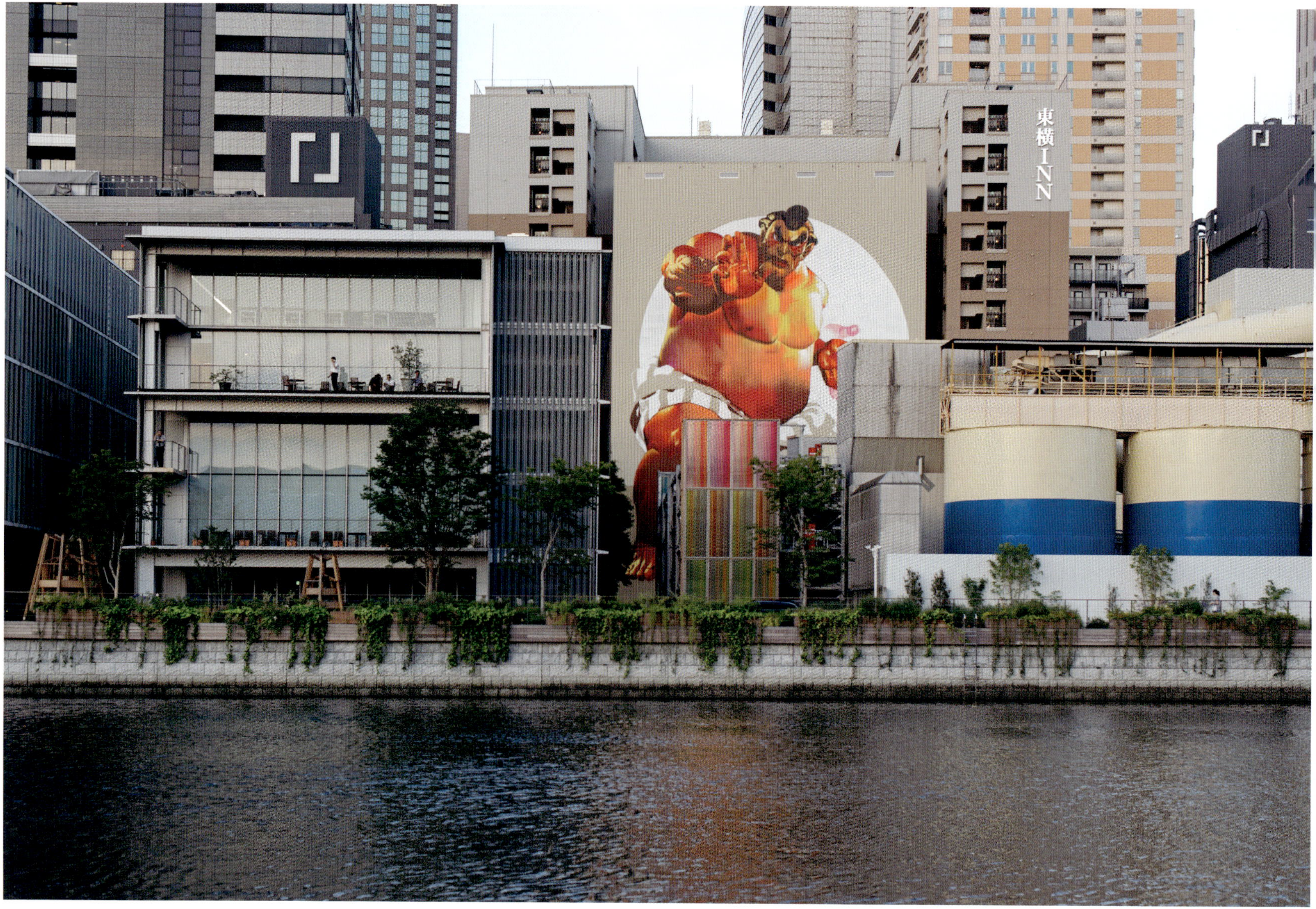

Case Maclaim

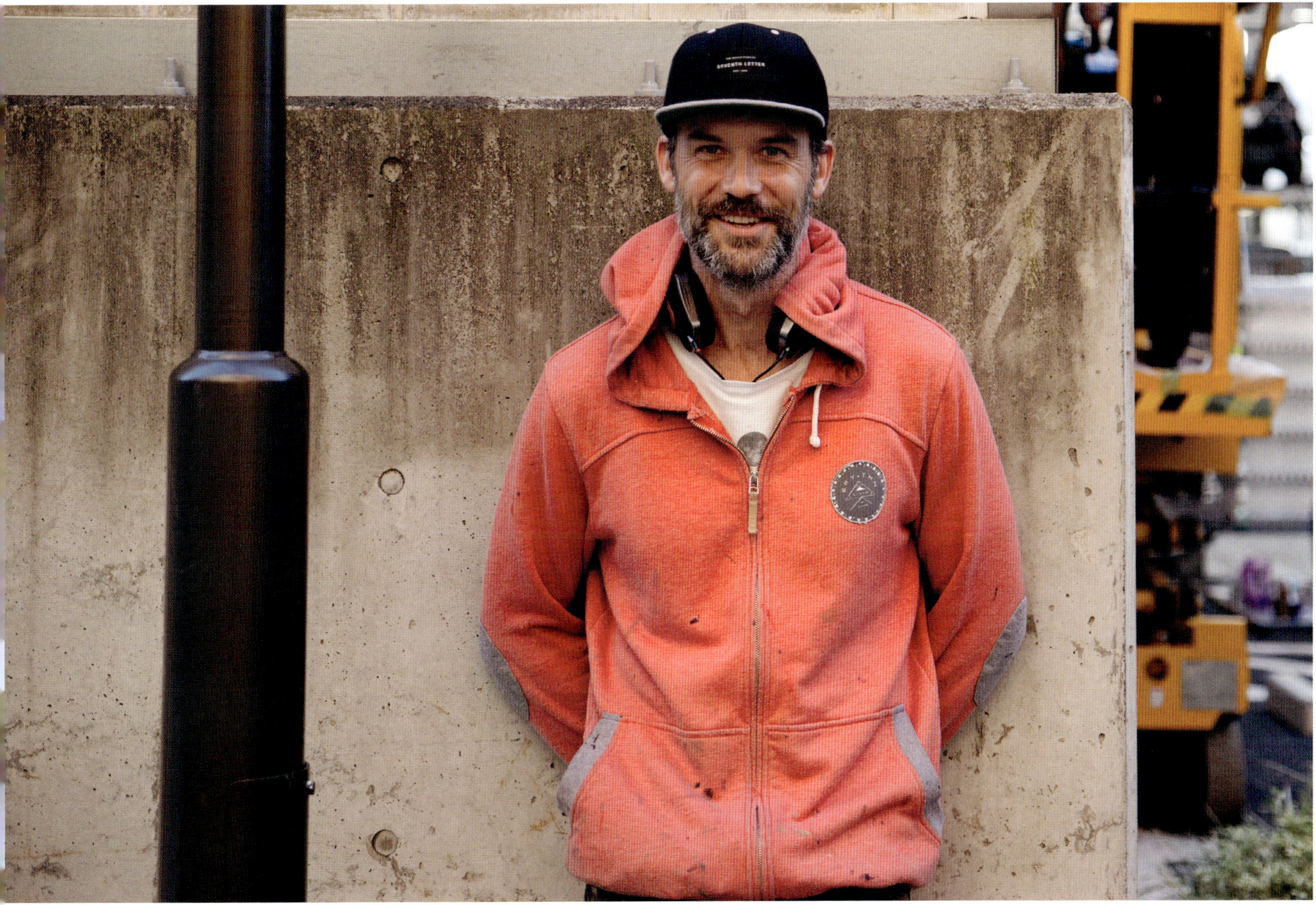

Case Maclaim

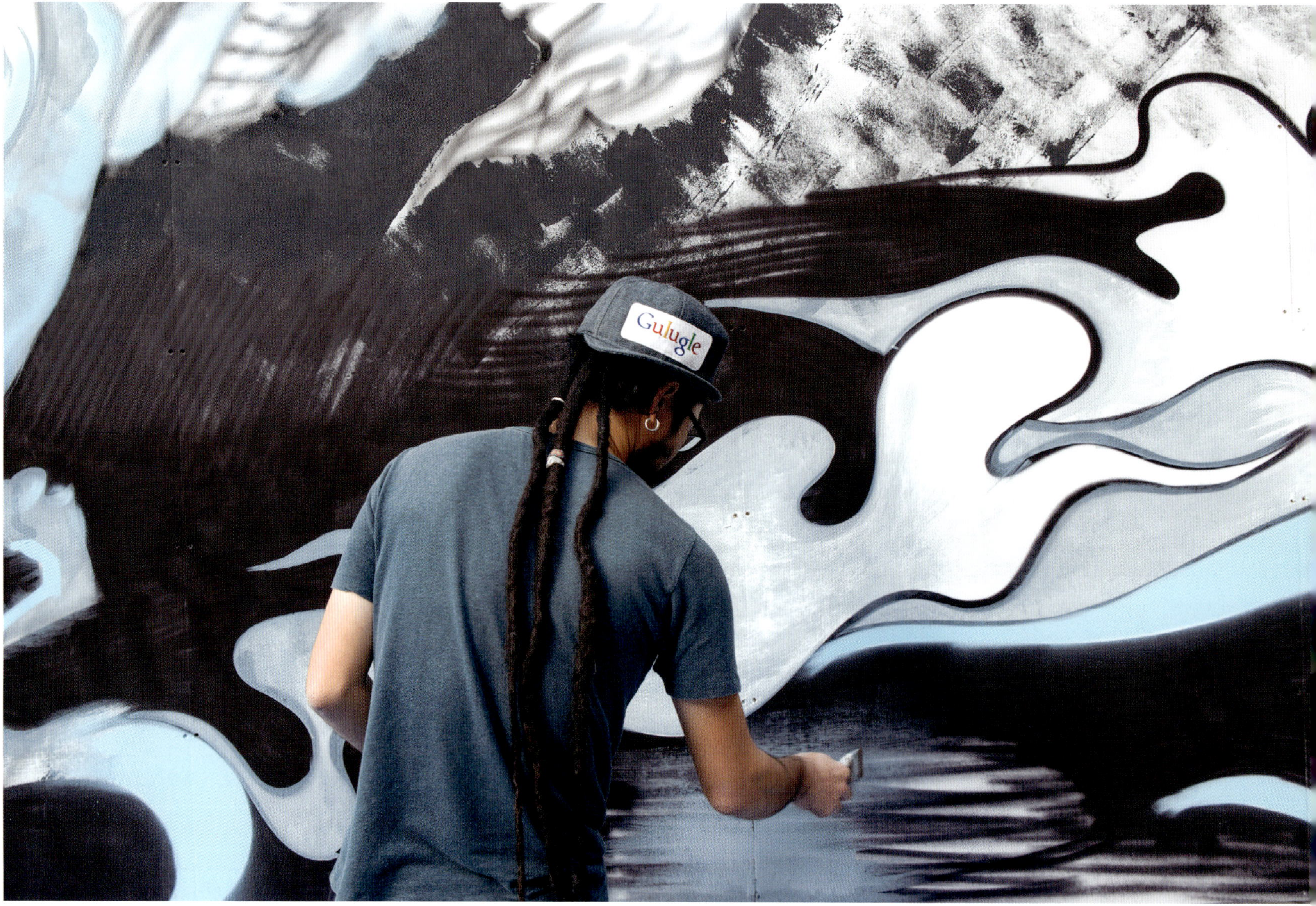

Mon

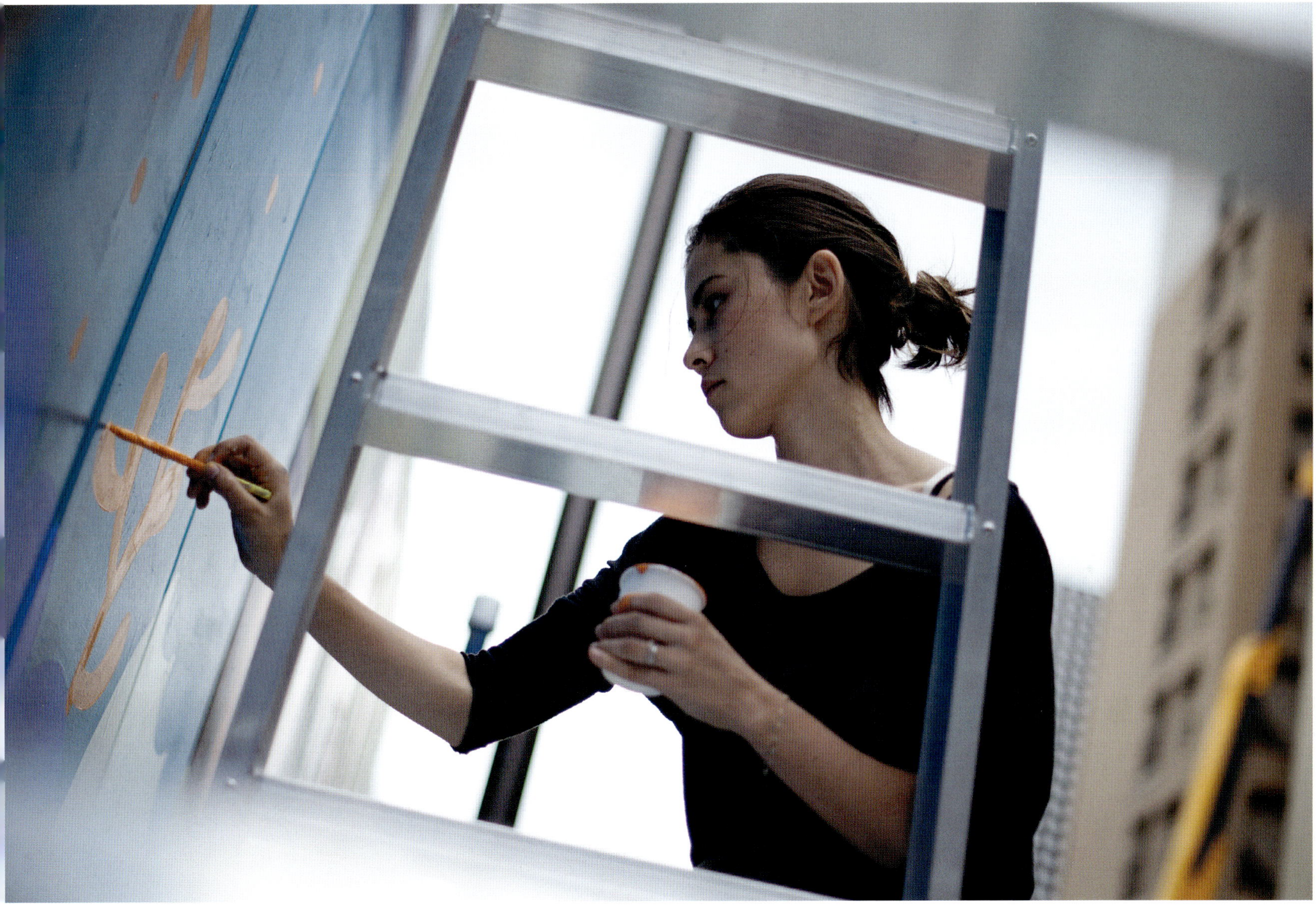

Frankie Cihi

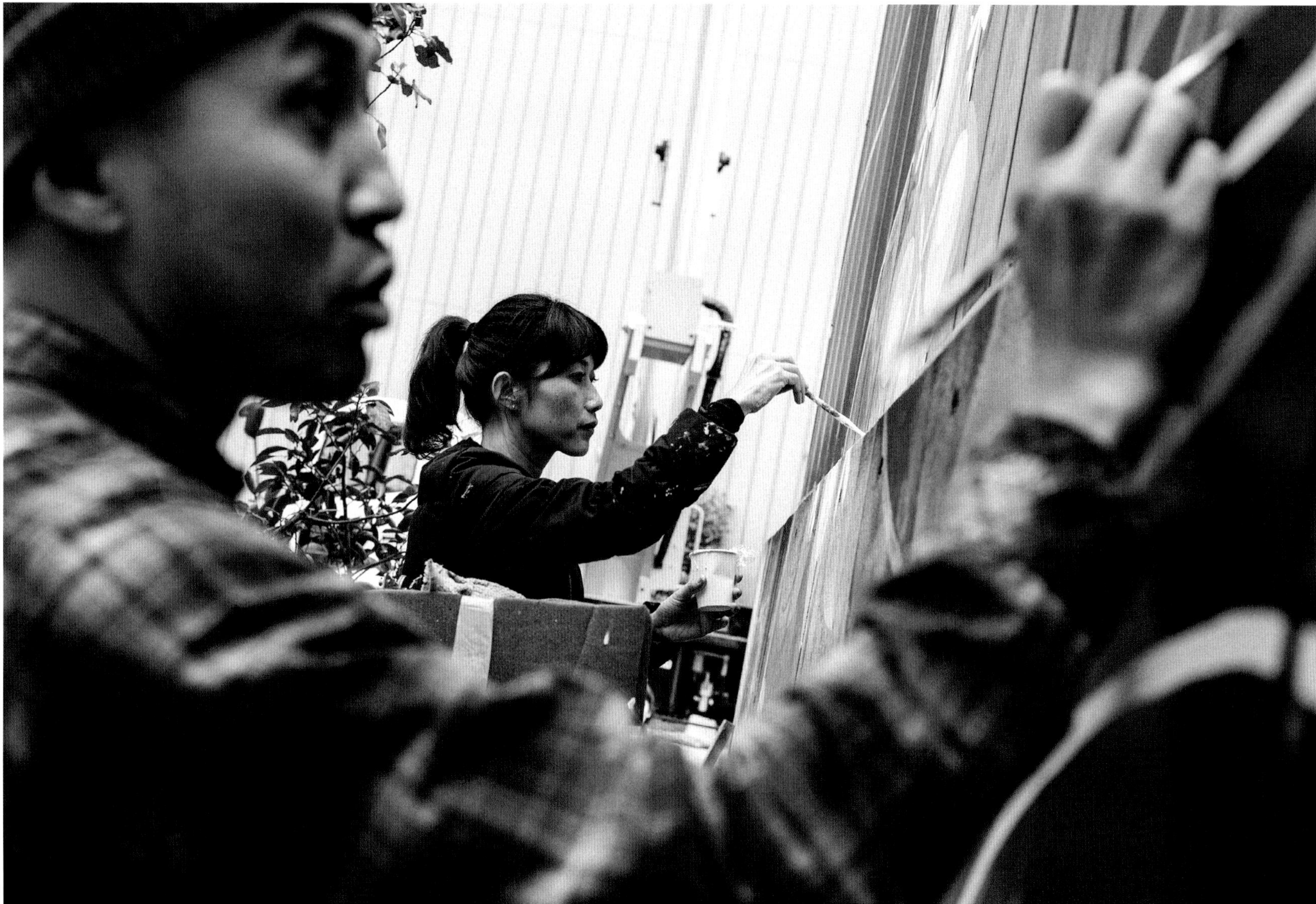

Kami & Sasu (Hitotzuki)

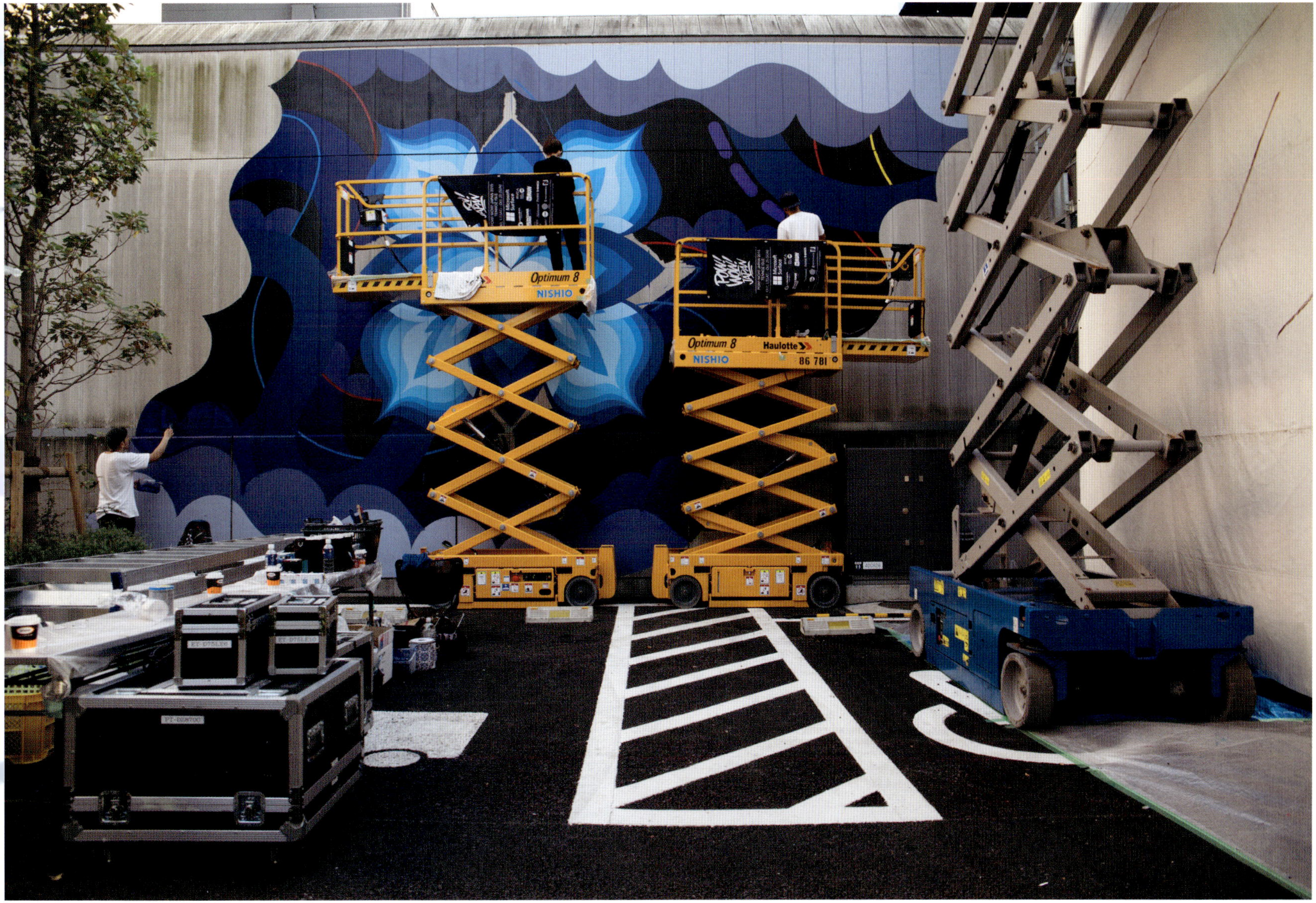

Kami & Sasu (Hitotzuki)

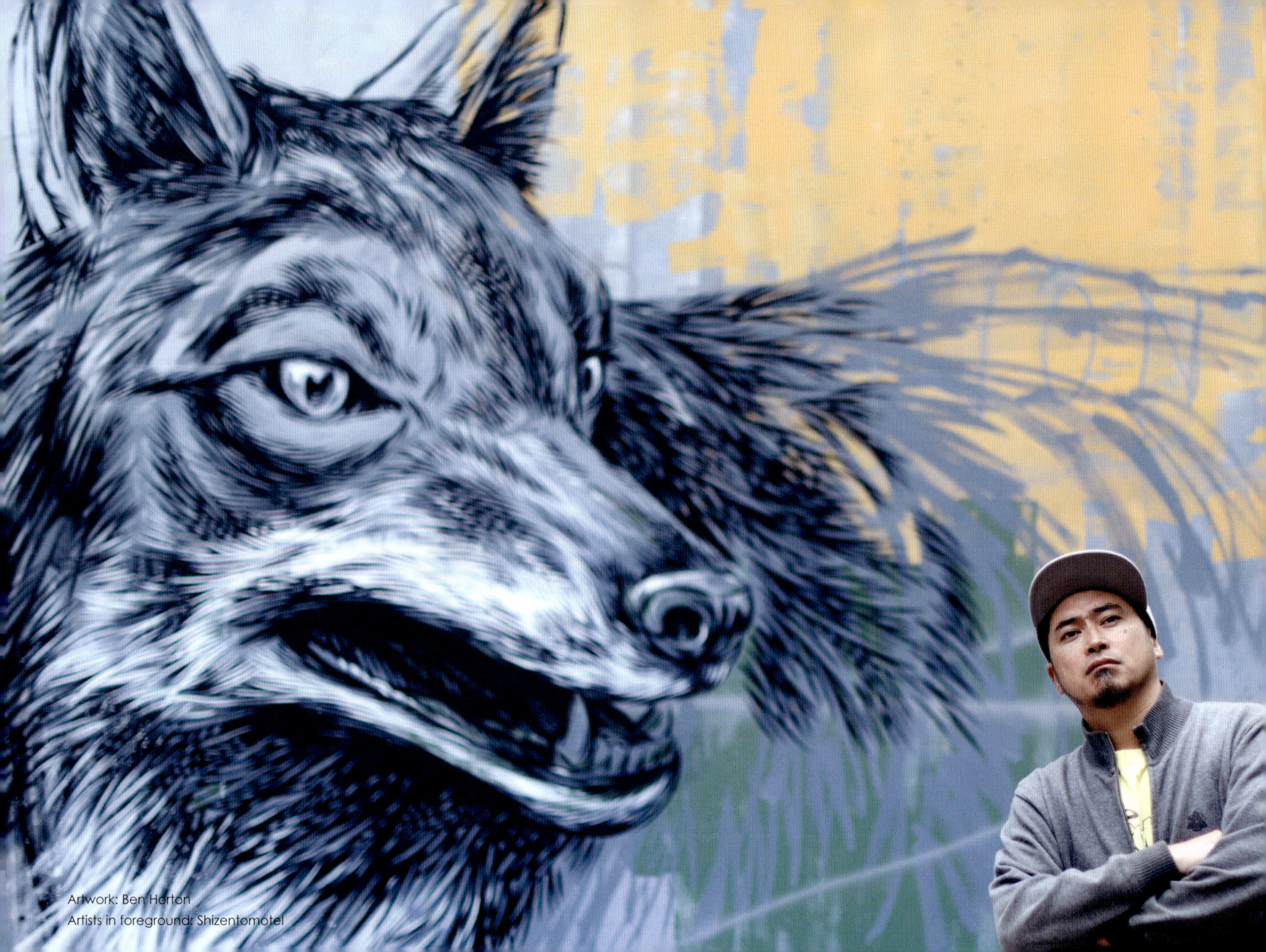

Artwork: Ben Horton
Artists in foreground: Shizentomotel

Tokyo by night is like no other place on the planet and offers an endless menu of clubs, bars, restaurants, karaoke bars, live music, and themed experiences of every kind. Whether in a skyscraper with seven floors of entertainment, or a hidden snack bar down an unmarked street, all offer an authentic and unforgettable time. Shibuya Crossing, famous for its all-way intersection, extends from one of the busiest train stations in Tokyo. Like most large stations in the city, a network of all-night shopping, drinking, and dancing creep below and above ground. Popular club nights feature neon-lit live painting accompanied by a DJ or performer. Similarly, galleries tucked away atop department stores, or behind popular clothing shops offer street artists and painters a venue to exhibit their work to a captive audience.

Similar to some Scandinavian countries, Japan shifted from traditional styles to a simpler, functional, more democratic sense of design in the twentieth century. Post WWII Japan was a fertile environment for redefining Japanese modernity. The use of characters to identify brands and market products or services became ubiquitous and is now reflected in the city's street art. Popular cartoon and anime characters offer a huge amount of distraction and escape for young and old alike and are often featured in the work of fine artists like Takahashi Murakami. Yoko Ono and Yayoi Kusama utilize this polished, clean style, rejecting the archaic symbolism of classic Japan while simultaneously coining a new Japanese individuality.

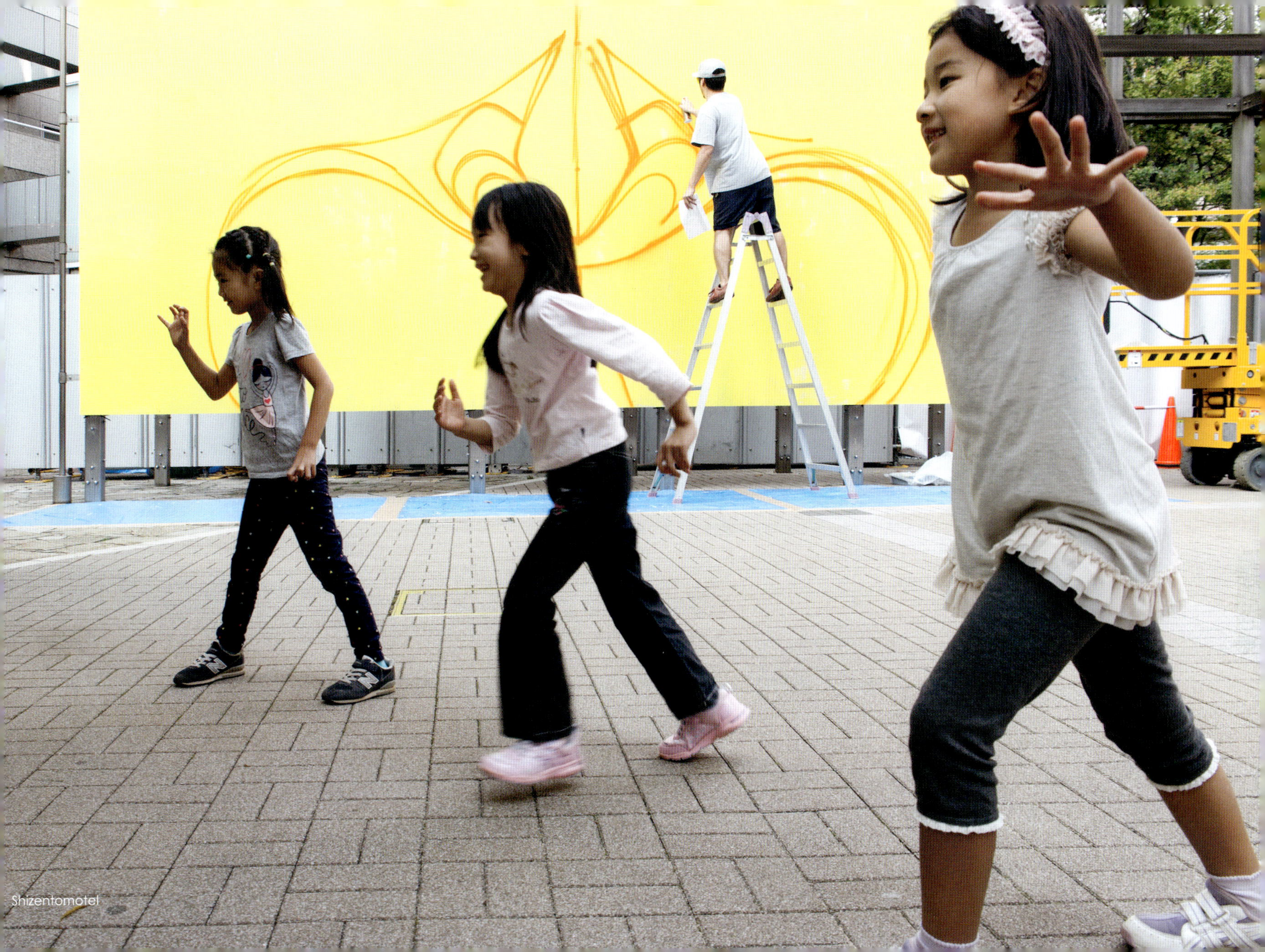

Shizentomotel

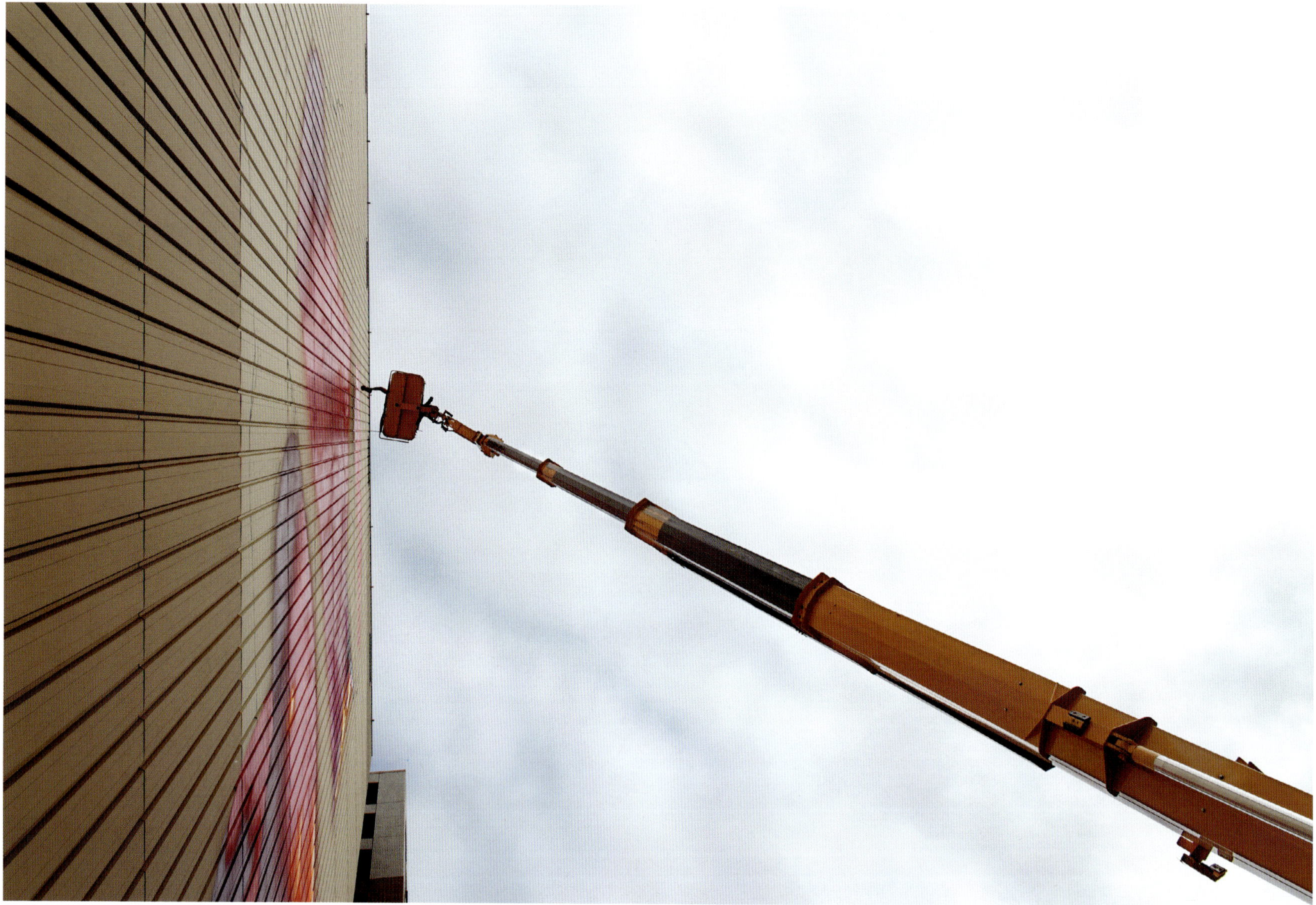
Case Maclaim

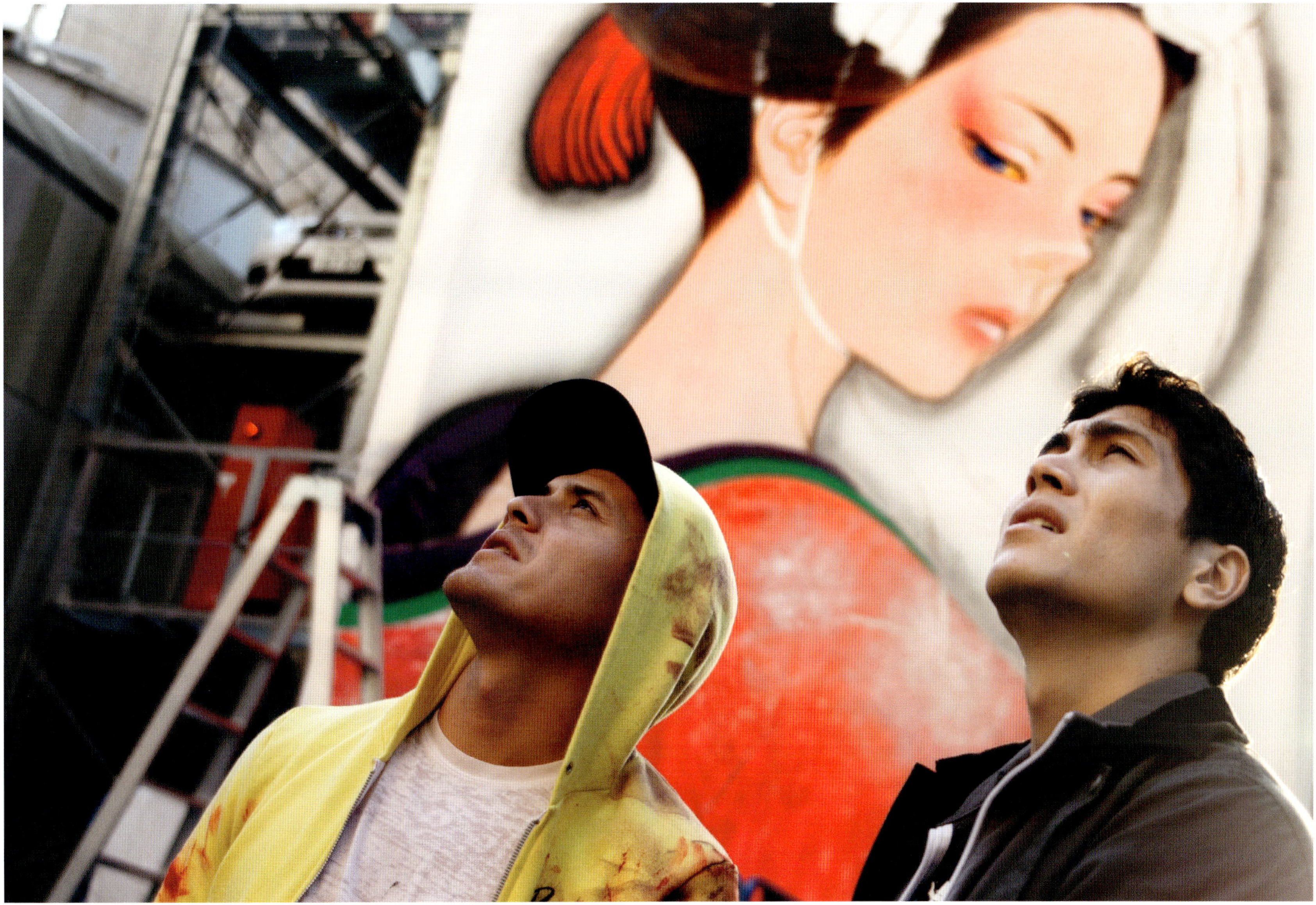

Kamea Hadar & Barr Hadar

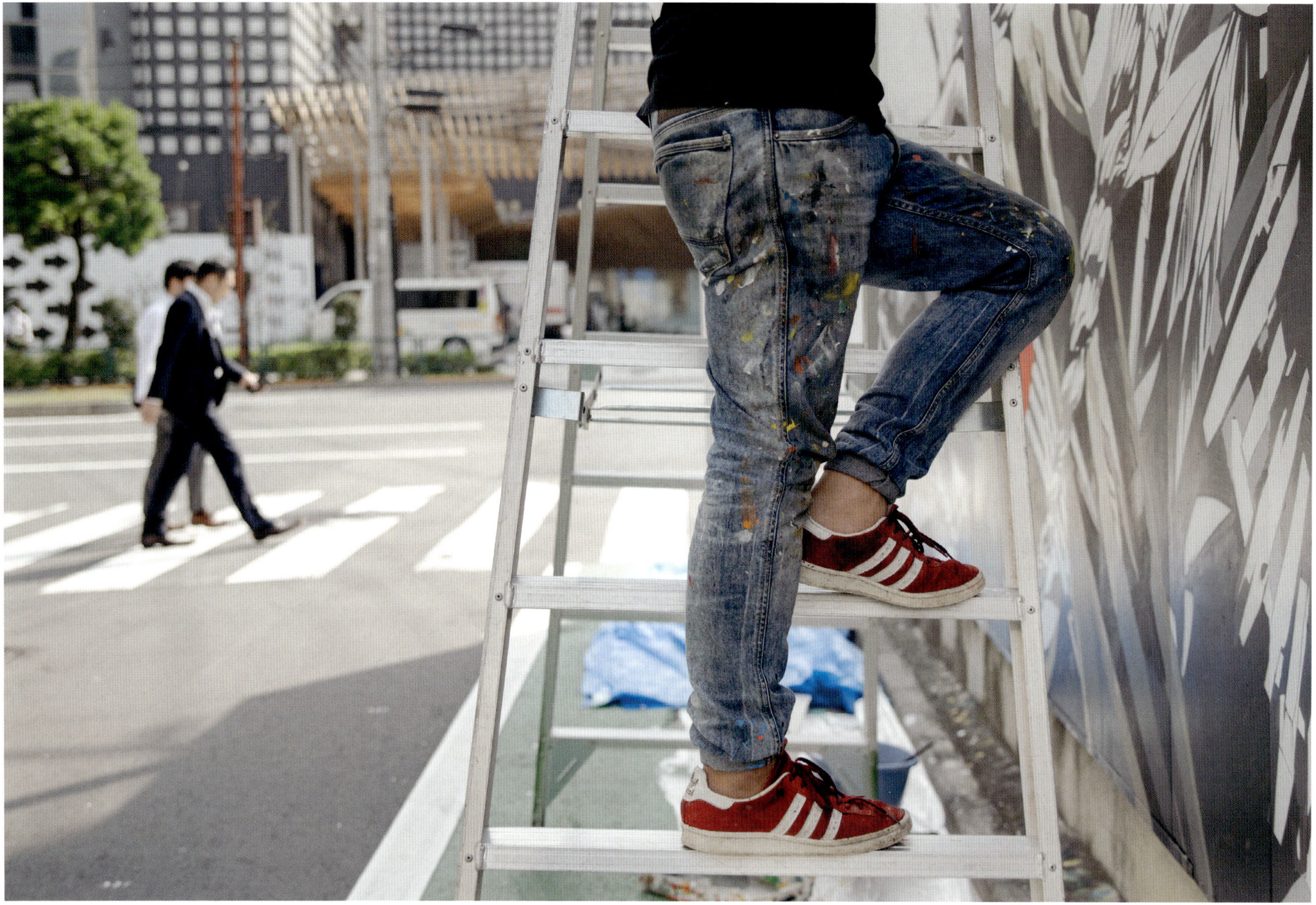

Dragon76

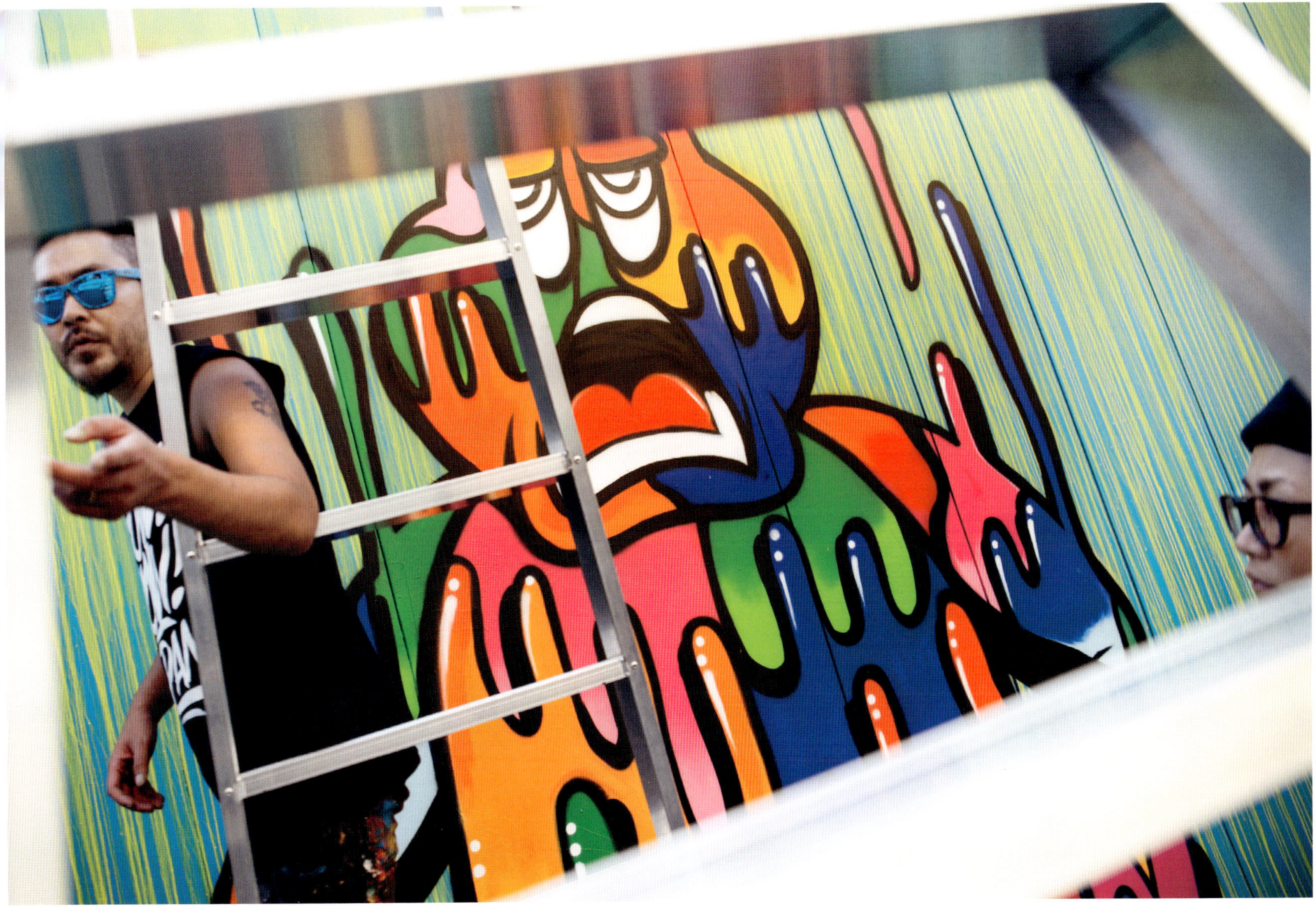

Jay Shogo

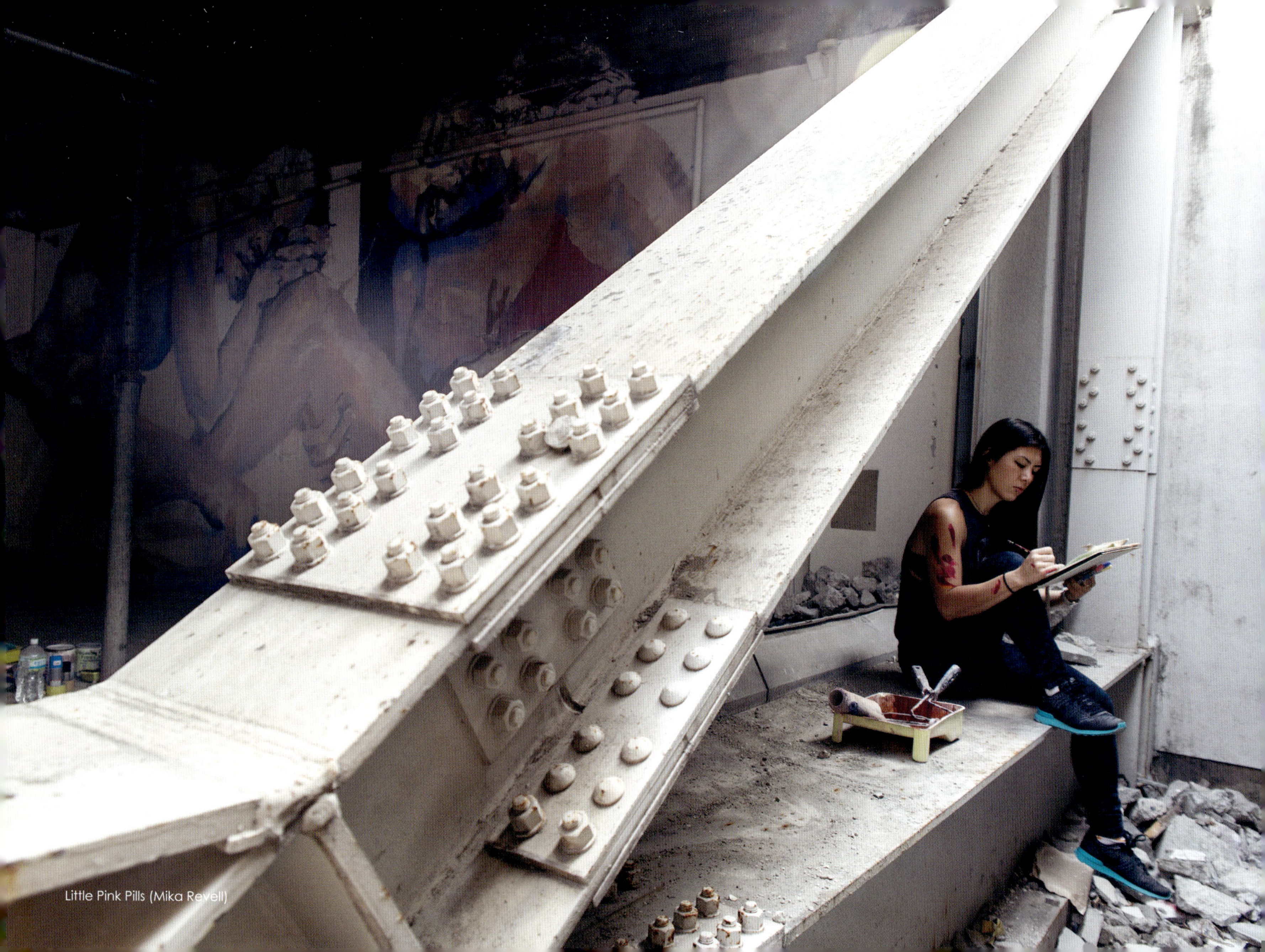

Little Pink Pills (Mika Revell)

After the 1950s, Japan's economy began to flourish. Industries like electronics, car manufacturing, and textiles made Japan the third wealthiest country in the world, despite being one of the smallest. Because of this Japan and its culture also blossomed. Even though Japan's industrial and international reputation changed rapidly, a strong desire to uphold the essence of this great civilization remained. The intrinsic cultural qualities that inform concepts of balance and beauty are still of pinnacle importance. In a world that constantly demands competition and progress, Tokyo finds space beneath the surface to uphold tradition and honor its foundations.

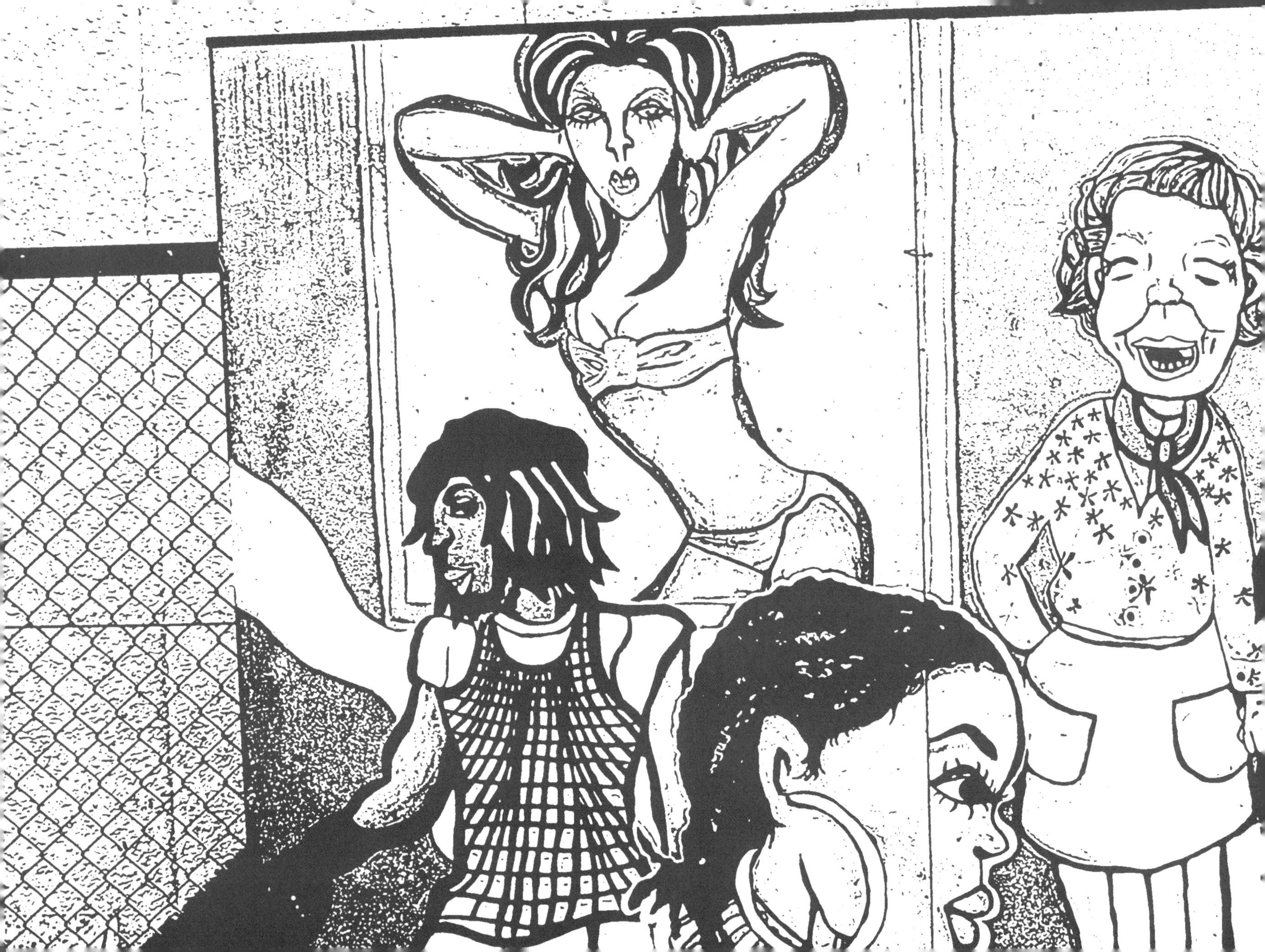

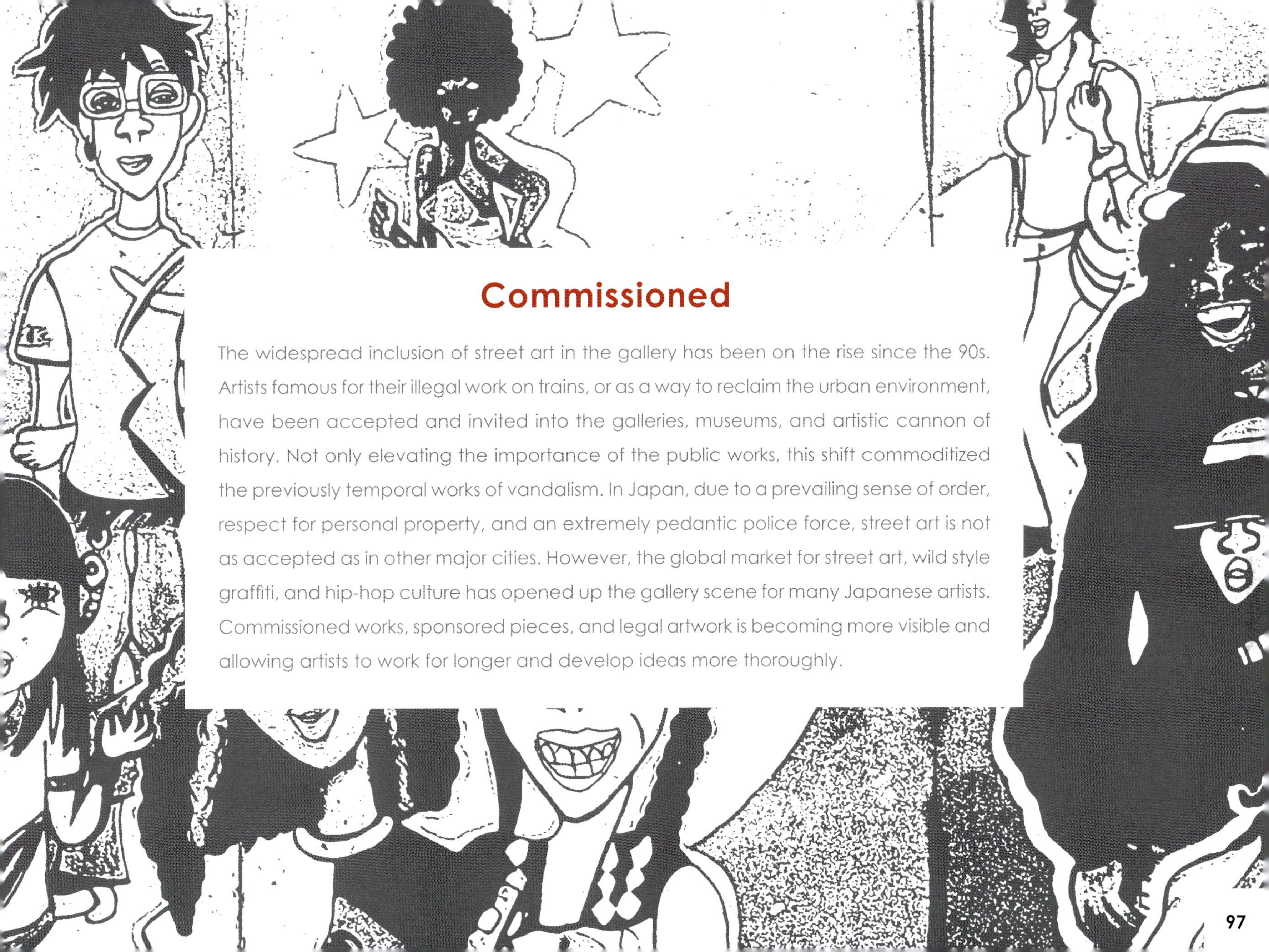

Commissioned

The widespread inclusion of street art in the gallery has been on the rise since the 90s. Artists famous for their illegal work on trains, or as a way to reclaim the urban environment, have been accepted and invited into the galleries, museums, and artistic cannon of history. Not only elevating the importance of the public works, this shift commoditized the previously temporal works of vandalism. In Japan, due to a prevailing sense of order, respect for personal property, and an extremely pedantic police force, street art is not as accepted as in other major cities. However, the global market for street art, wild style graffiti, and hip-hop culture has opened up the gallery scene for many Japanese artists. Commissioned works, sponsored pieces, and legal artwork is becoming more visible and allowing artists to work for longer and develop ideas more thoroughly.

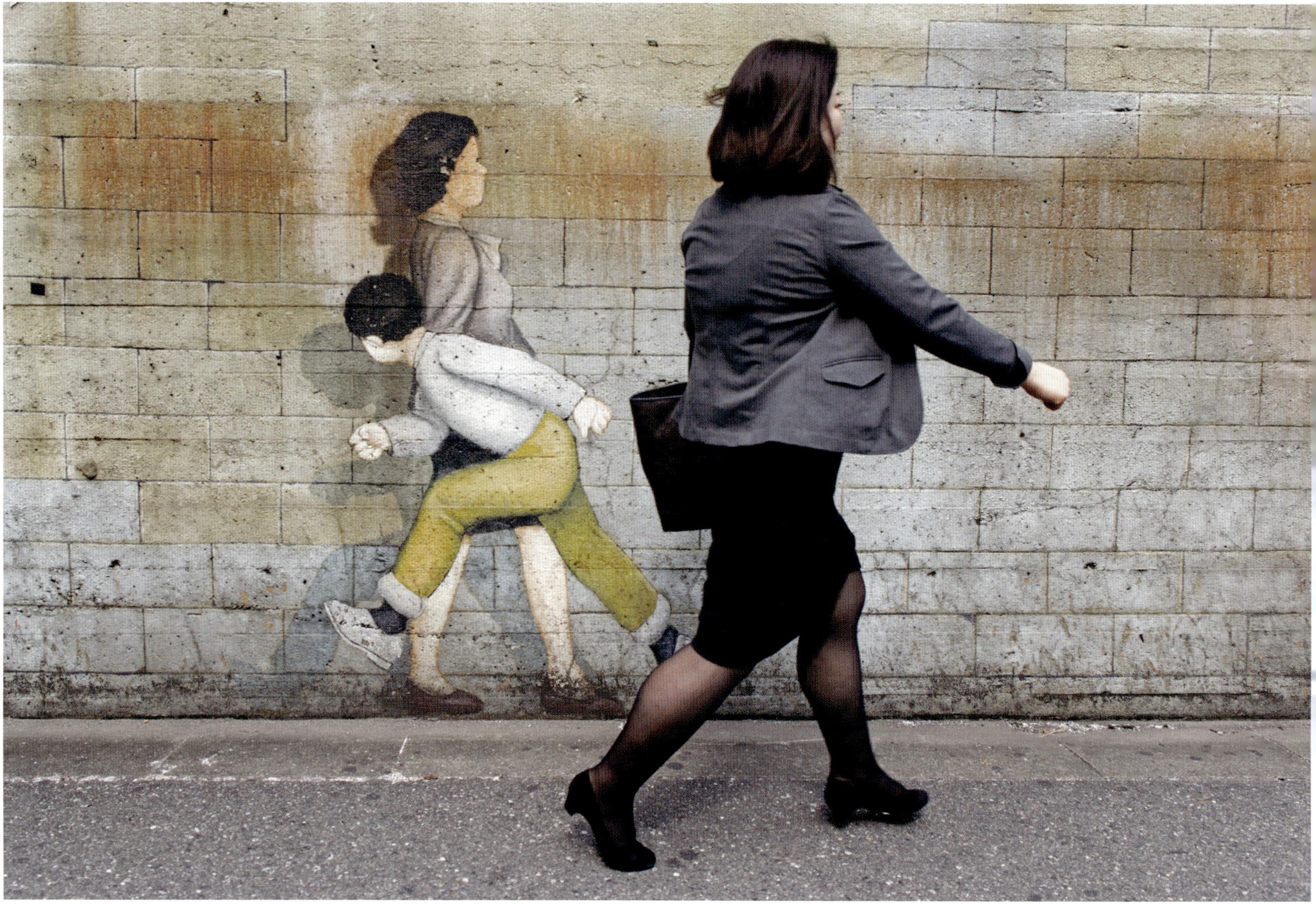

Location: Ryogoku

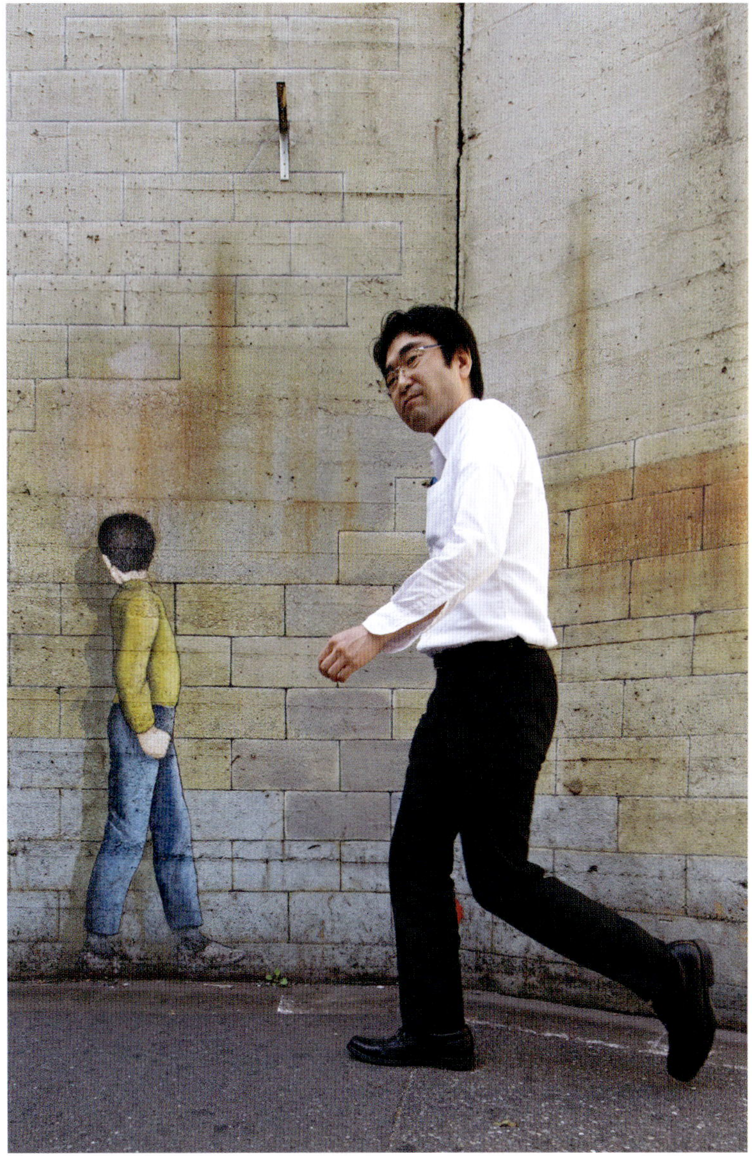

Location: Ryogoku

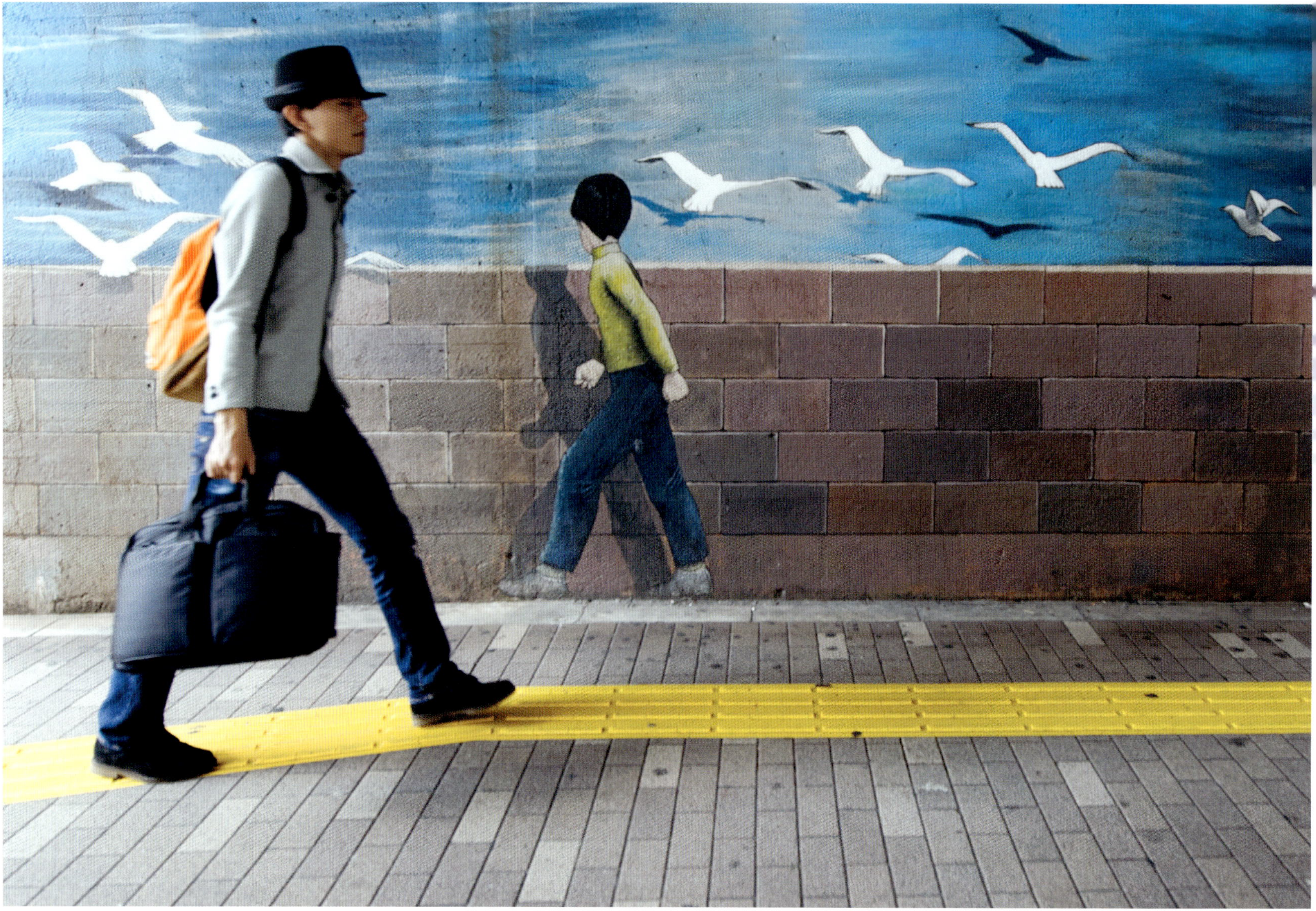

Location: Ryogoku

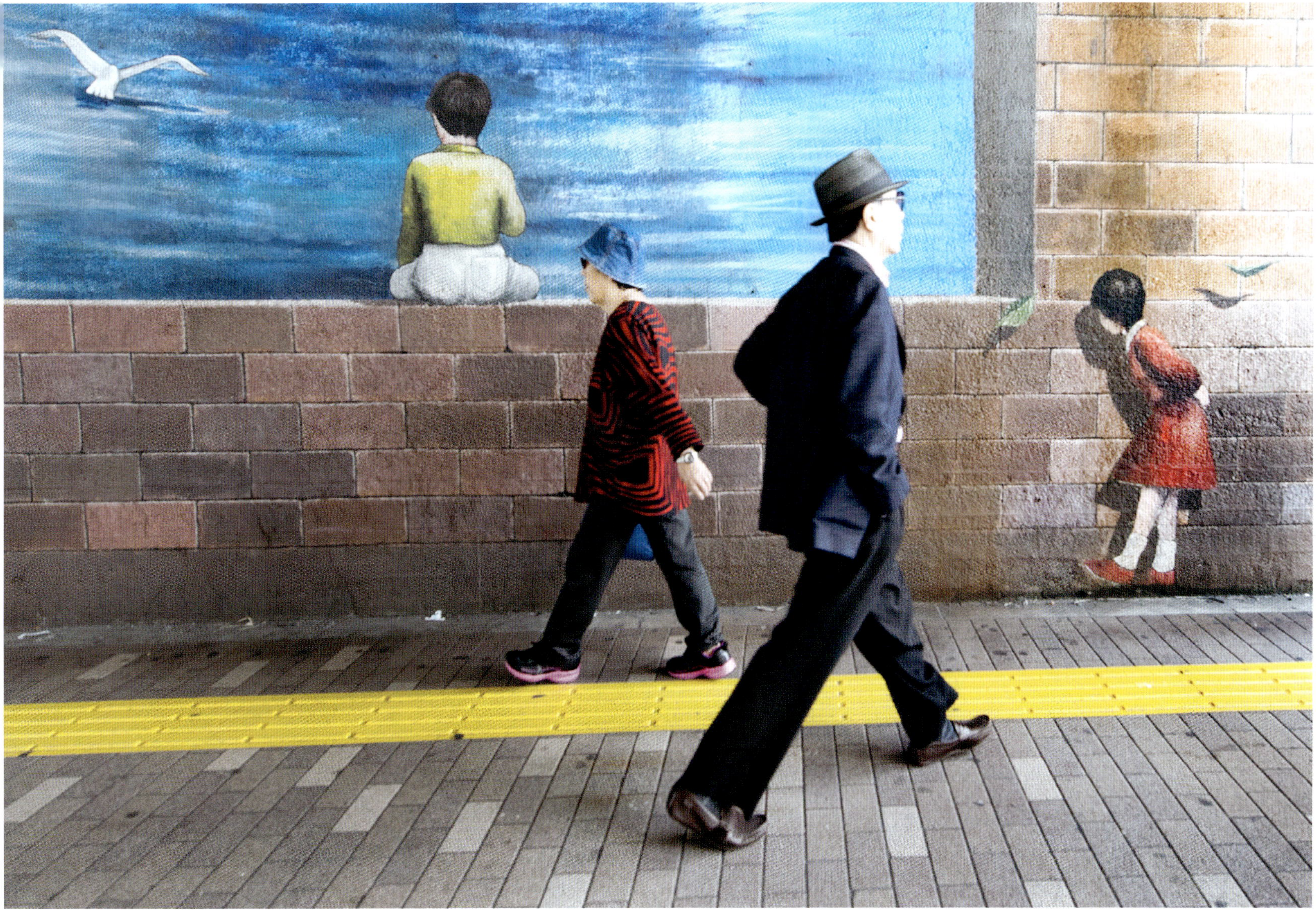

Location: Ryogoku

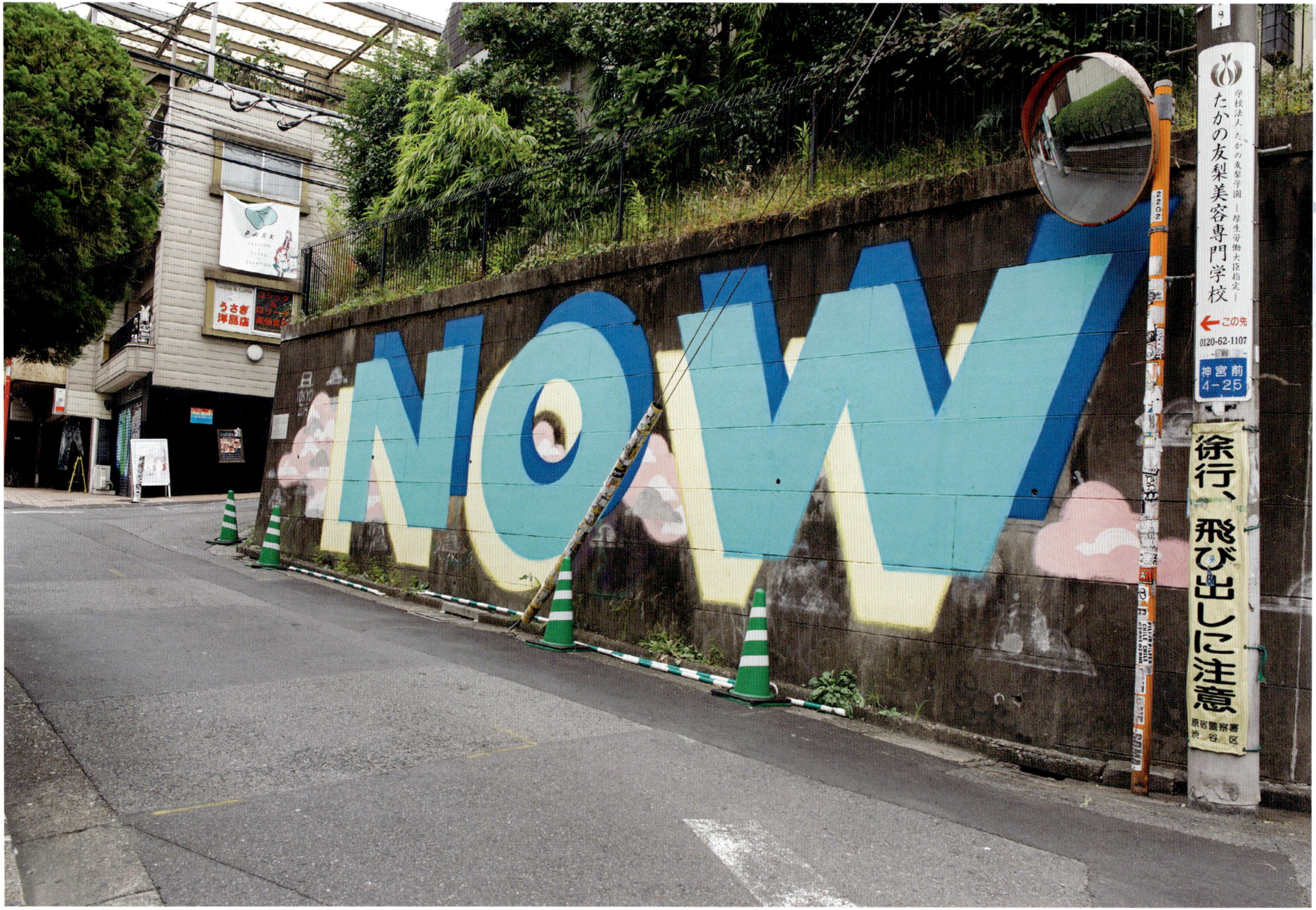

Stephen Powers

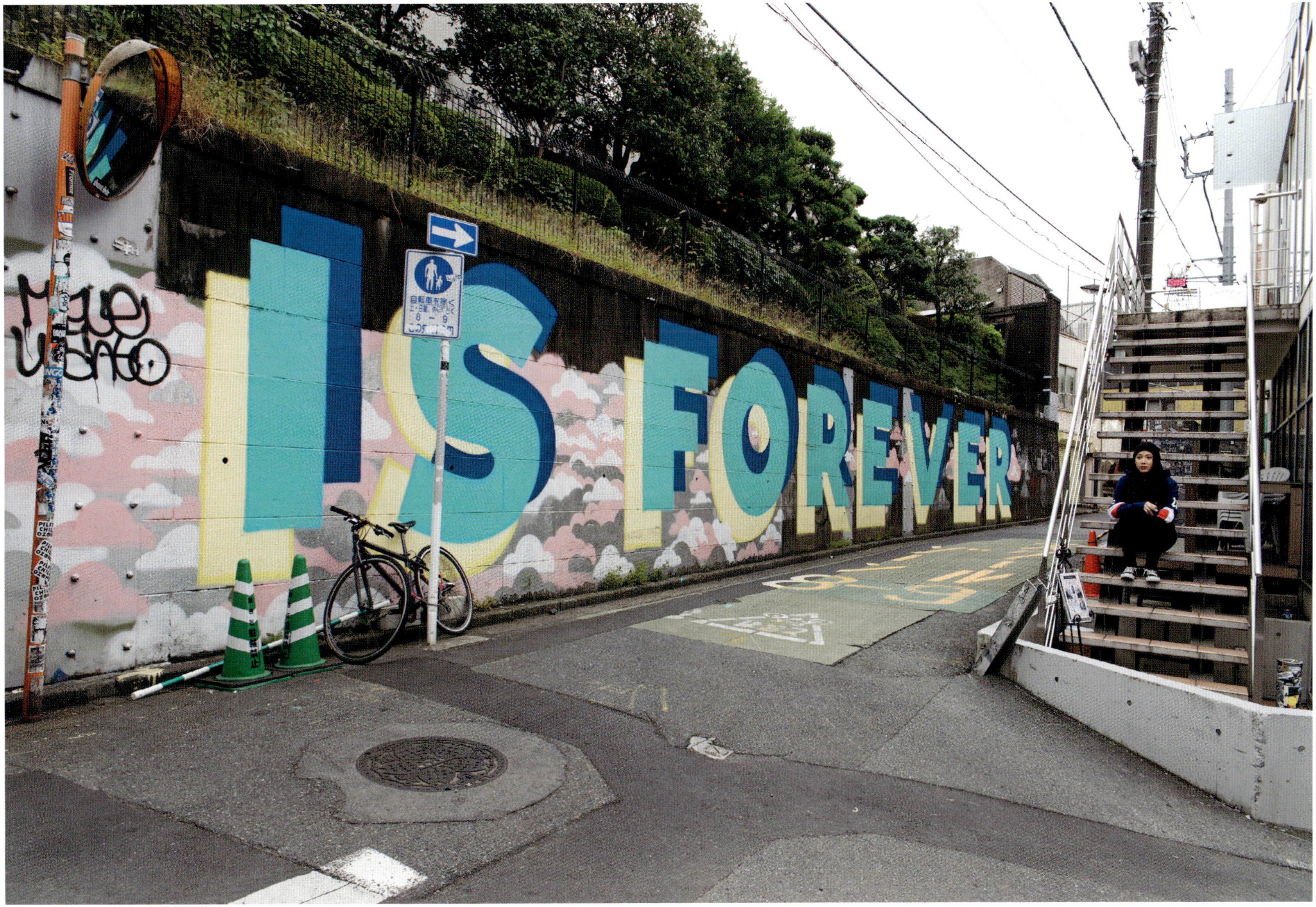

Stephen Powers

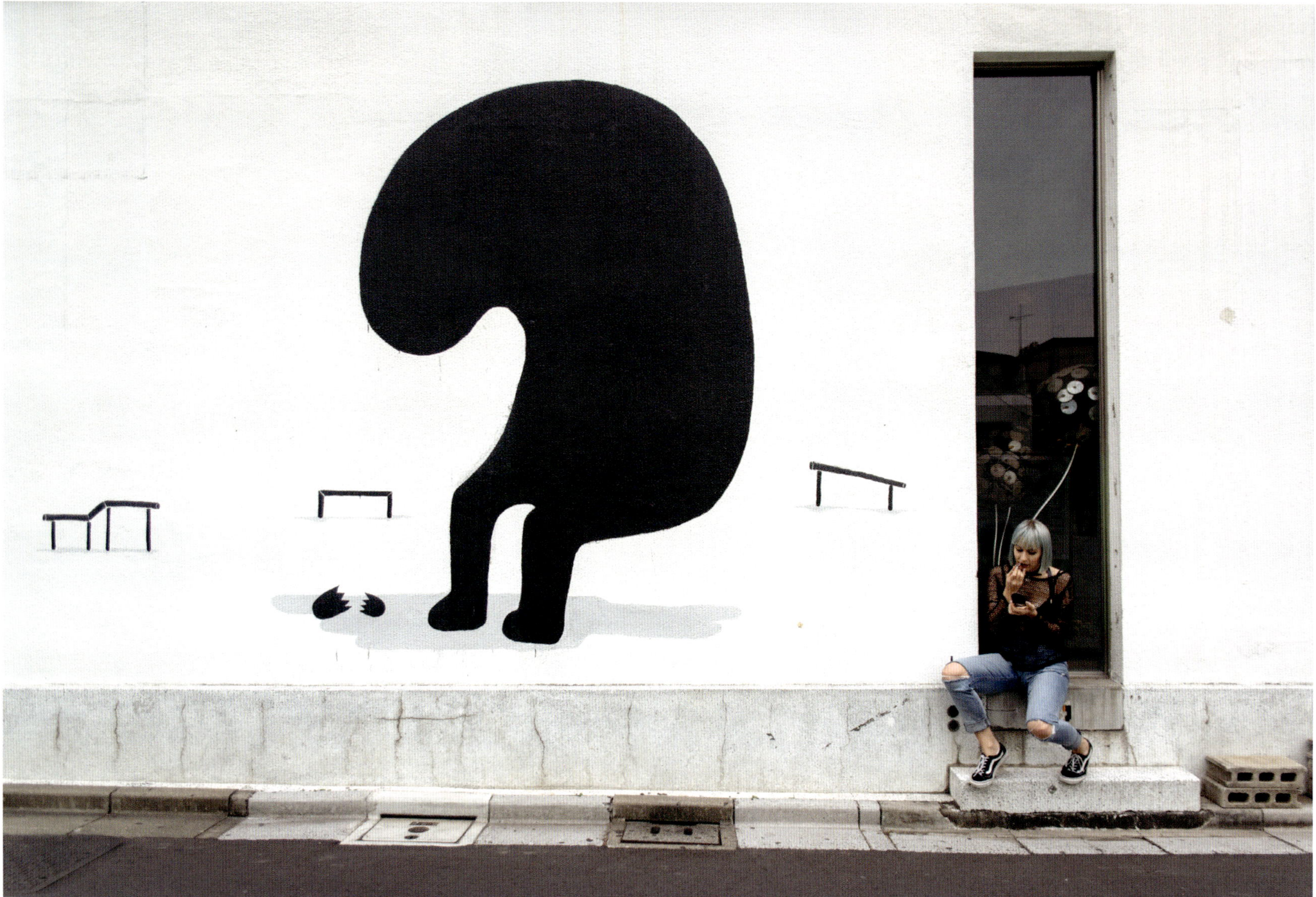

Ly

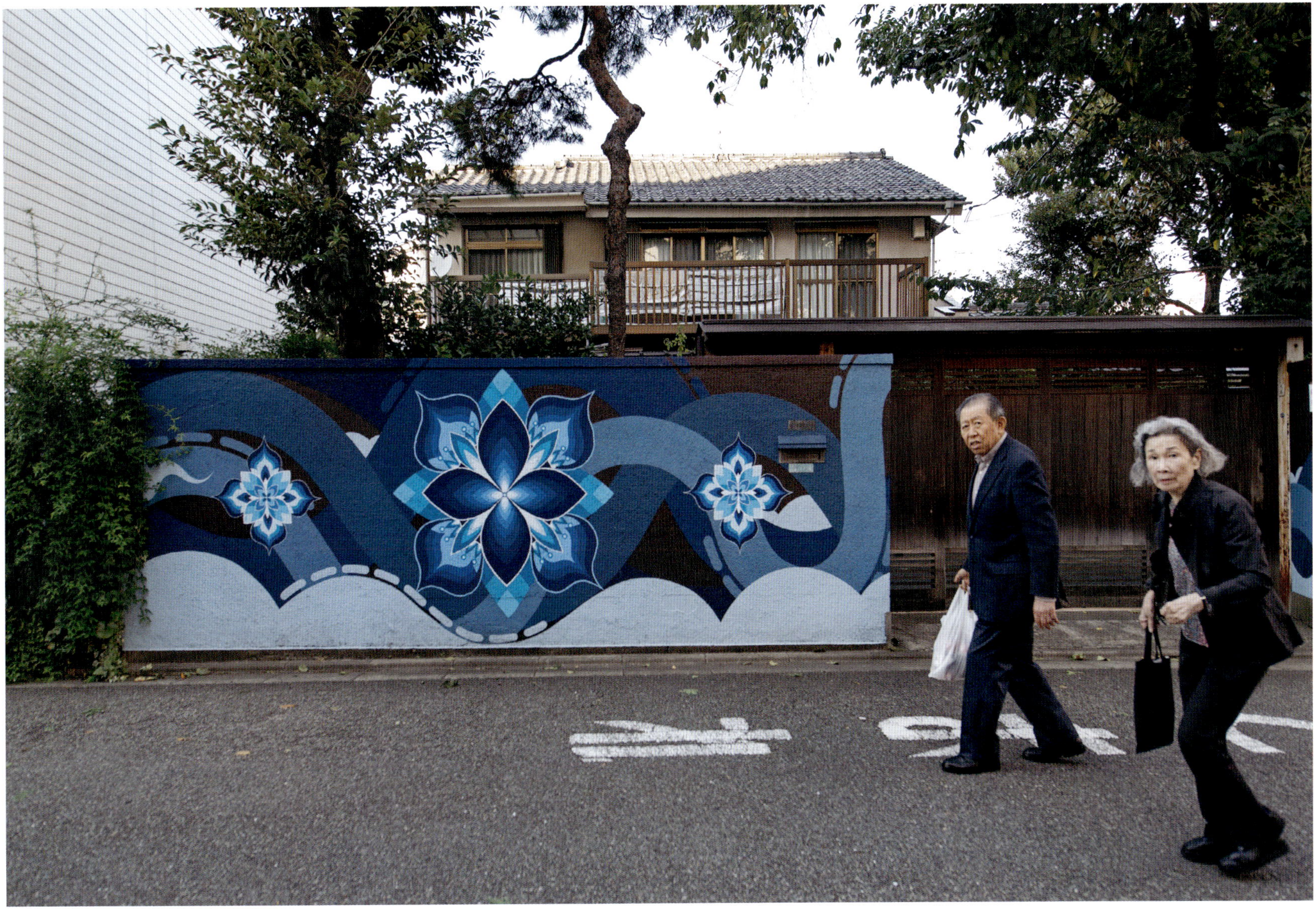

Hitotzuki

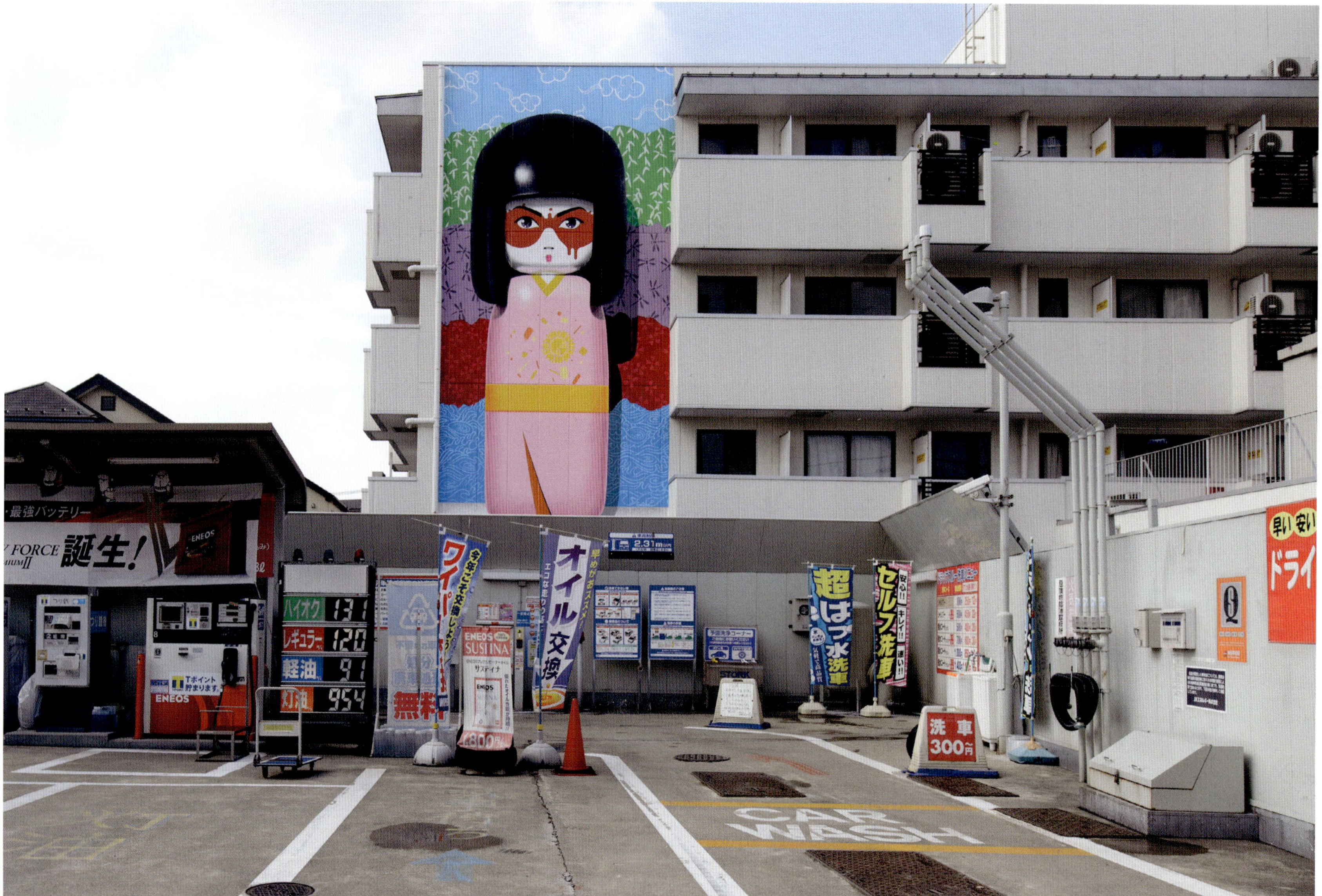
最強バッテリー
誕生!
ENEOS
ハイオク 131
レギュラー 120
軽油 91
灯油 954
Tポイント貯まります。
オイル交換
早めがおススメ!
ENEOS SUSTINA
超はっ水洗車
セルフ洗車
安心!! キレイ!! 速い!!
洗車 300円~
早い 安い
ドライ
CAR WASH

Fin DAC

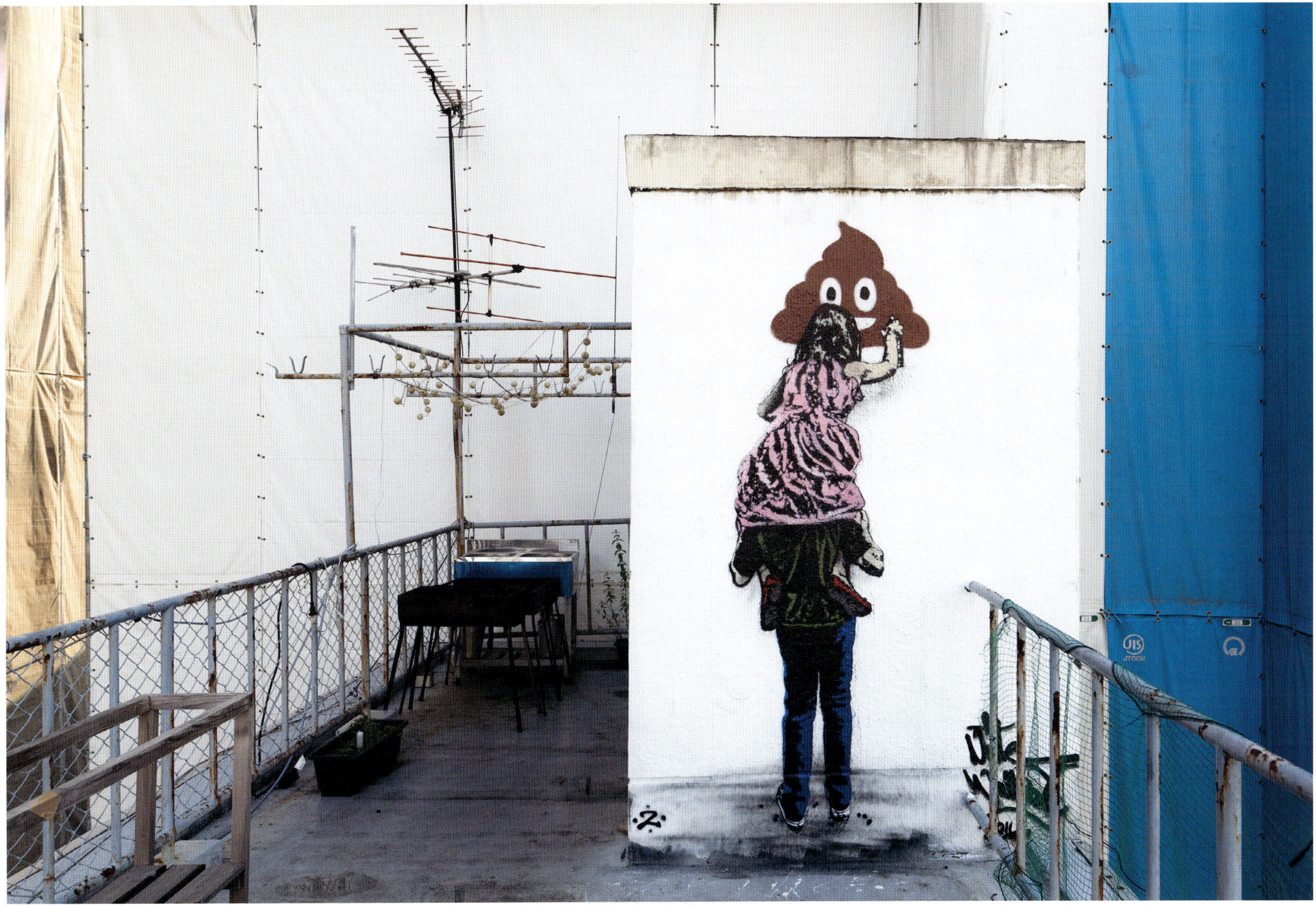

Nick Walker

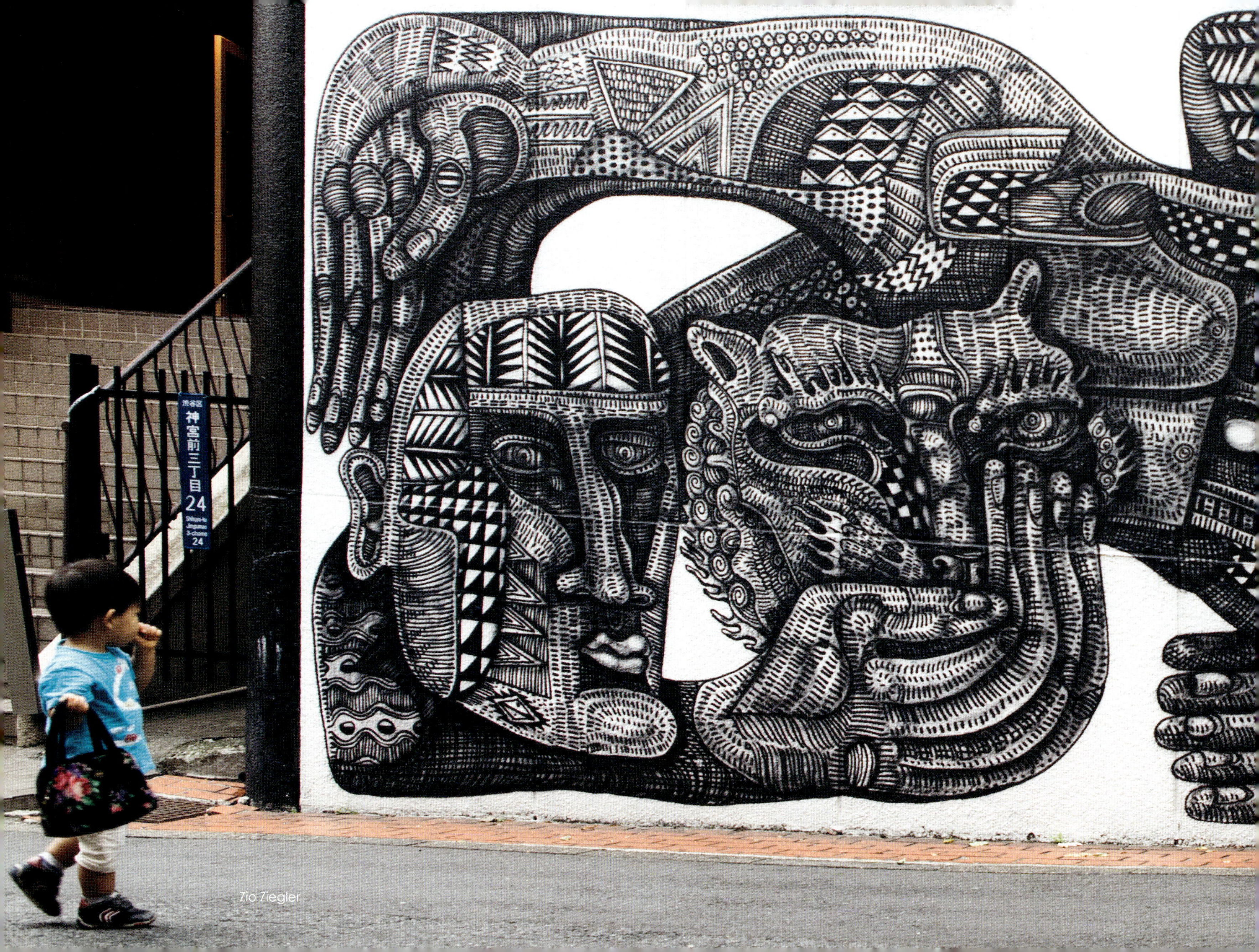

Zio Ziegler

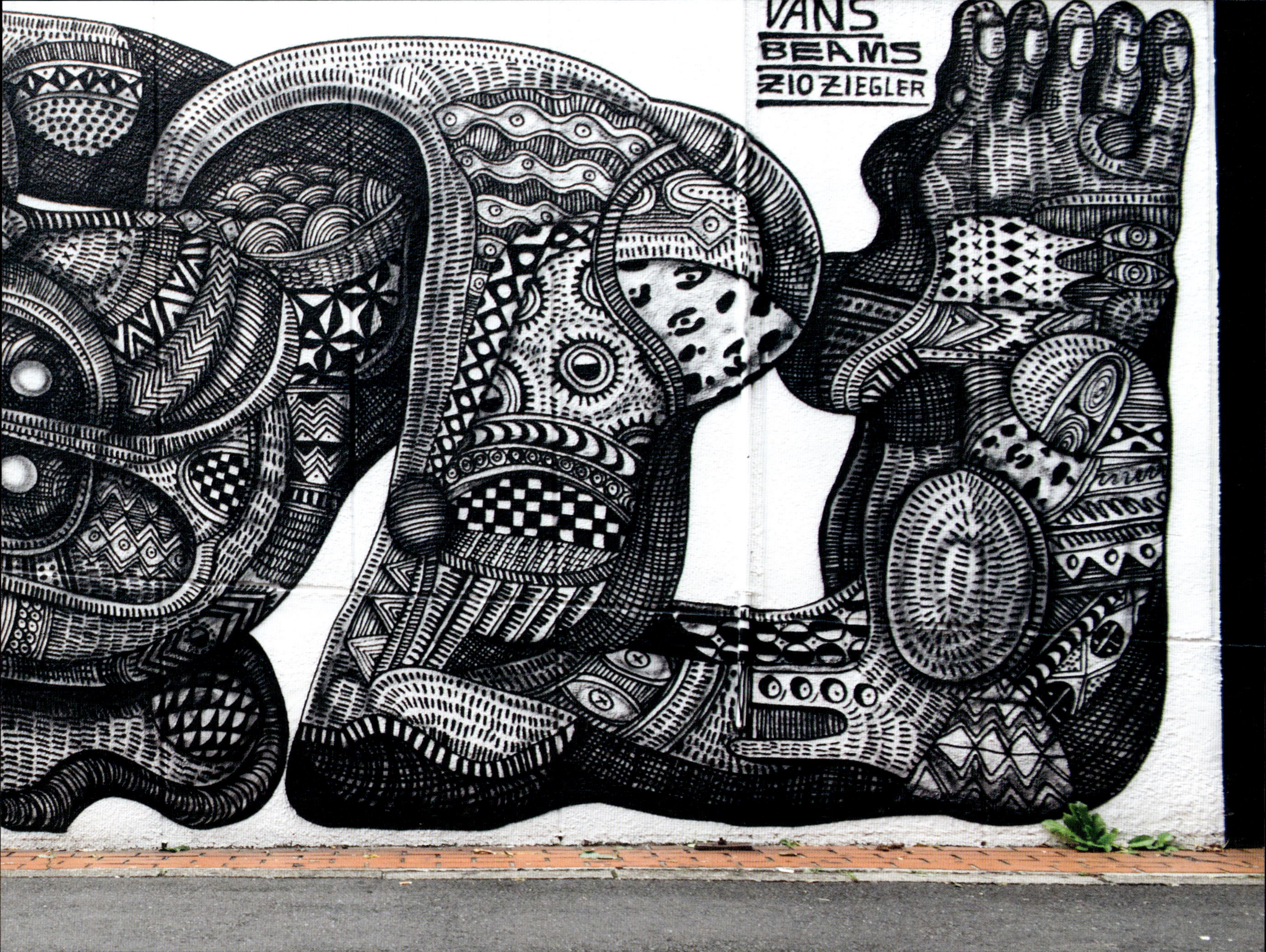
VANS
BEAMS
ZIO ZIEGLER

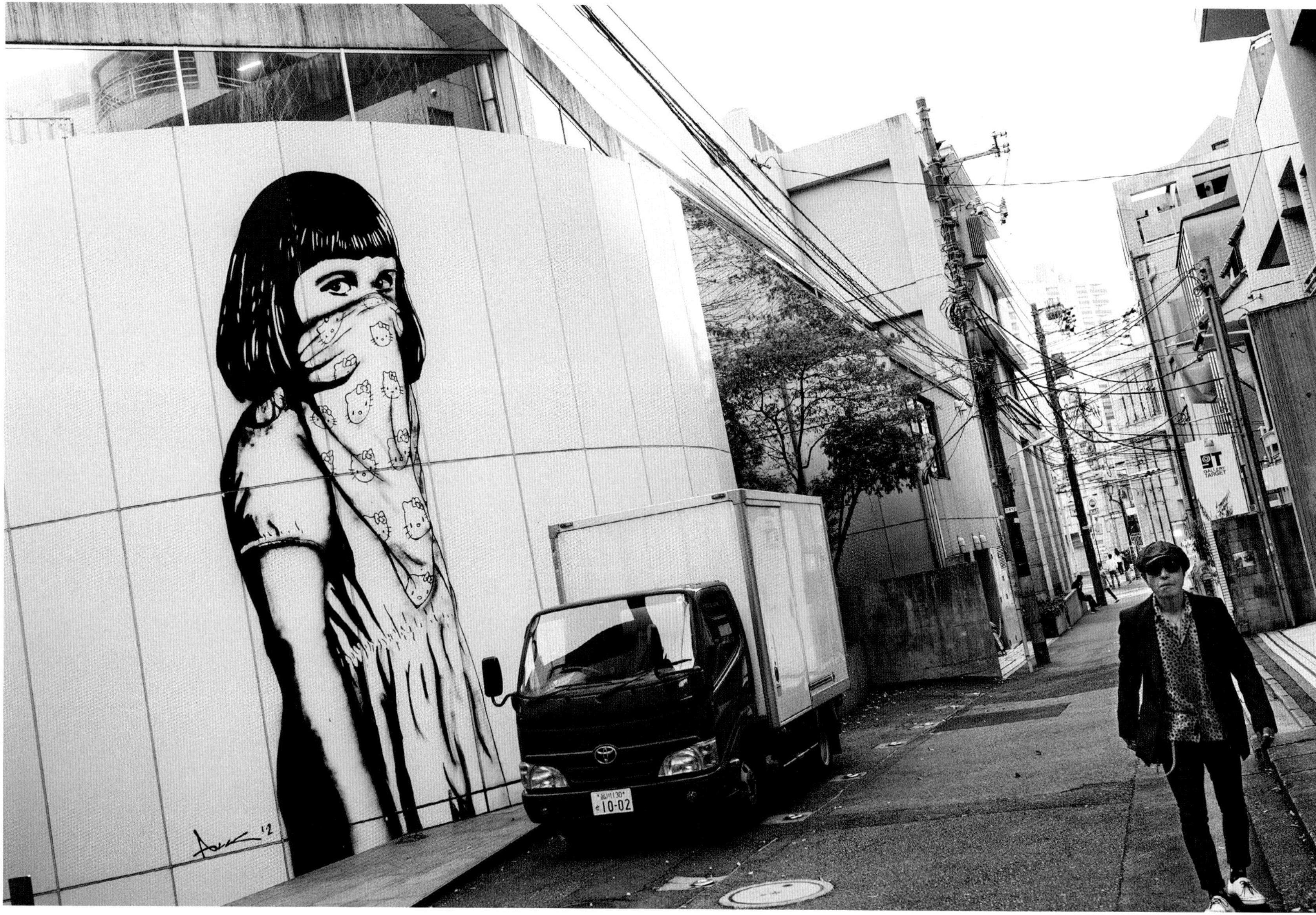

Dolk

Today in Tokyo more businesses and creative enterprises are commissioning murals and interior accents that incorporate traditional style graffiti techniques. The up-market department store Isetan even held a graffiti art show on its top floor this year, incorporating the medium into its cannon of priceless antique and classical works. The spread of street art into the mainstream continues to creep into Japanese visual culture, while also elevating its status in the art world. Social media and peer sharing have become one of the most beneficial forms of advertising, and what better way to prove you are progressive than through art and a little bit of playful controversy?

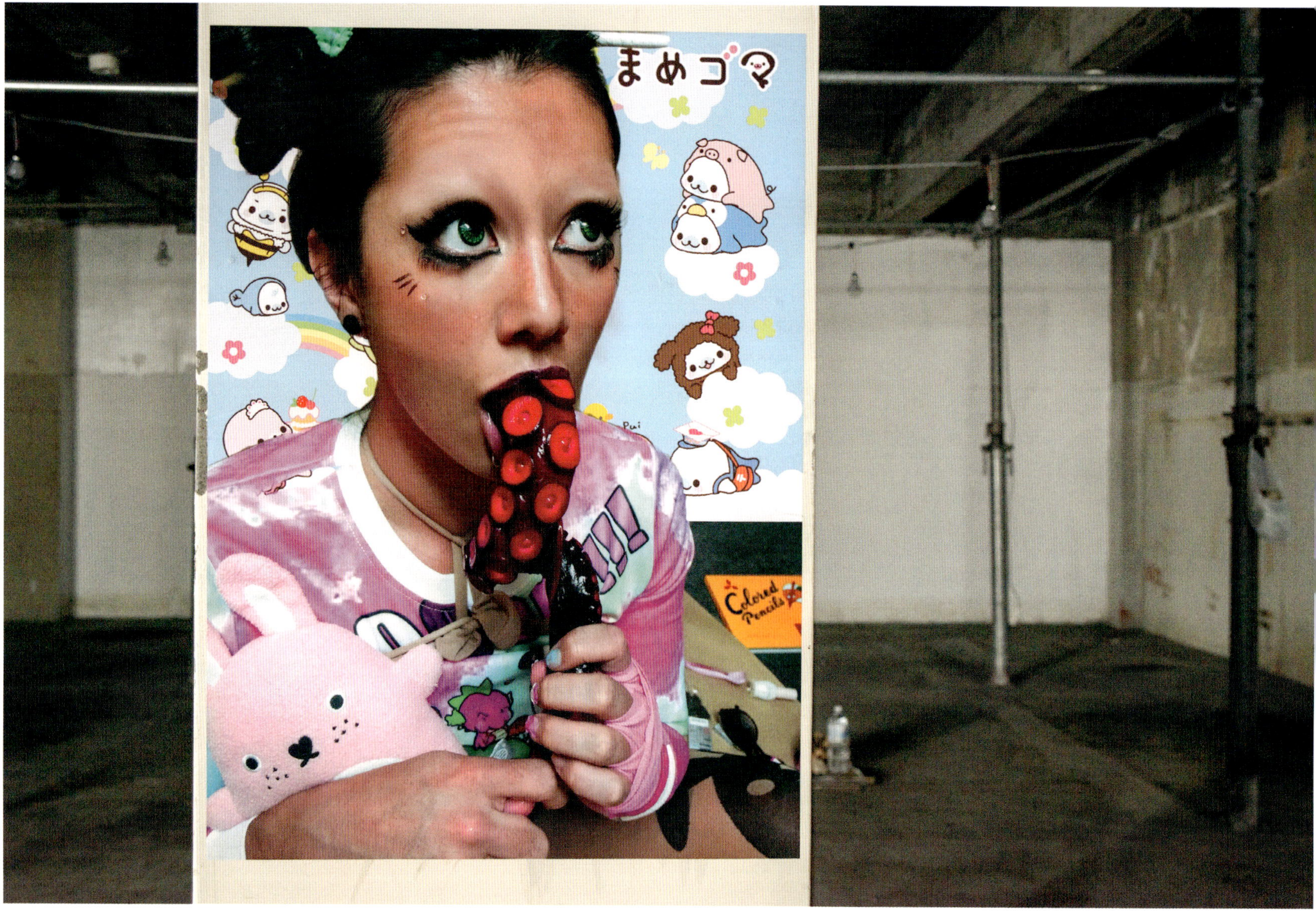

Little Pink Pills (Mika Revell)

Perhaps as a means of engaging in the global art market and the ideas of creative discourse, Japan seems to be making efforts to incorporate new perspectives. However, there is a visible battle between old and new Japan—people who understand the need for reform versus those who are steadfast and bound to their traditions. Elements of Japanese design principles, balance, harmony, and simplicity, exist in these commissioned artworks alongside graffiti style fonts, dripping spray paint, and cartoonish eyes. A post-modern hybrid street art style, perhaps "post-graffiti," is emerging from the contradictory base of Japanese culture.

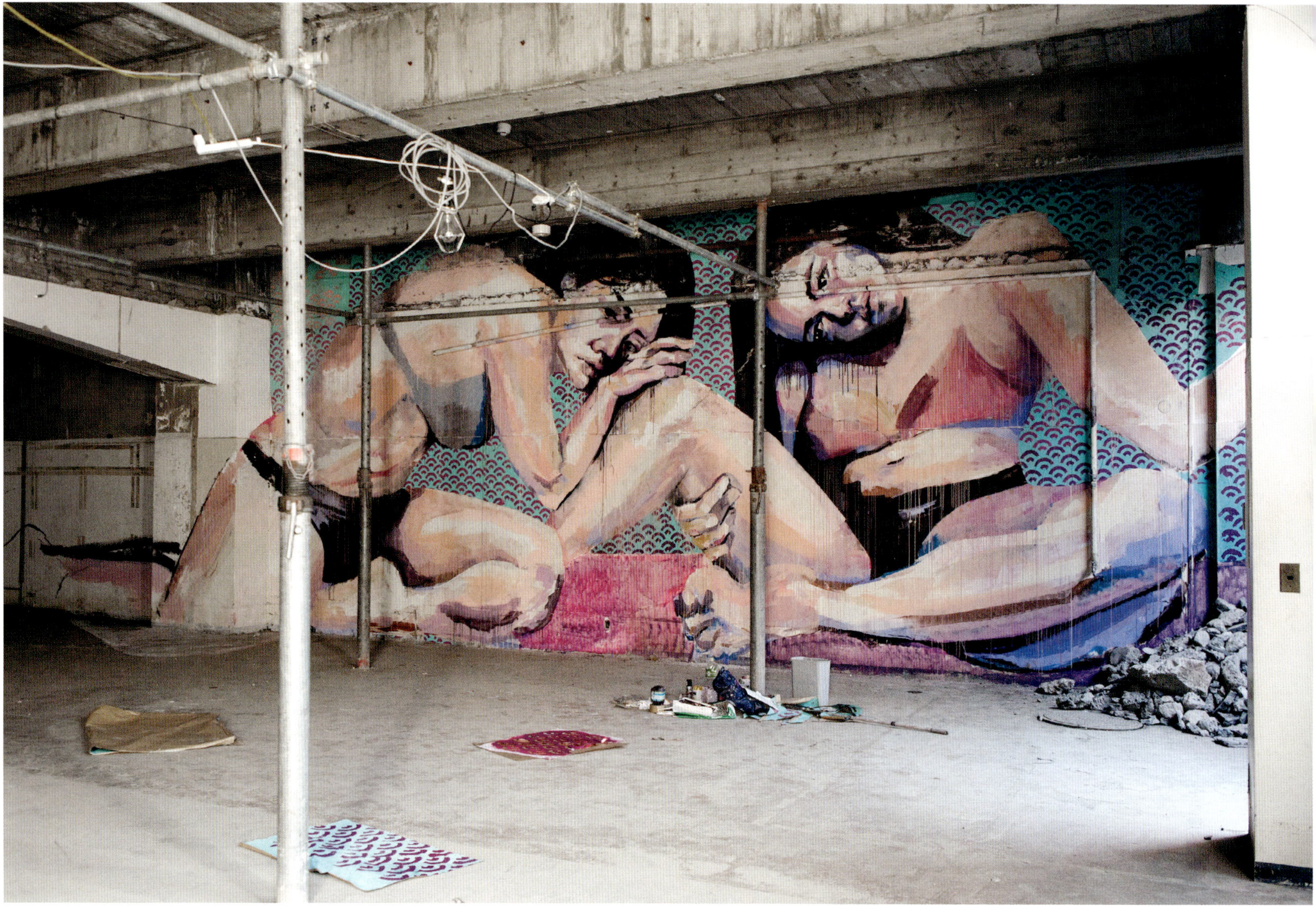

Digesting artwork from all around the globe informs, influences, and incites creativity, culture, and the individual. A chart depicting progress in the cultural sense does not look like a steady incline but rather an intricate web. Walking the streets on a hunt for urban art, this web of connectivity is tangible. Seeing the secret marks of taggers while stumbling upon shrines and ancient gardens reveals the significance of a people and their environment. In a sea of advertisements, traffic signals, and rushing people, the moments and opportunities to view and appreciate a place are priceless.

Little Pink Pills (Mika Revell)

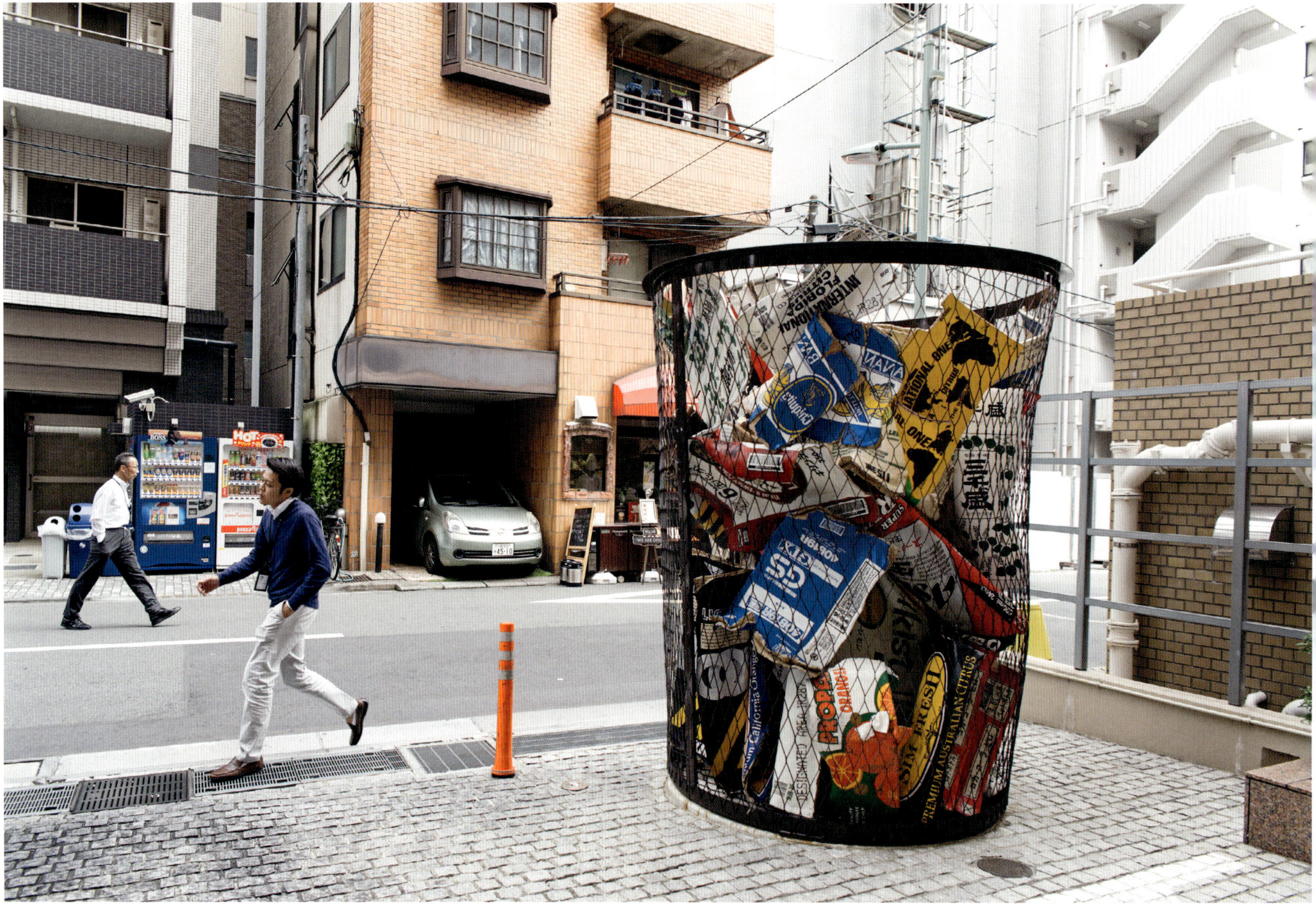

Kimiyo Mishima

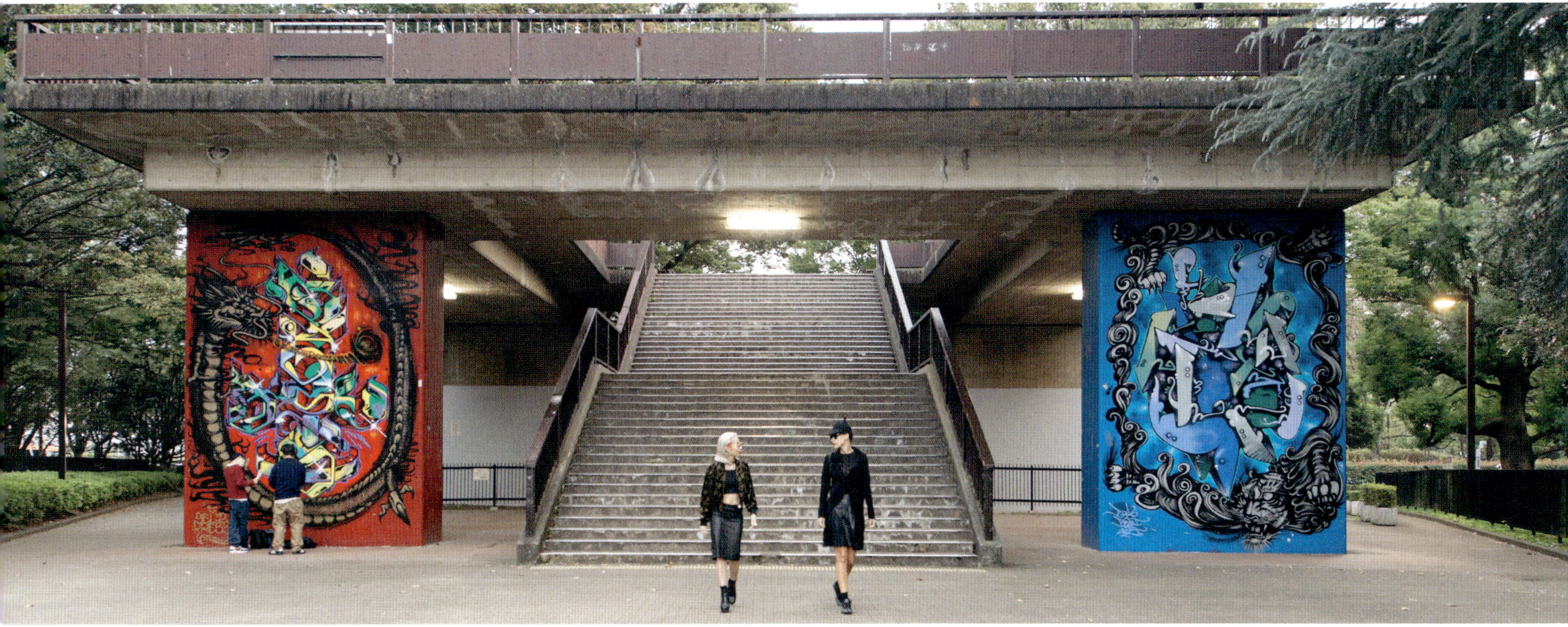

Seiko 1

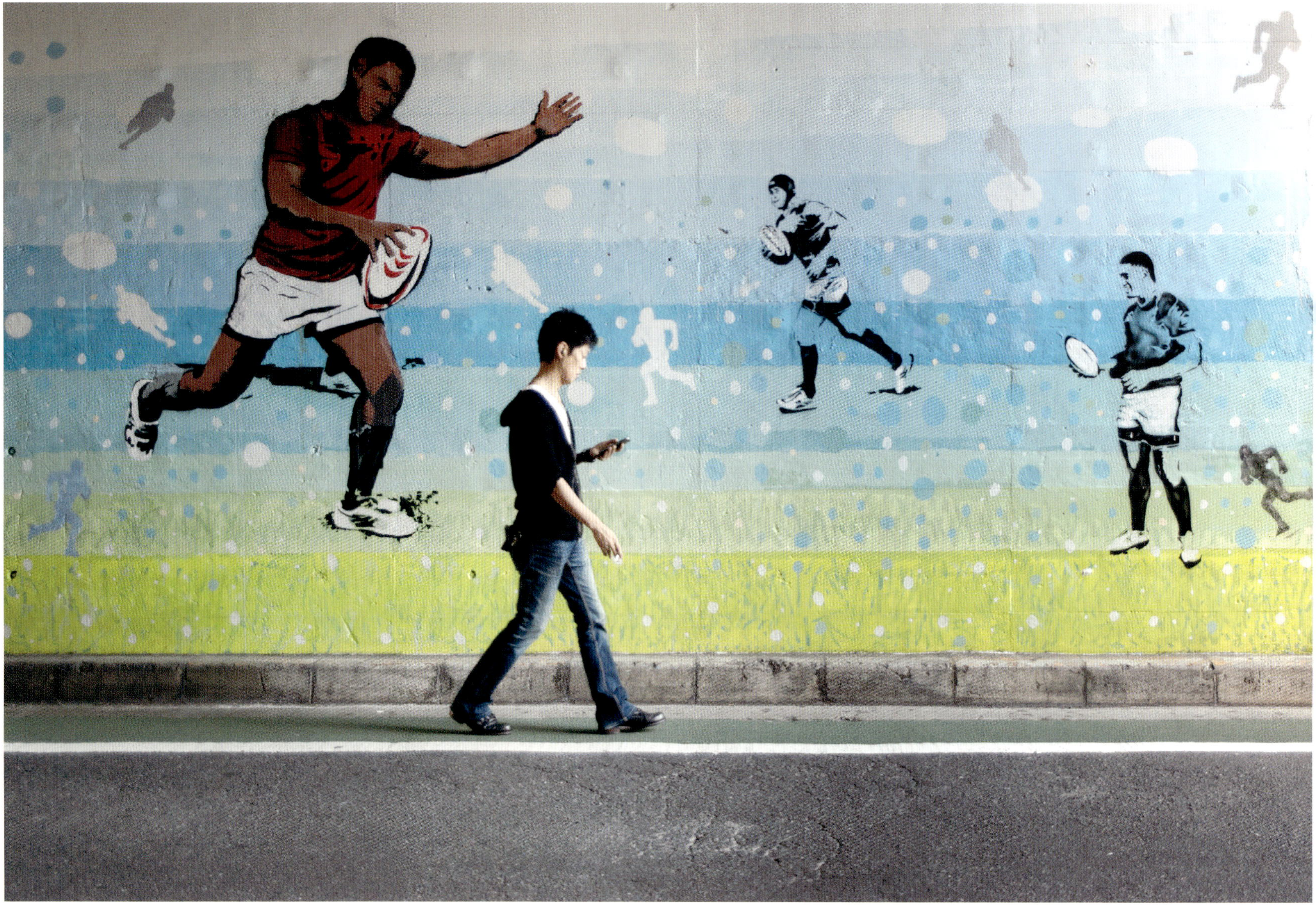

Location: Aobadai

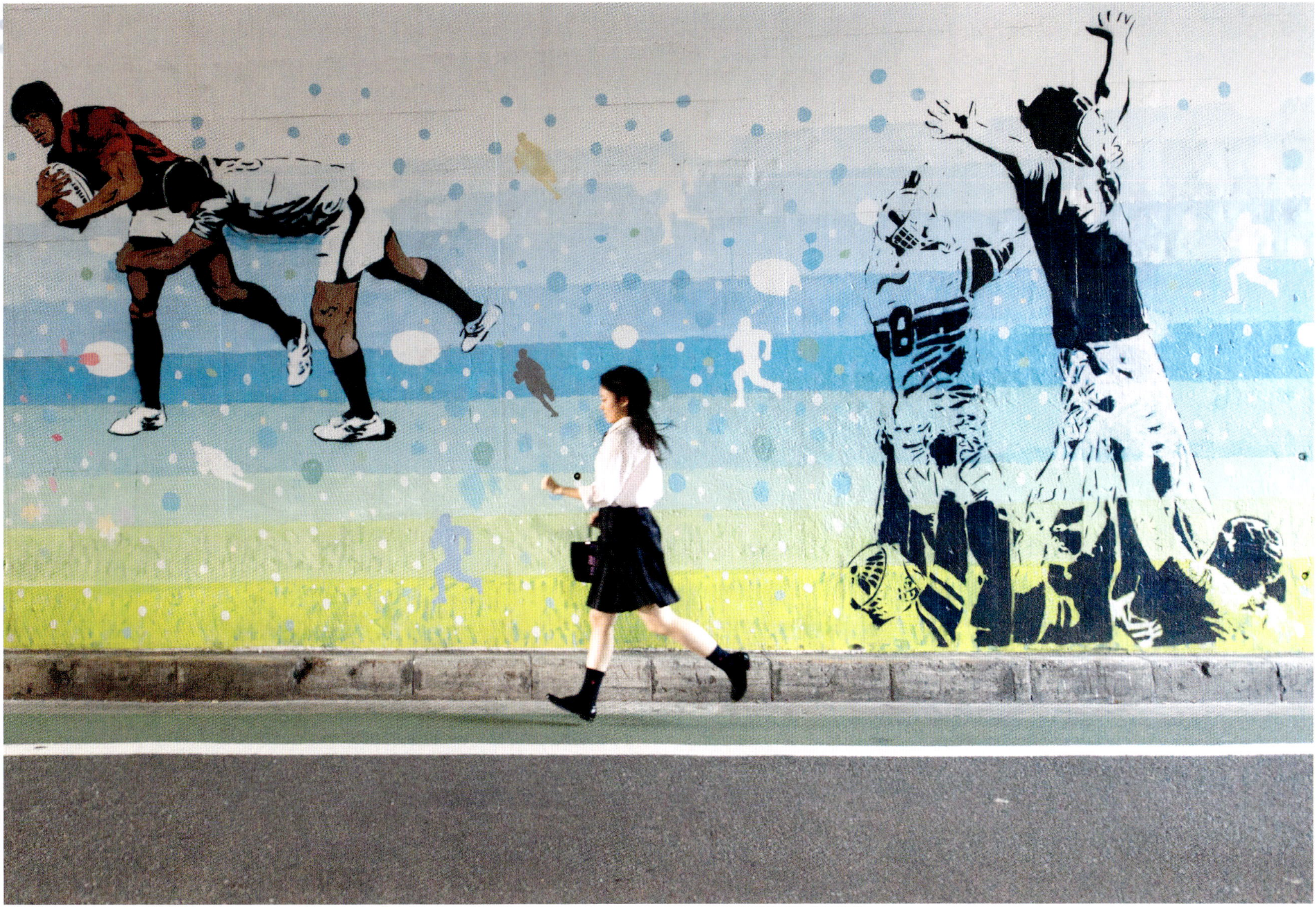

Location: Aobadai

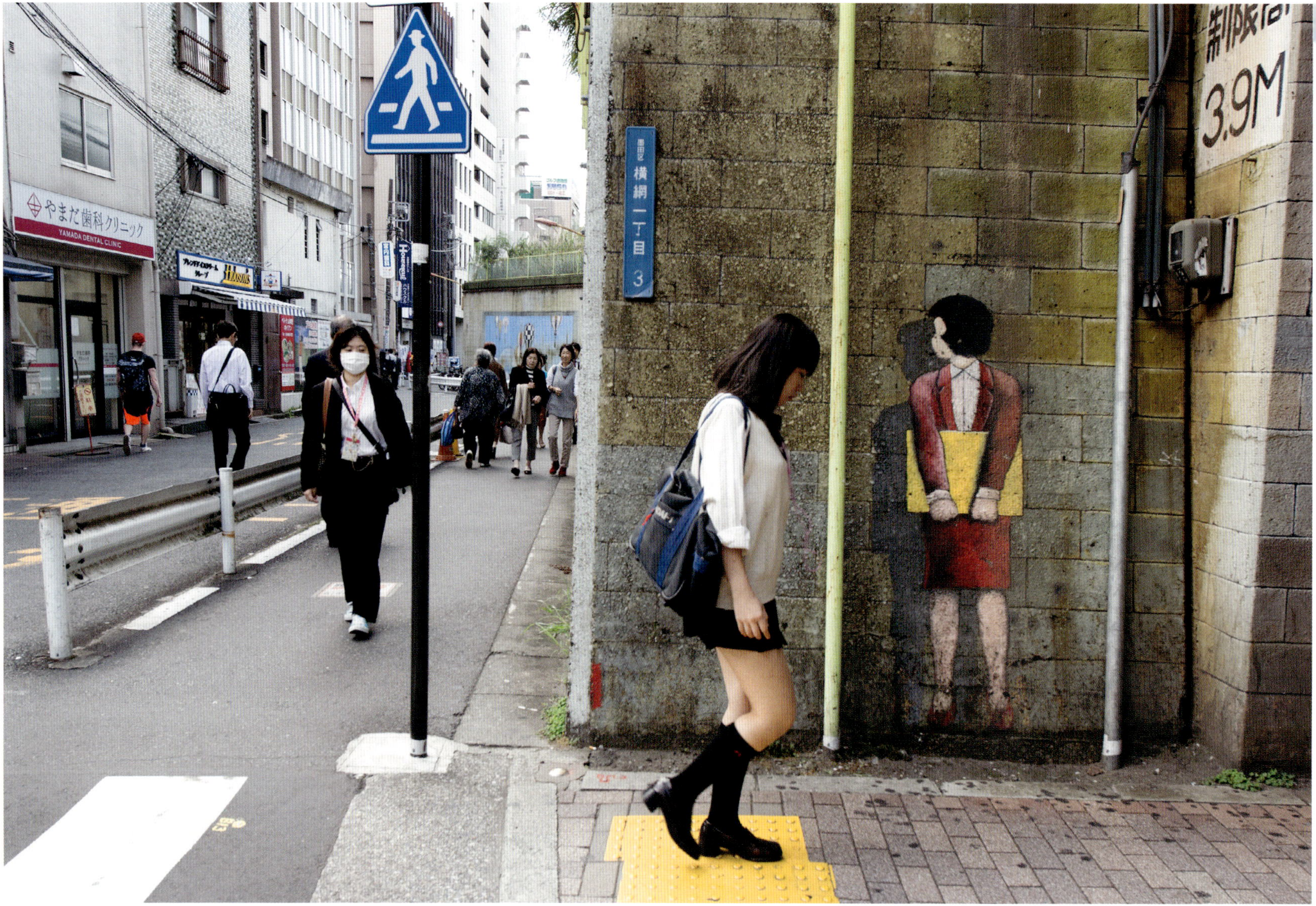

Location: Ryogoku

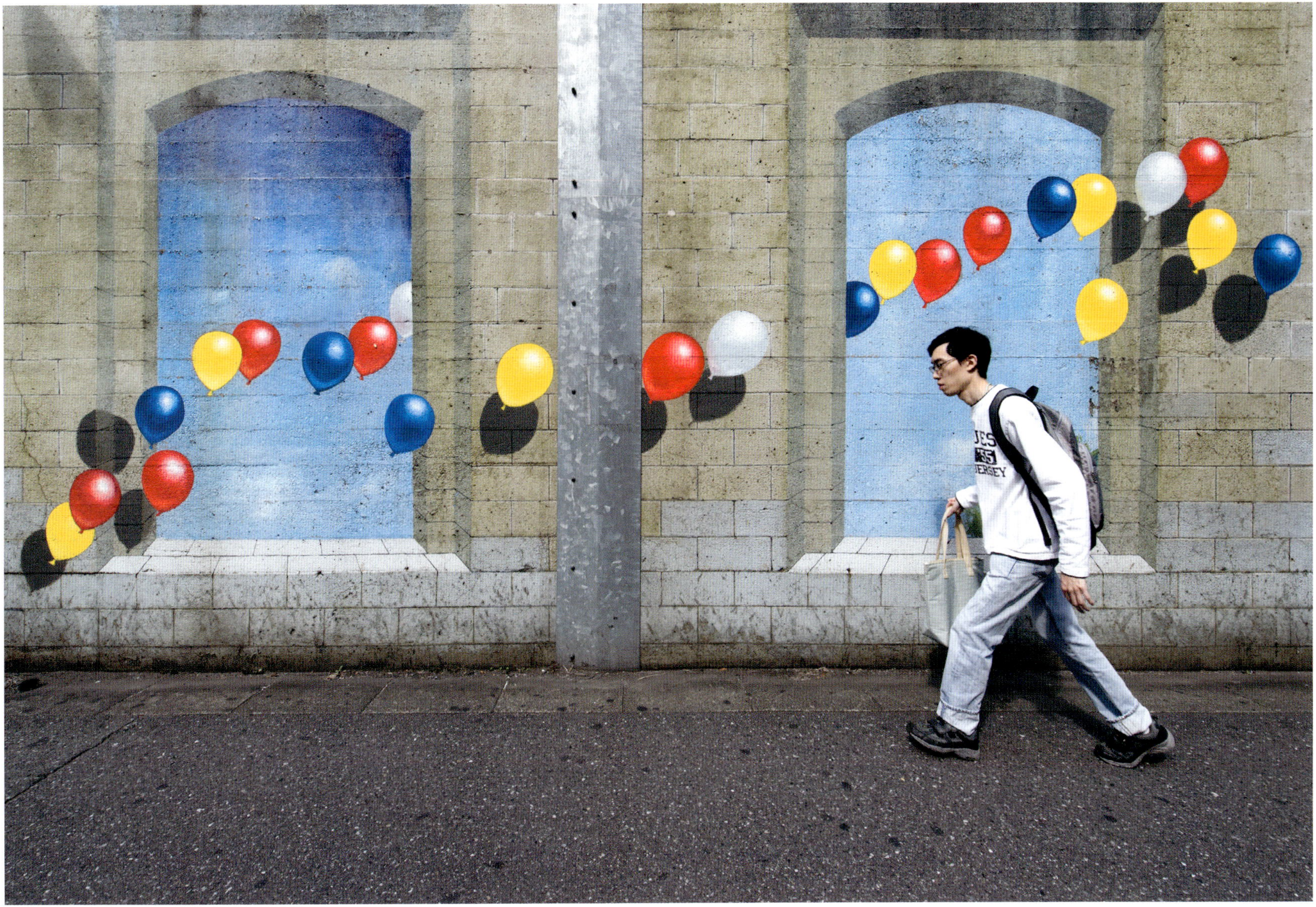

Location: Ryogoku

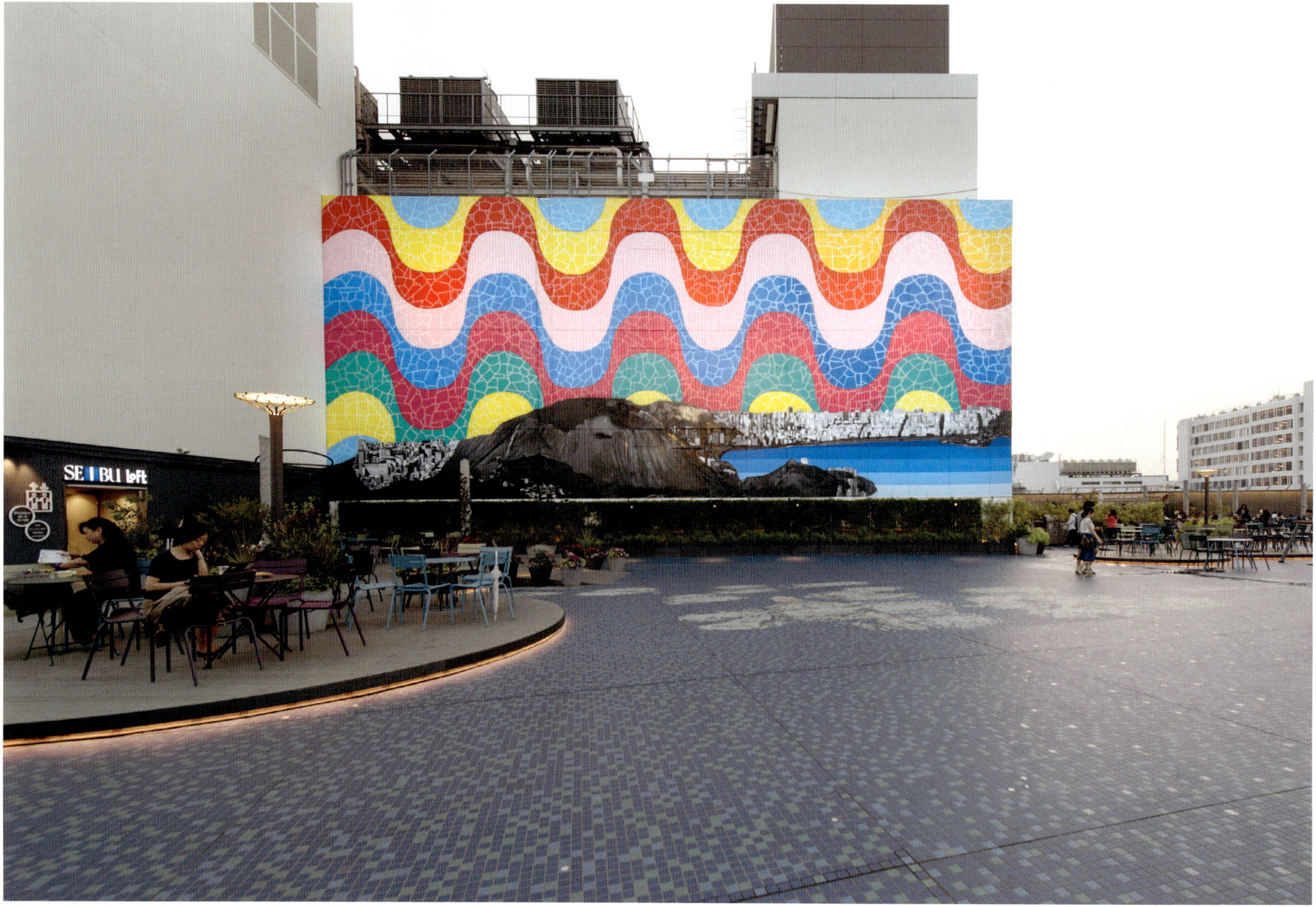

Kobra

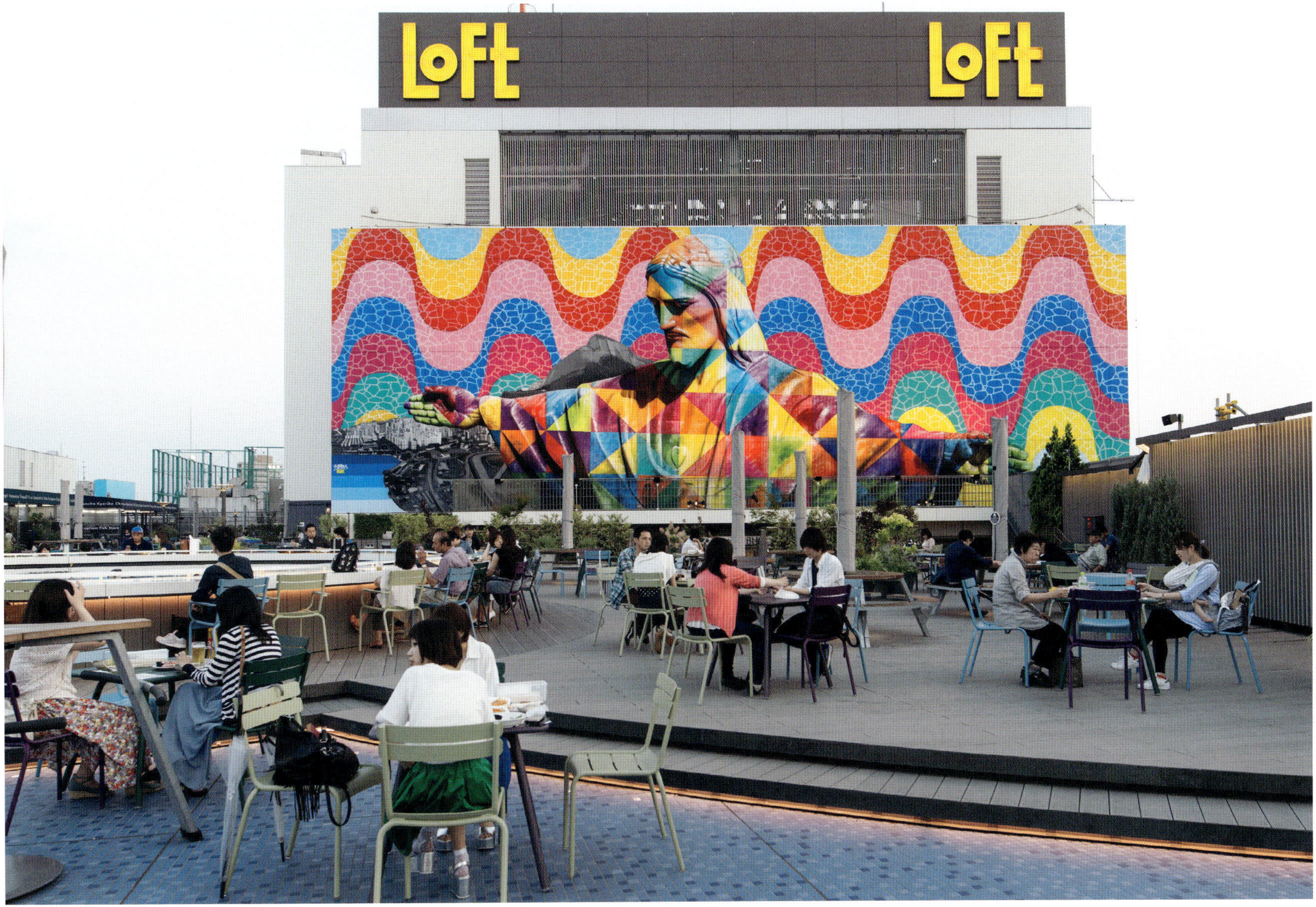

Kobra

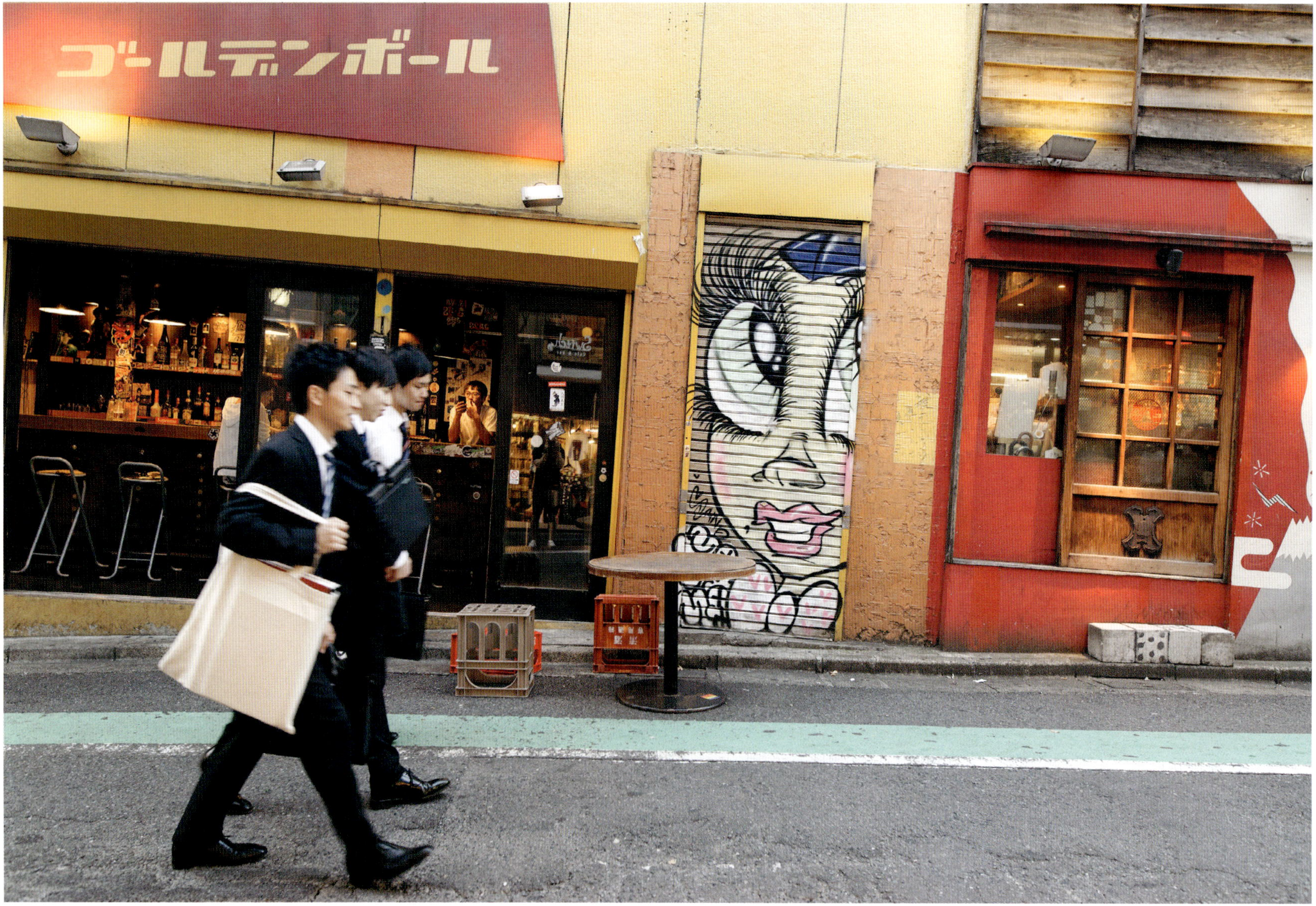

SAND ONE

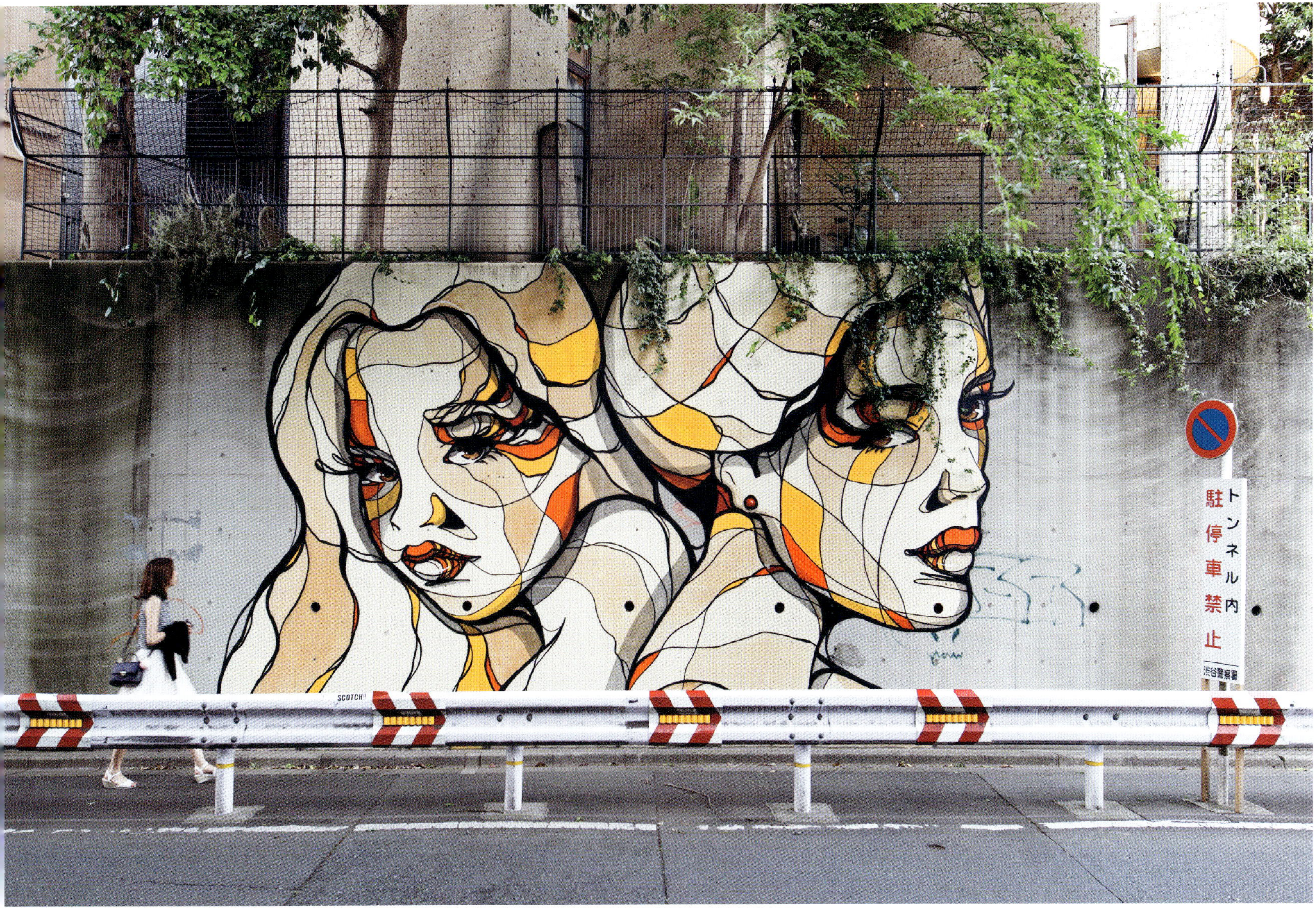

El Bocho

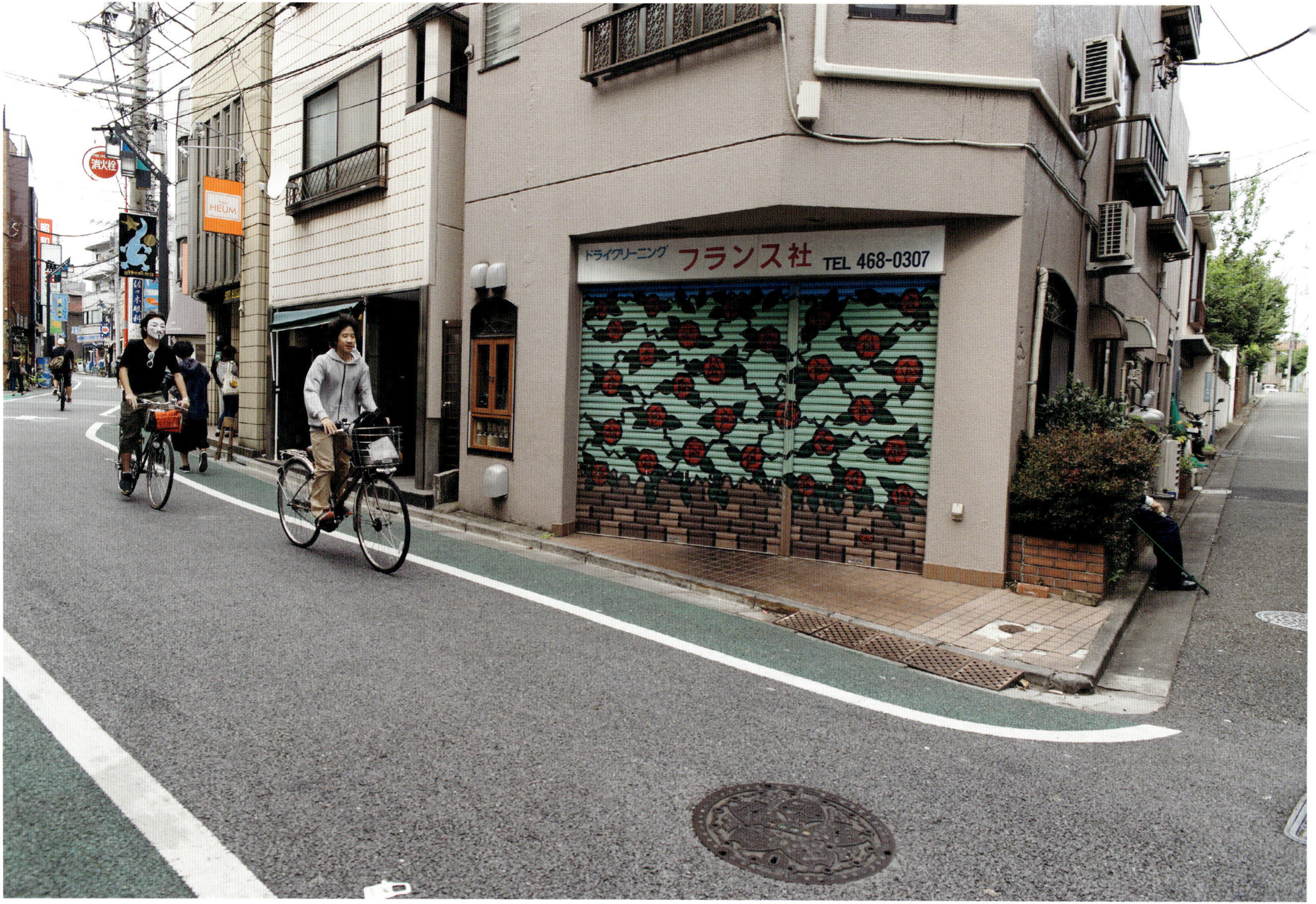

Location: Shimokitazawa

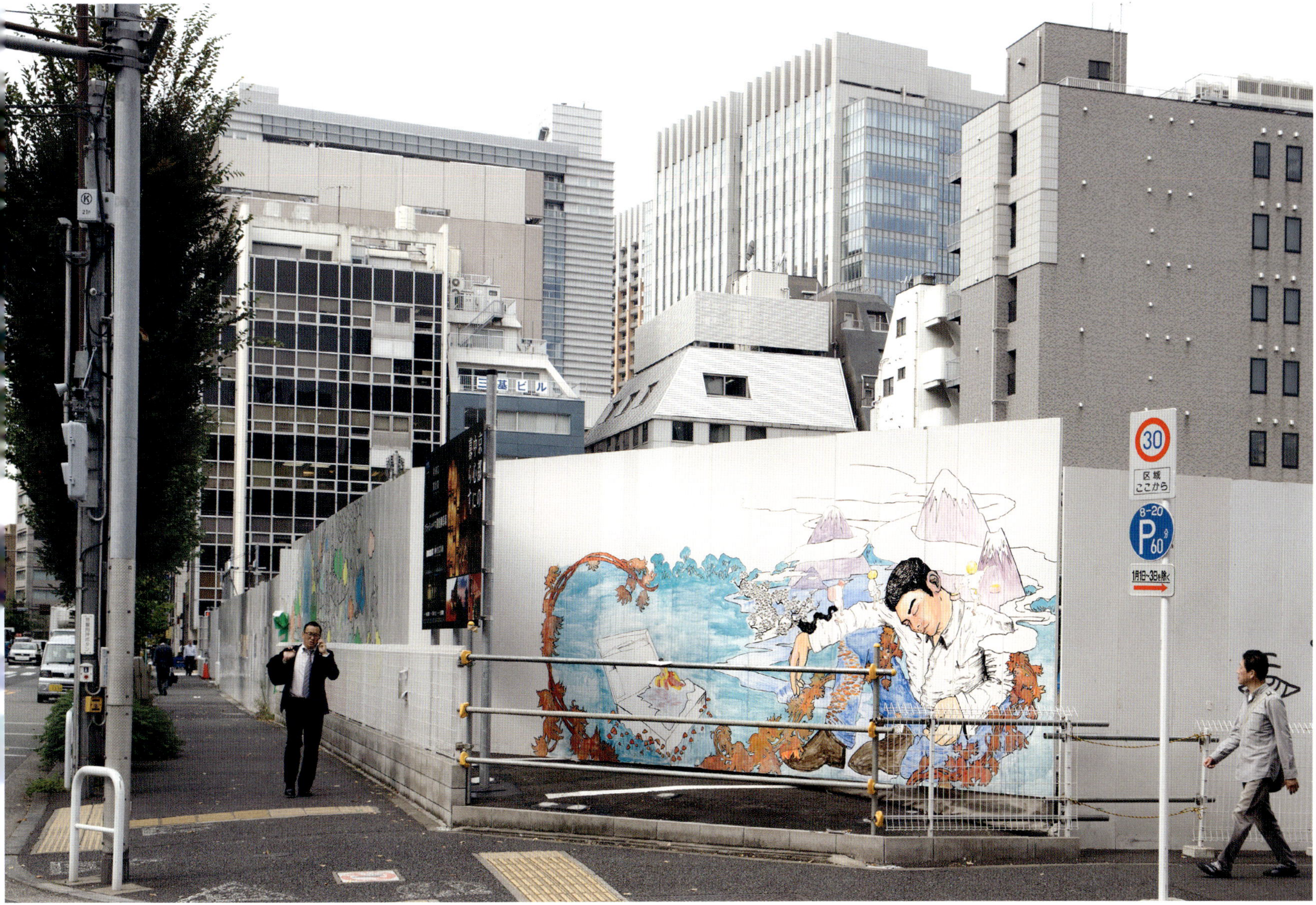

Little Pink Pills (Mika Revell)

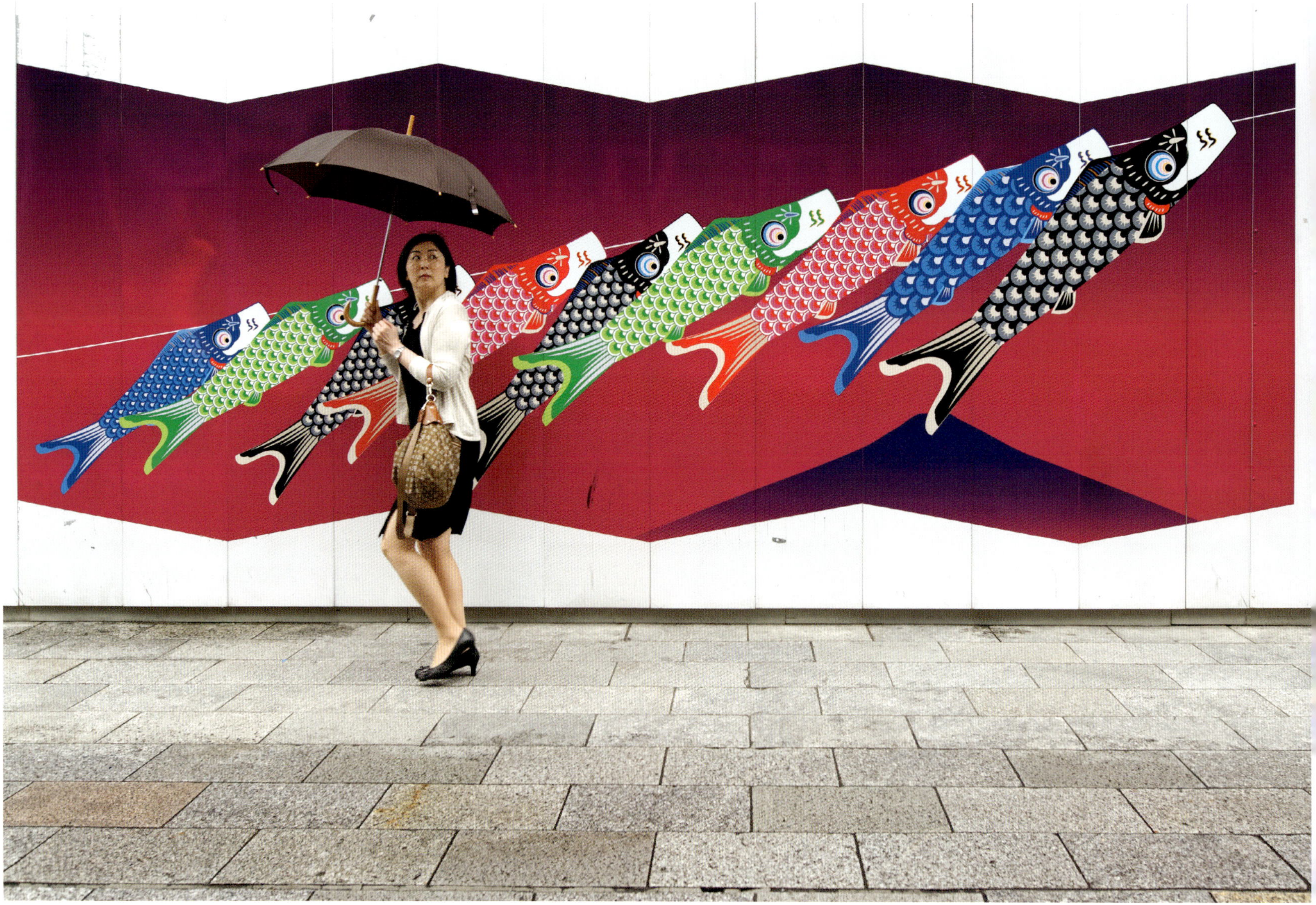

Junko Koshino

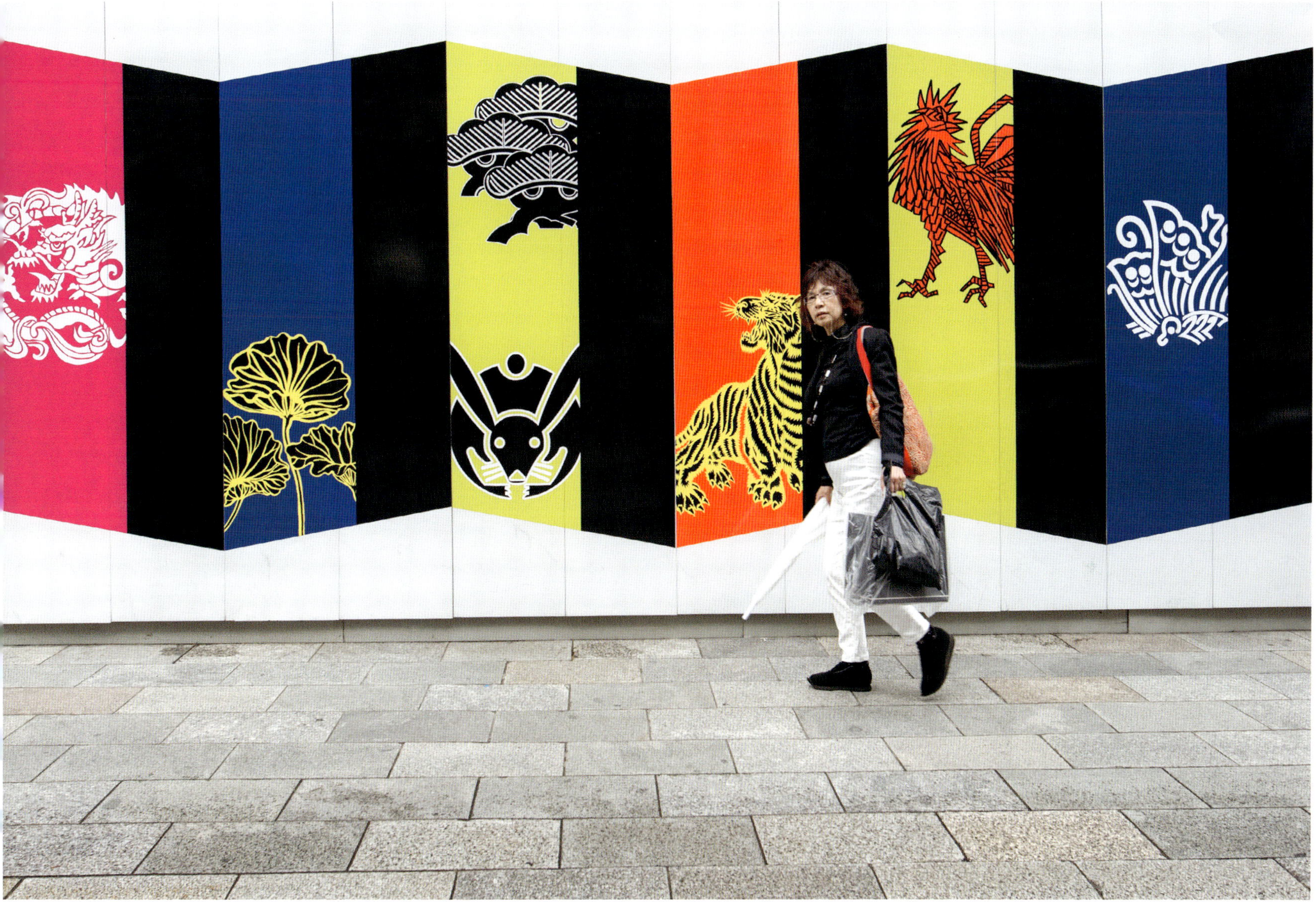

Junko Koshino

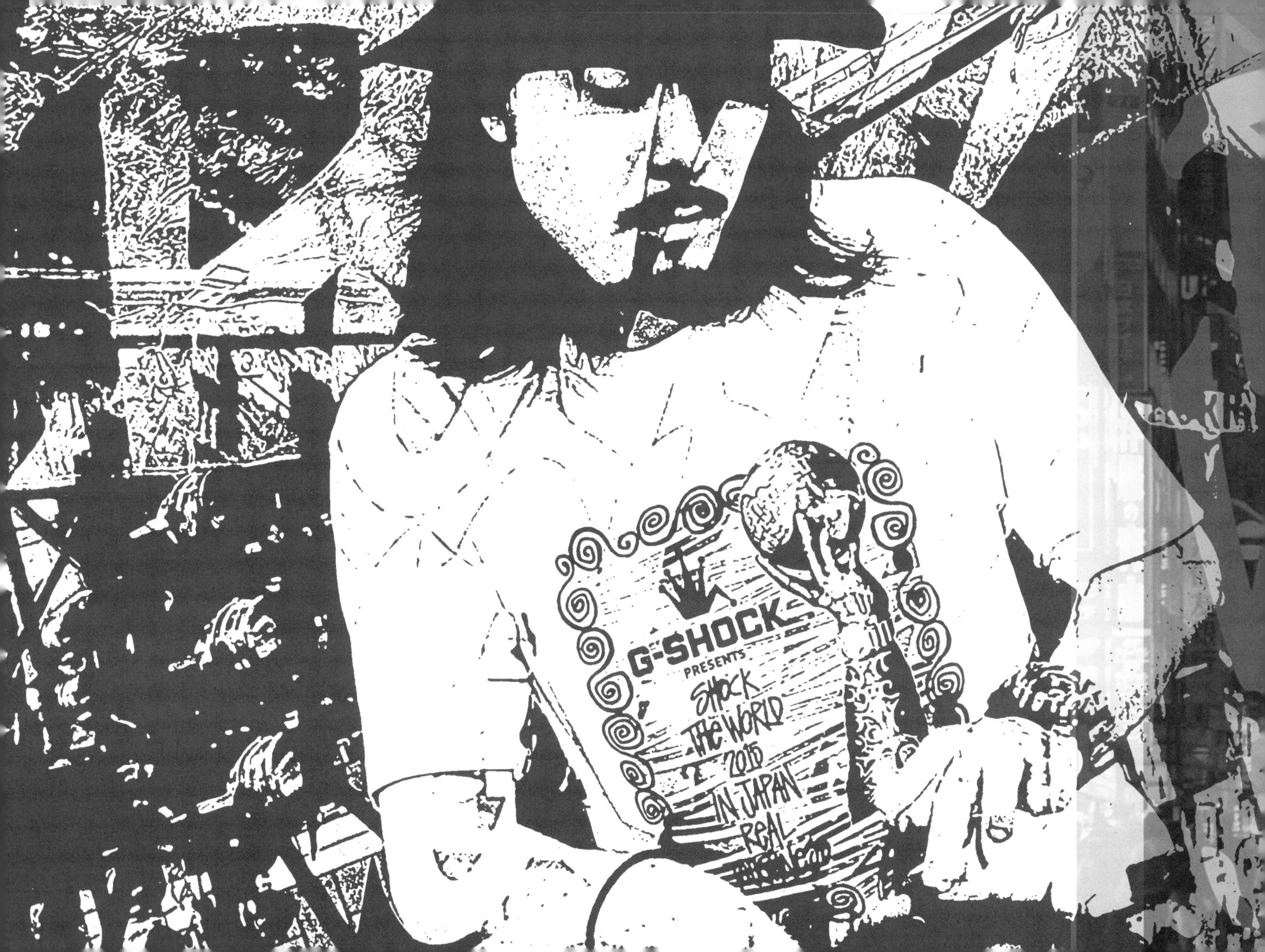
G-SHOCK
PRESENTS
SHOCK
THE WORLD
2015
IN JAPAN
REAL

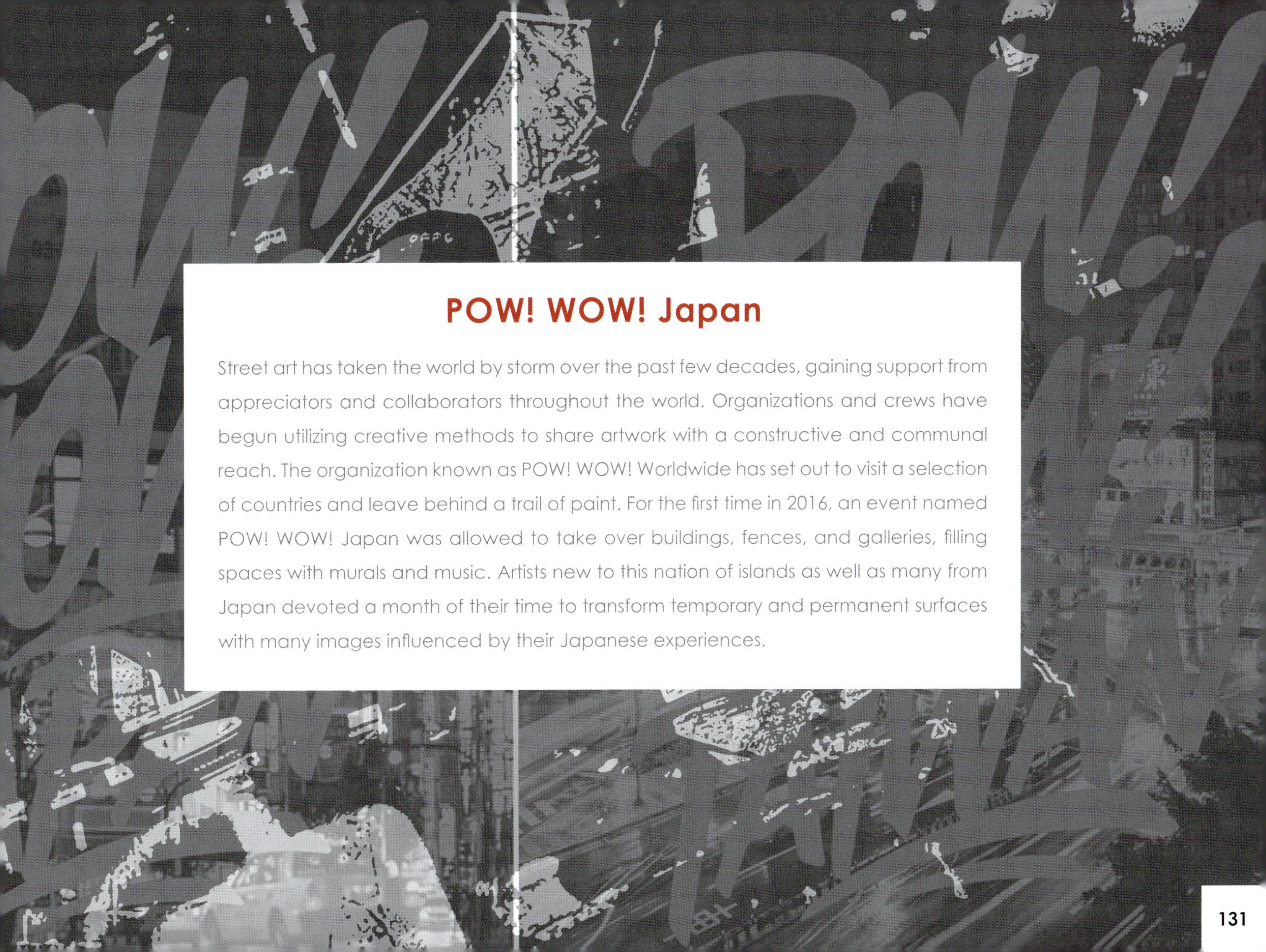

POW! WOW! Japan

Street art has taken the world by storm over the past few decades, gaining support from appreciators and collaborators throughout the world. Organizations and crews have begun utilizing creative methods to share artwork with a constructive and communal reach. The organization known as POW! WOW! Worldwide has set out to visit a selection of countries and leave behind a trail of paint. For the first time in 2016, an event named POW! WOW! Japan was allowed to take over buildings, fences, and galleries, filling spaces with murals and music. Artists new to this nation of islands as well as many from Japan devoted a month of their time to transform temporary and permanent surfaces with many images influenced by their Japanese experiences.

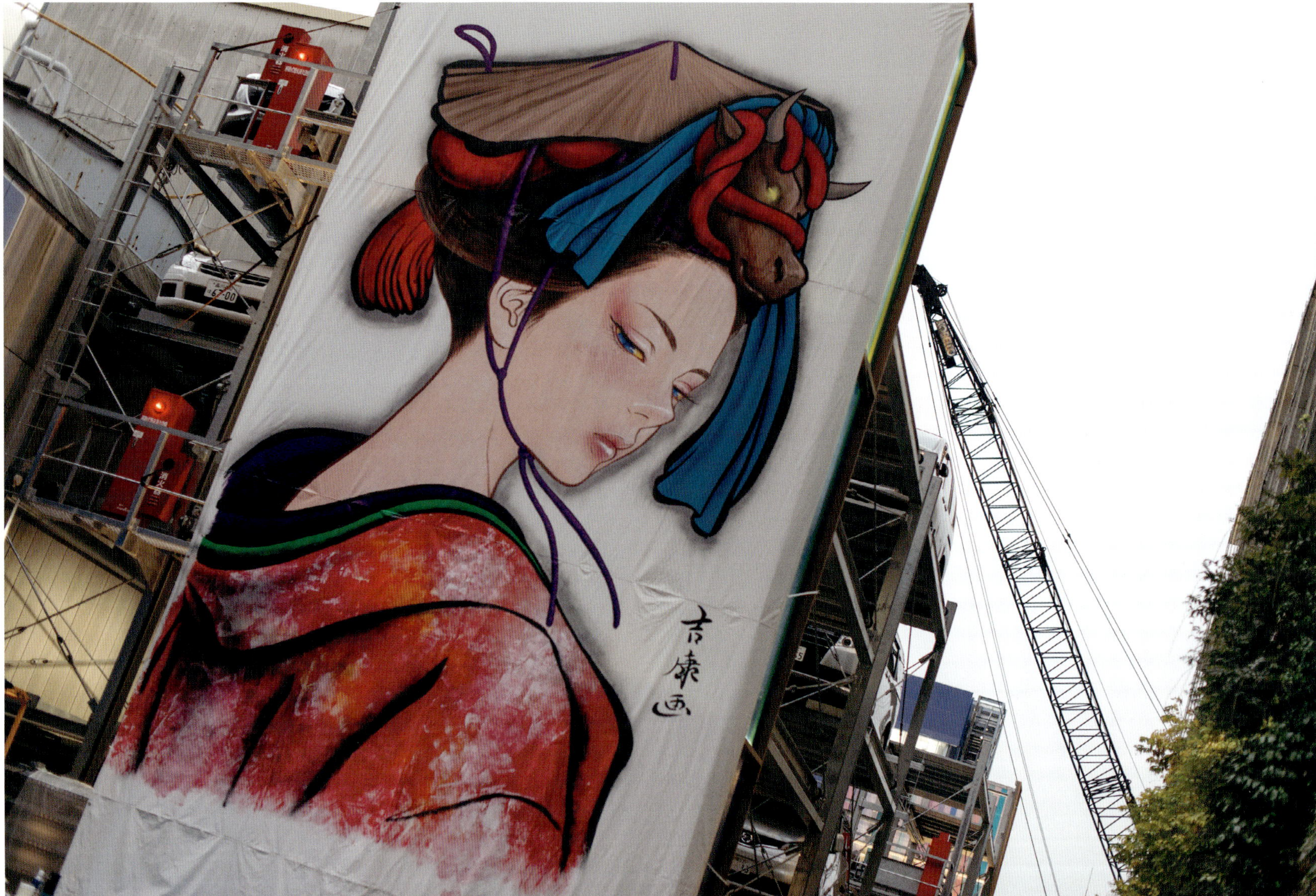

Tamura Yoshiyasu

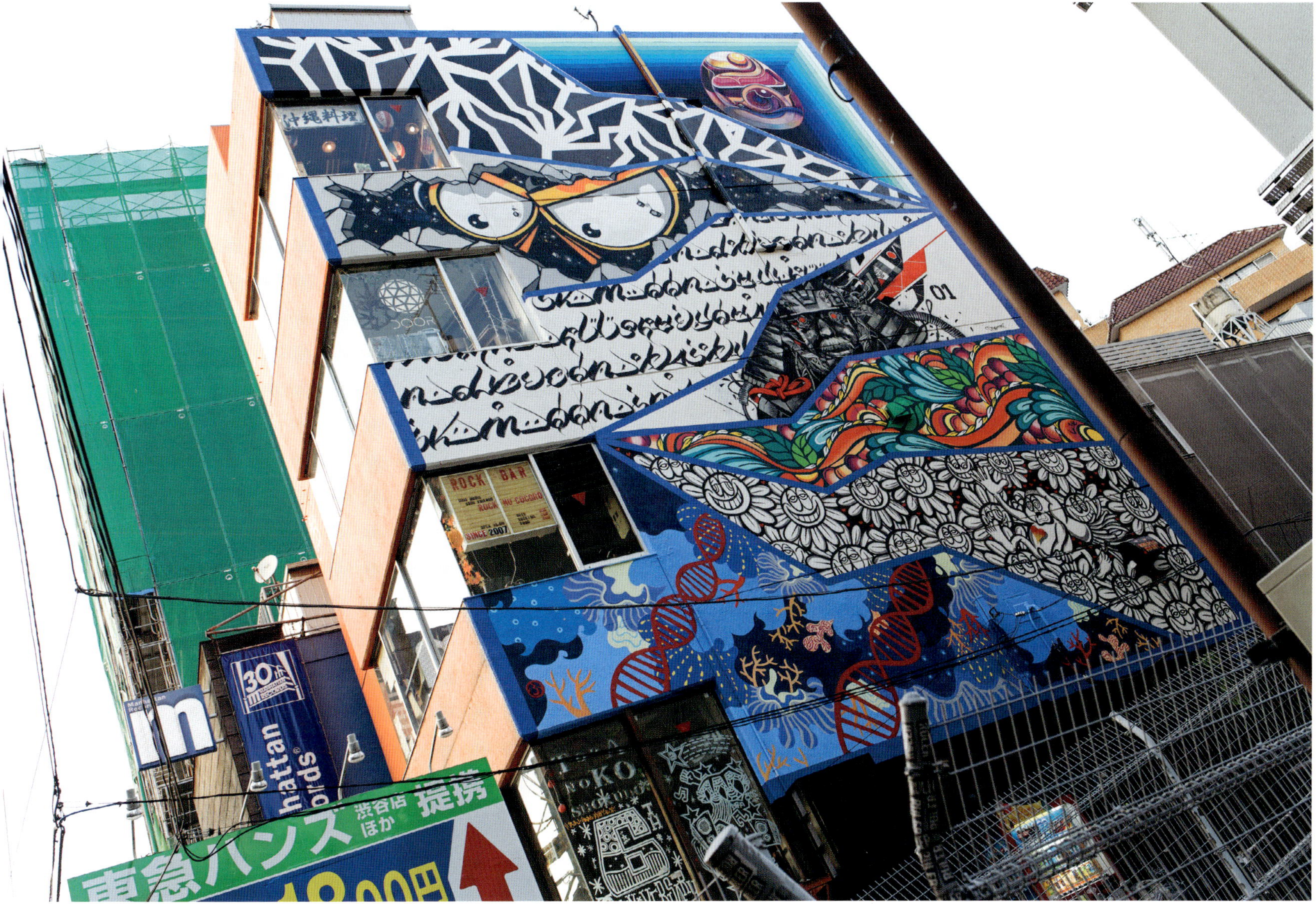

Jay Shogo, Frankie Cihi, Luise Ono, Dragon76, Cook1, Bakibaki, Mon

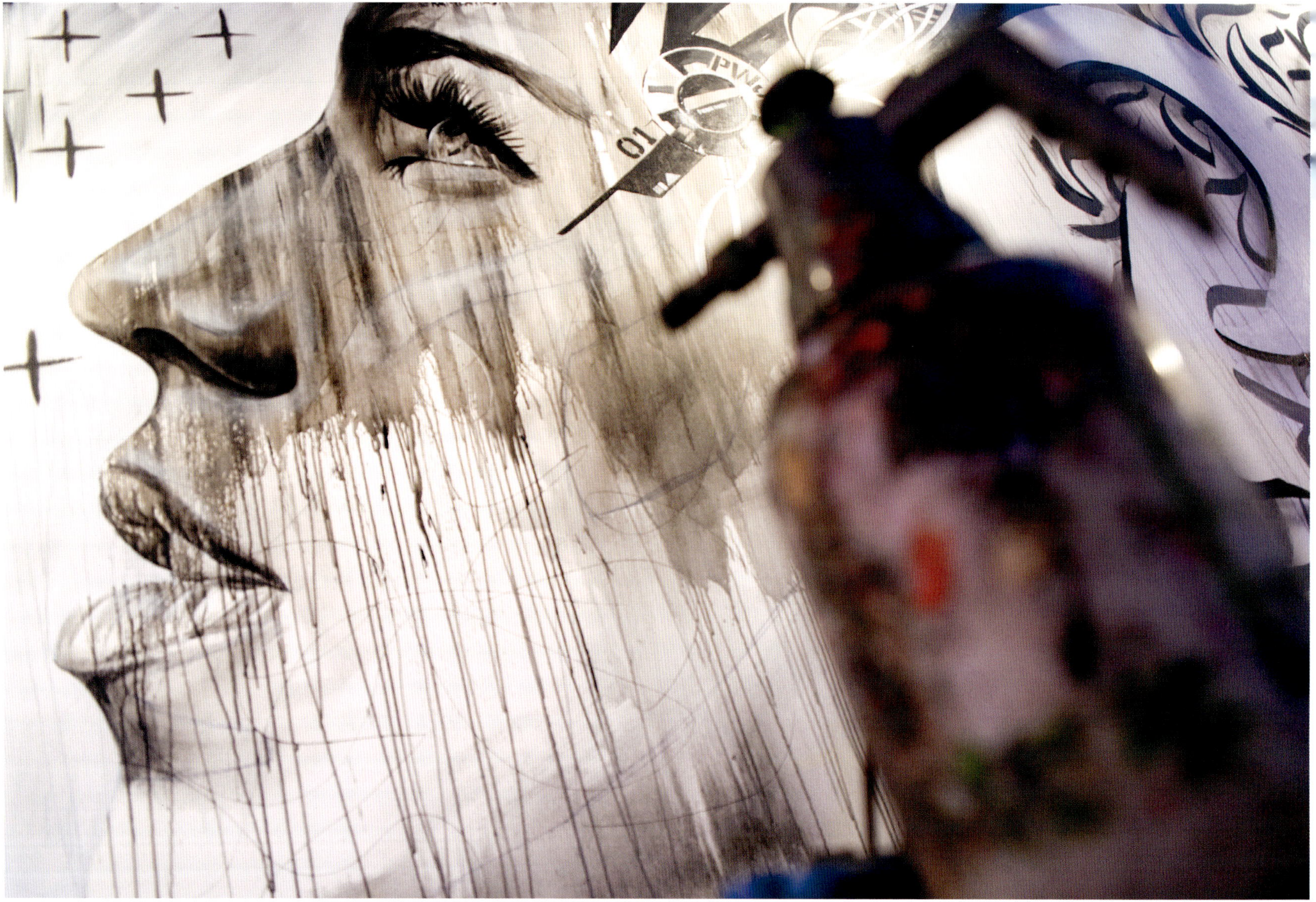

Kamea Hadar

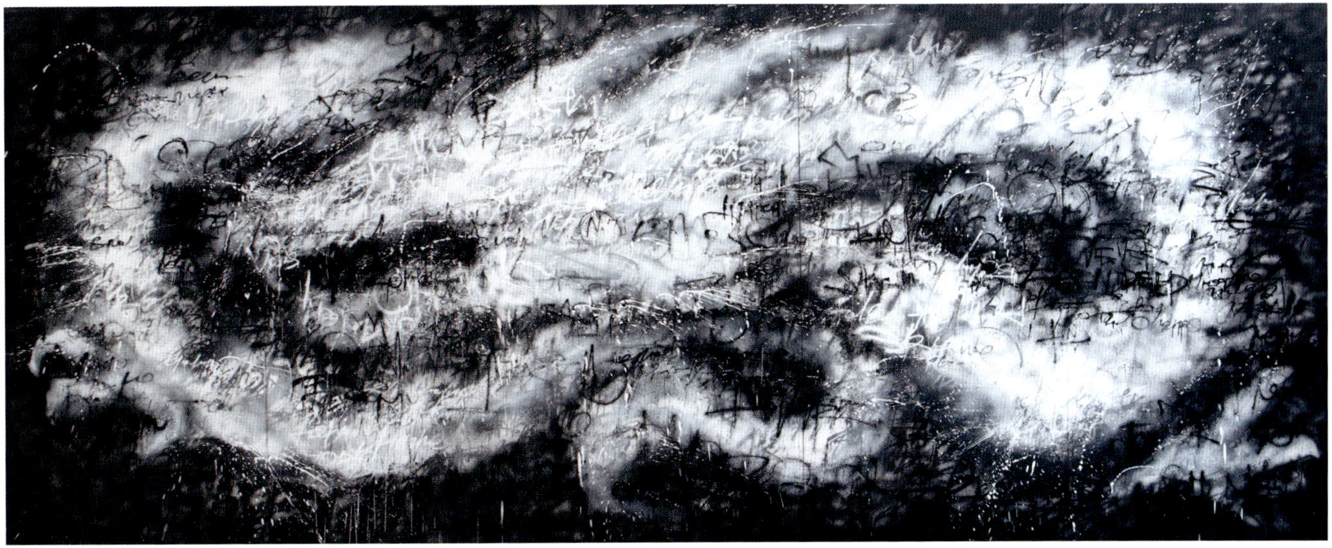

Colasa

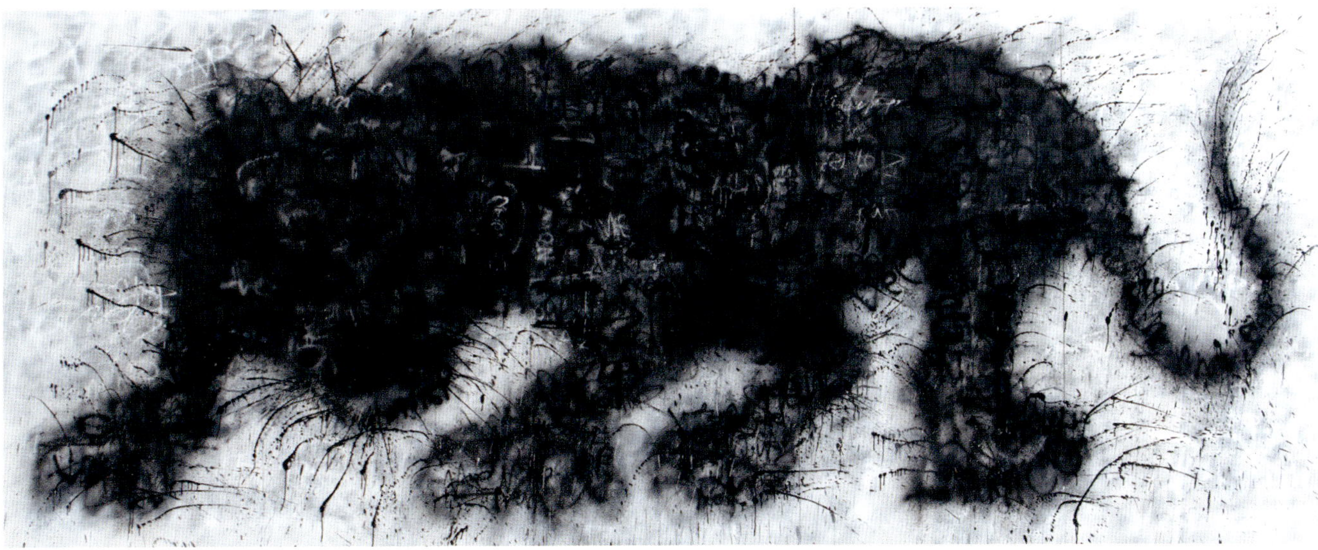

Colasa

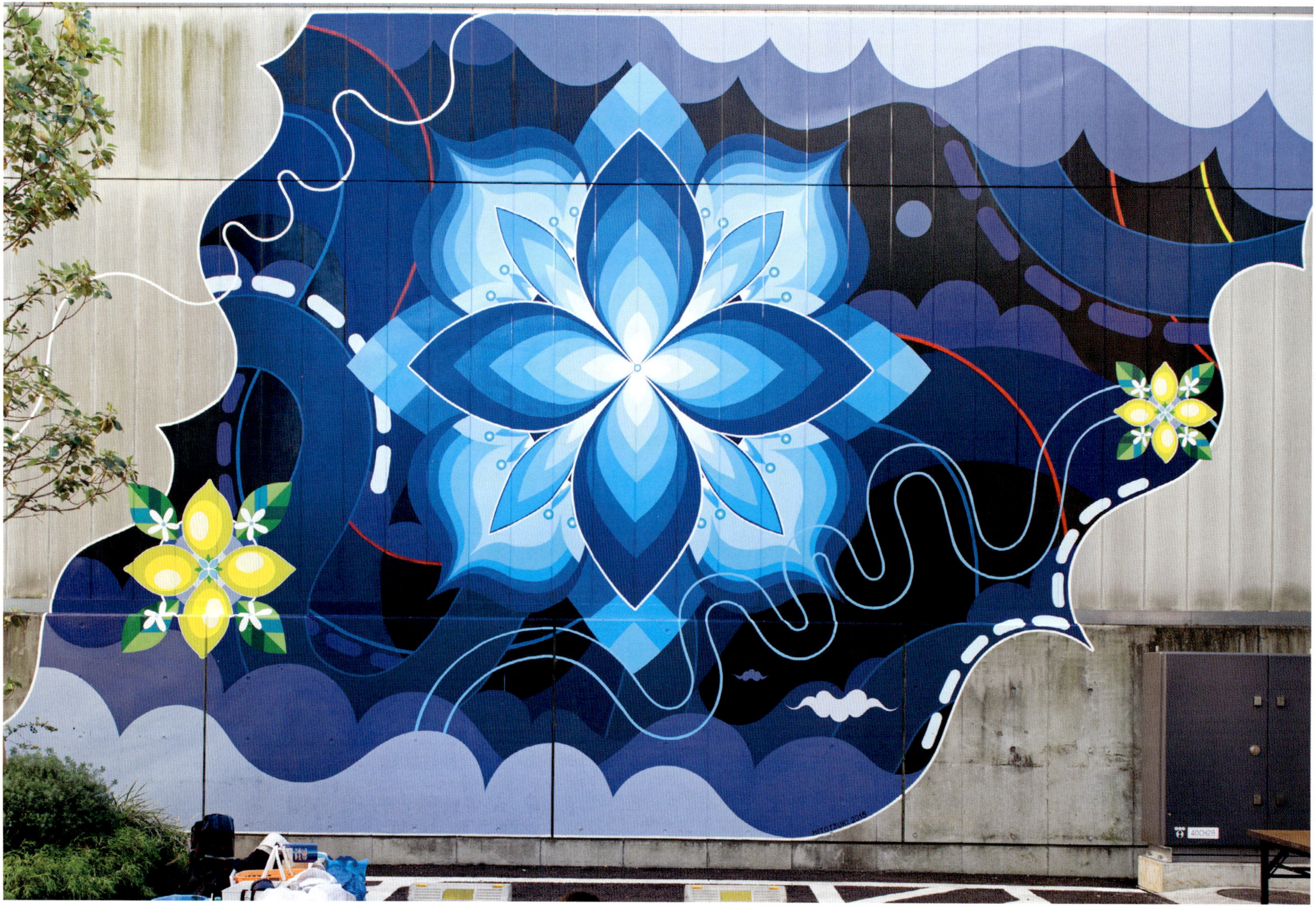

Hitotzuki

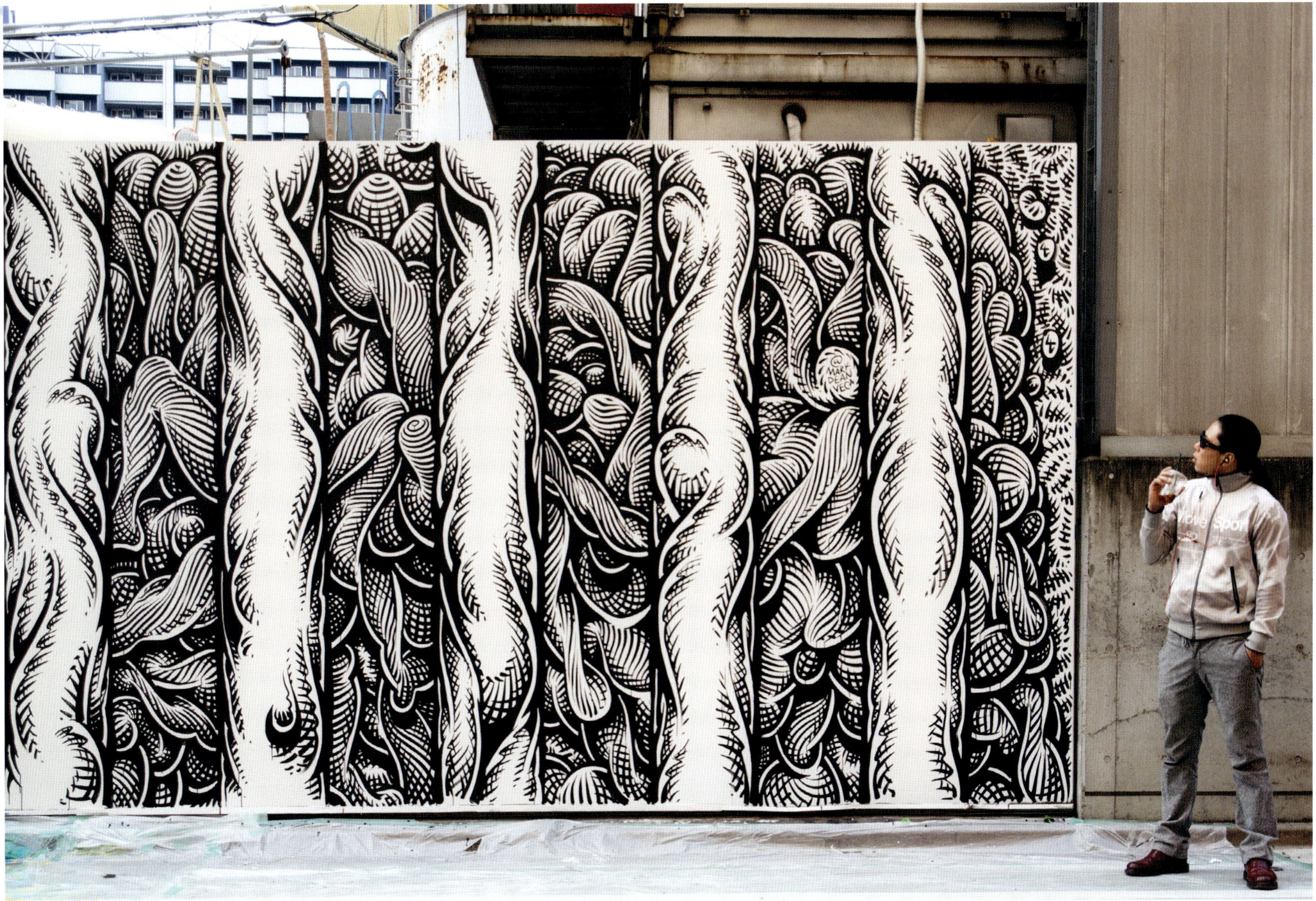

Mark Dean Veca

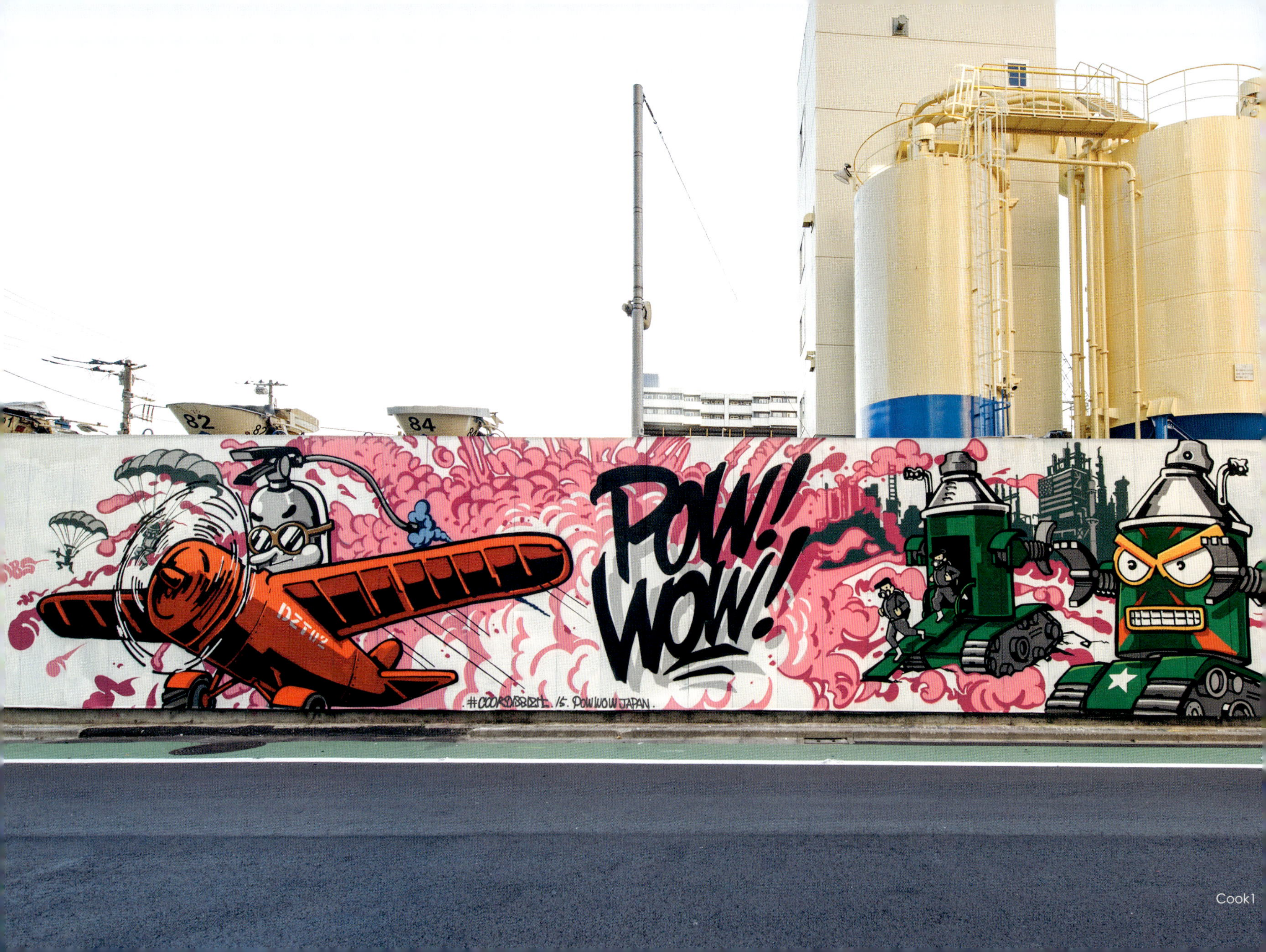

Cook1

Due to the popularization of graffiti styles, mural and street art organizations have begun to arrange events and commissioned pieces for artists all over the world. In many cities there are "free walls" where artists can paint, tag, and sticker without threat of being arrested. This is also a strategic way to deter people from defacing businesses or neighborhoods. In Tokyo, it is still uncommon to find many designated "free walls," however, temporary facades, construction walls, and interior walls are more often becoming opportunities for creativity. In the Harajuku shopping area, you can find art on the walls of eateries, tattoo parlors, and vintage shops, as well as temporary panels or canvases for live paint events. POW! WOW! Japan takes place during the month of October and brings artists from all over the world and Japan to collaborate and redesign the urban landscape from Shibuya to Tennozu Isle. Artists like Cook1 and Case Maclaim worked alongside one another to create massive murals, walls of color, and dramatic designs that injected something vibrant and new onto the scene.

Tokyo, the capital city of the land of the rising sun, presents a world of visual complexity and inspiration. It's not uncommon to see young girls with every color of hair, contact lenses, and iconoclastic fashions. Cafes selling pumpkin spice lattes sit adjacent to centuries-old shrines. What is known as *Kawaii*, or cute, style, most commonly seen in the Harajuku area, is a visual movement that originated in Japan. It is characterized by childish, decorative motifs such as hearts, stars, rainbows, and cute characters. As early as the 1970s with the development of Sanrio's Hello Kitty character, a shift occurred in the Japanese principles of design and culture. The importance of "beautiful" or "refined" attributes became "cute" and "neat." Today series like Pokemon, Dragon Ball Z, and One Piece are not only cultural institutions, they are now as revered and present in mainstream culture as religious or political figures and icons of industry. In a rapidly transforming city, the lines between ideology, advertising, and aesthetics are constantly blurring and redefining our visual language.

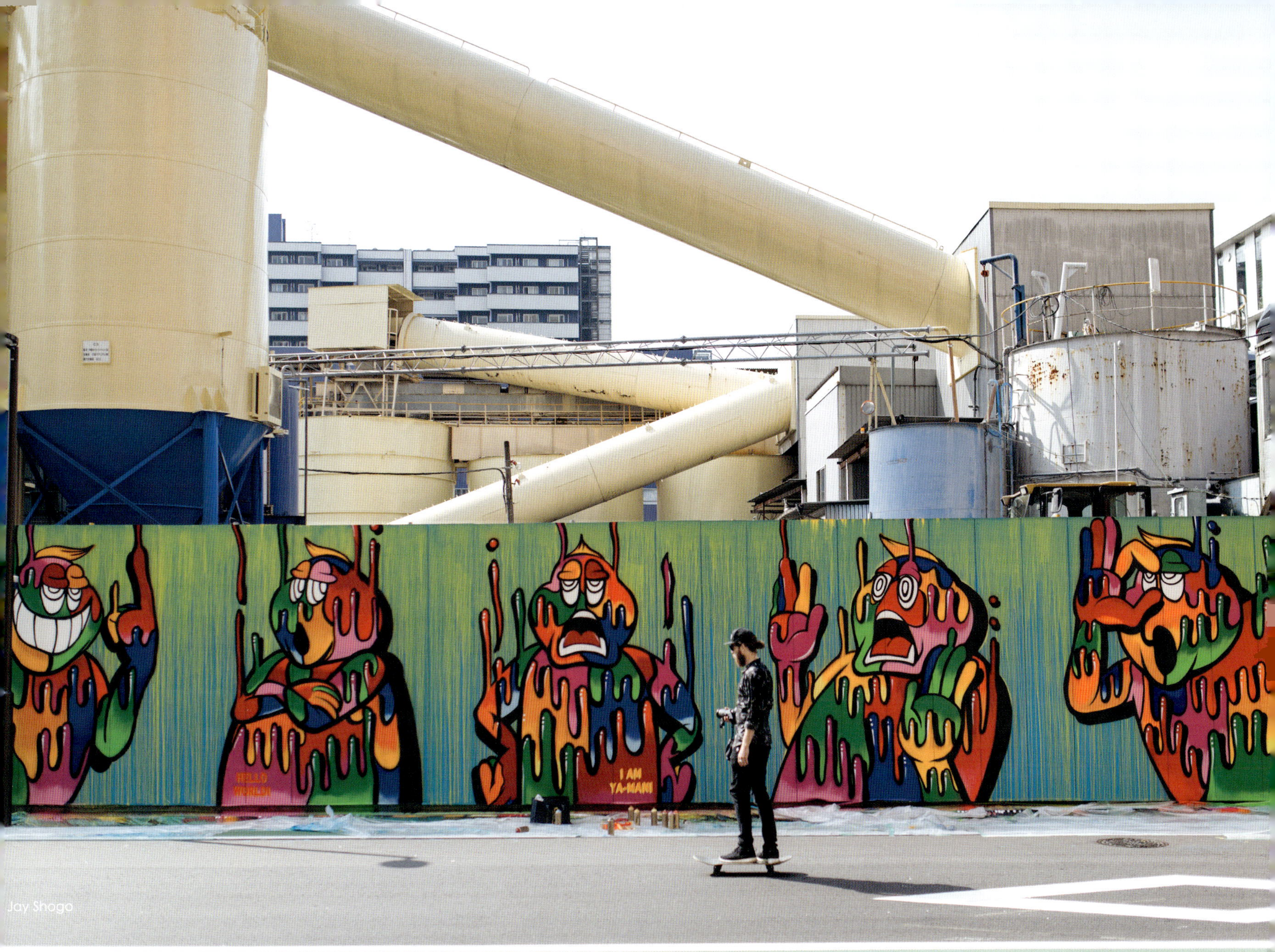

Jay Shogo

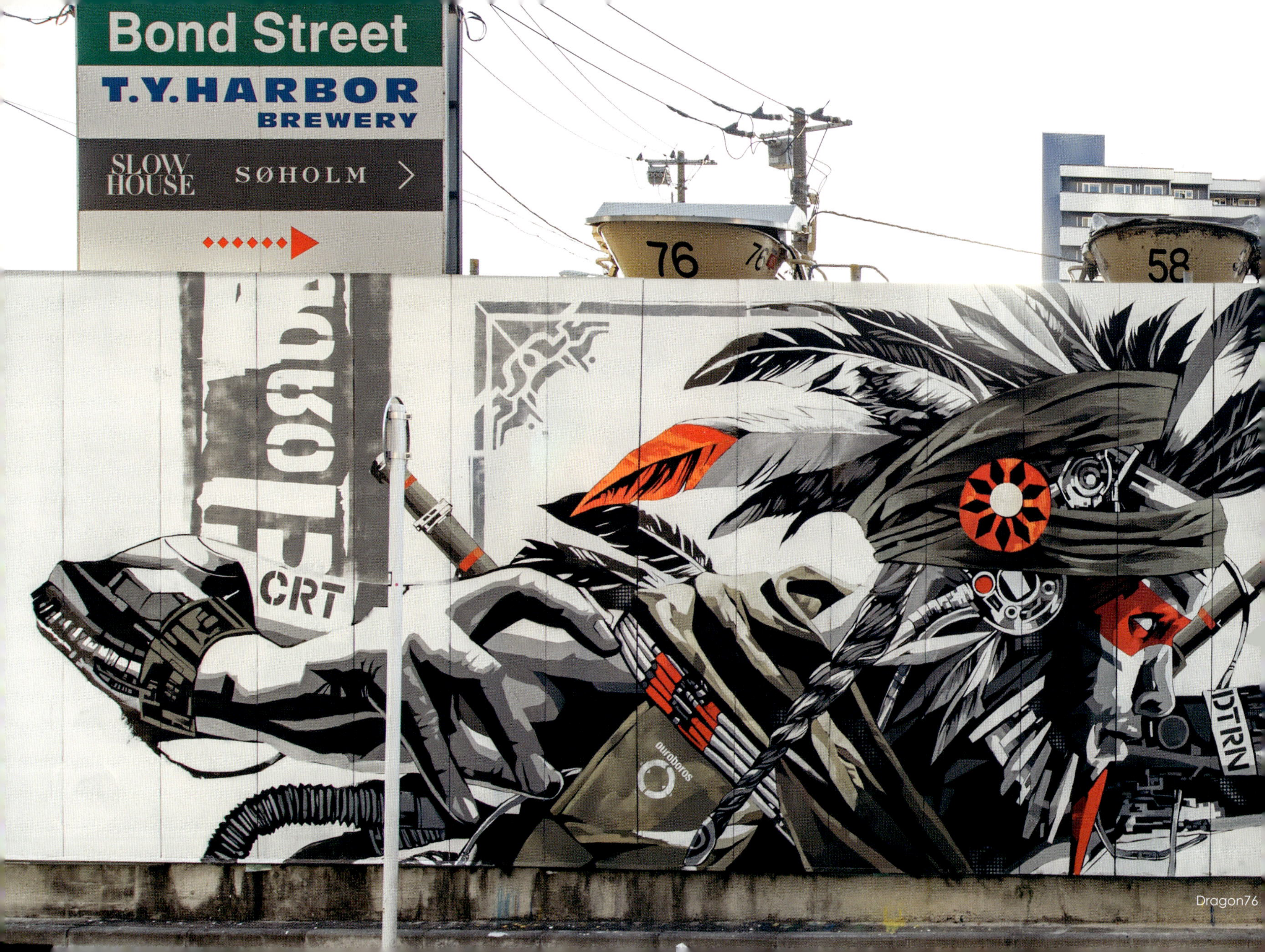
Bond Street
T.Y.HARBOR
BREWERY
SLOW HOUSE
SØHOLM
76
58
CRT
ouroboros
DTRN
Dragon76

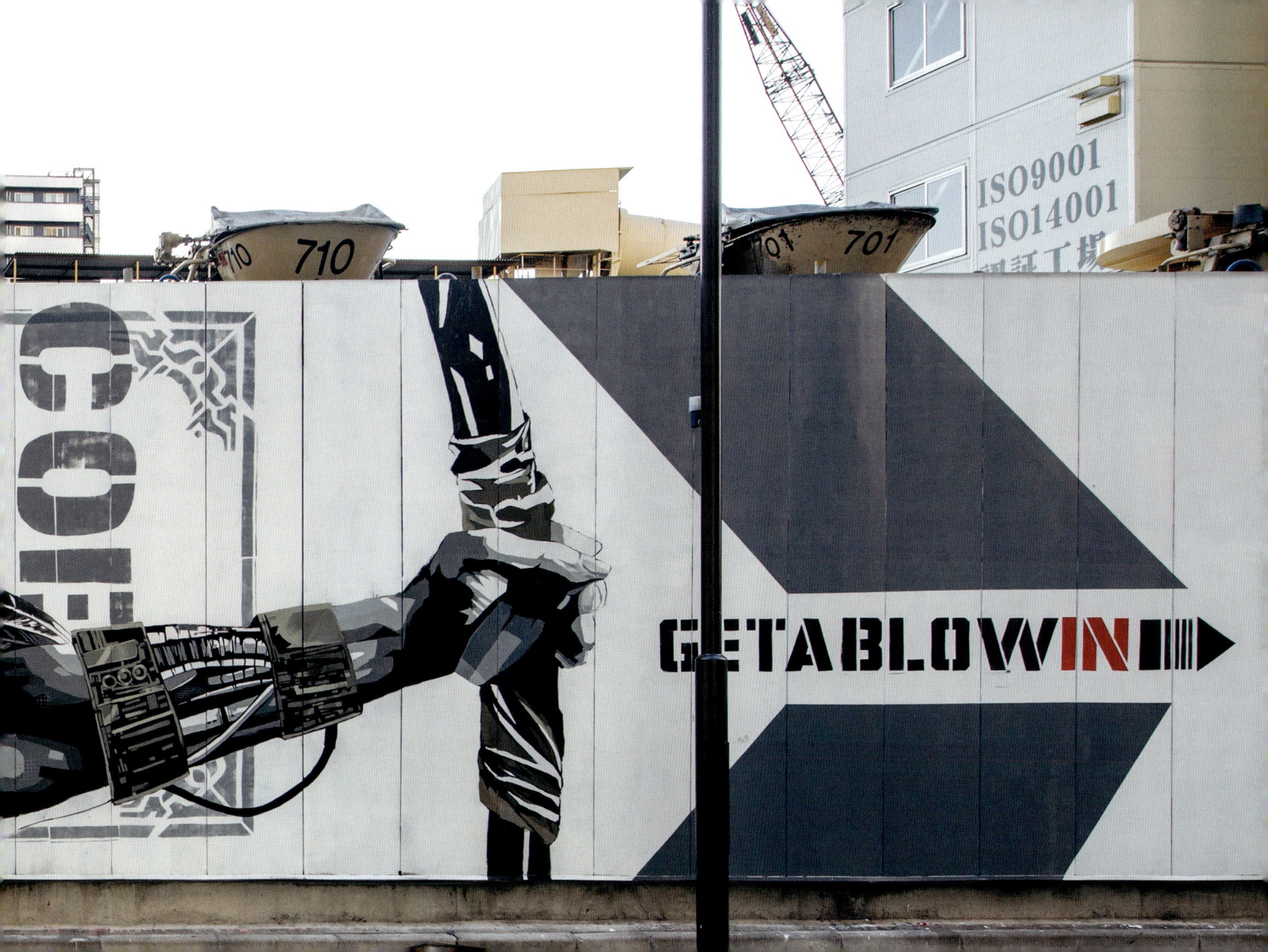
710
710
701
701
ISO9001
ISO14001
GETABLOWIN

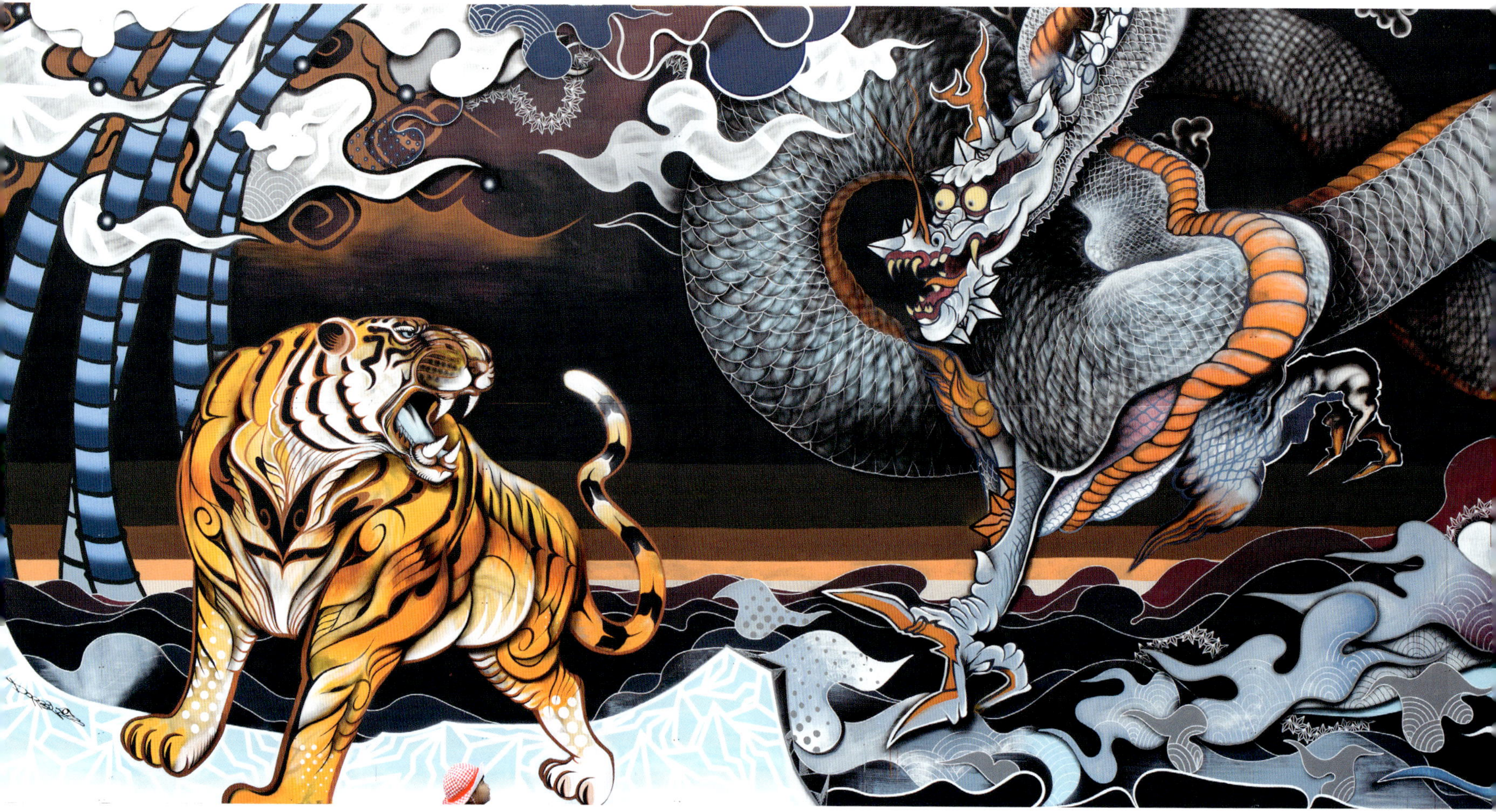

Doppel

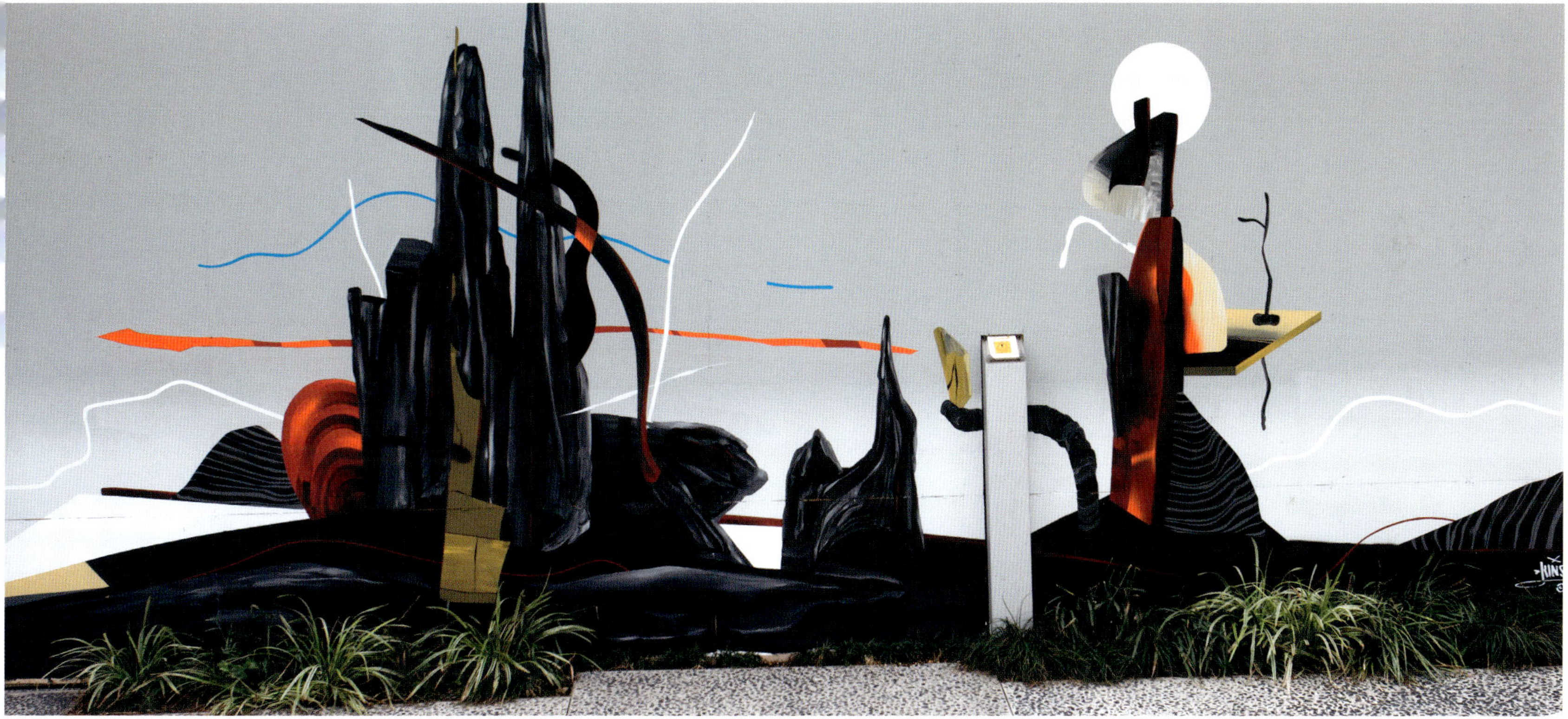

Kinsey

Shizentomotel

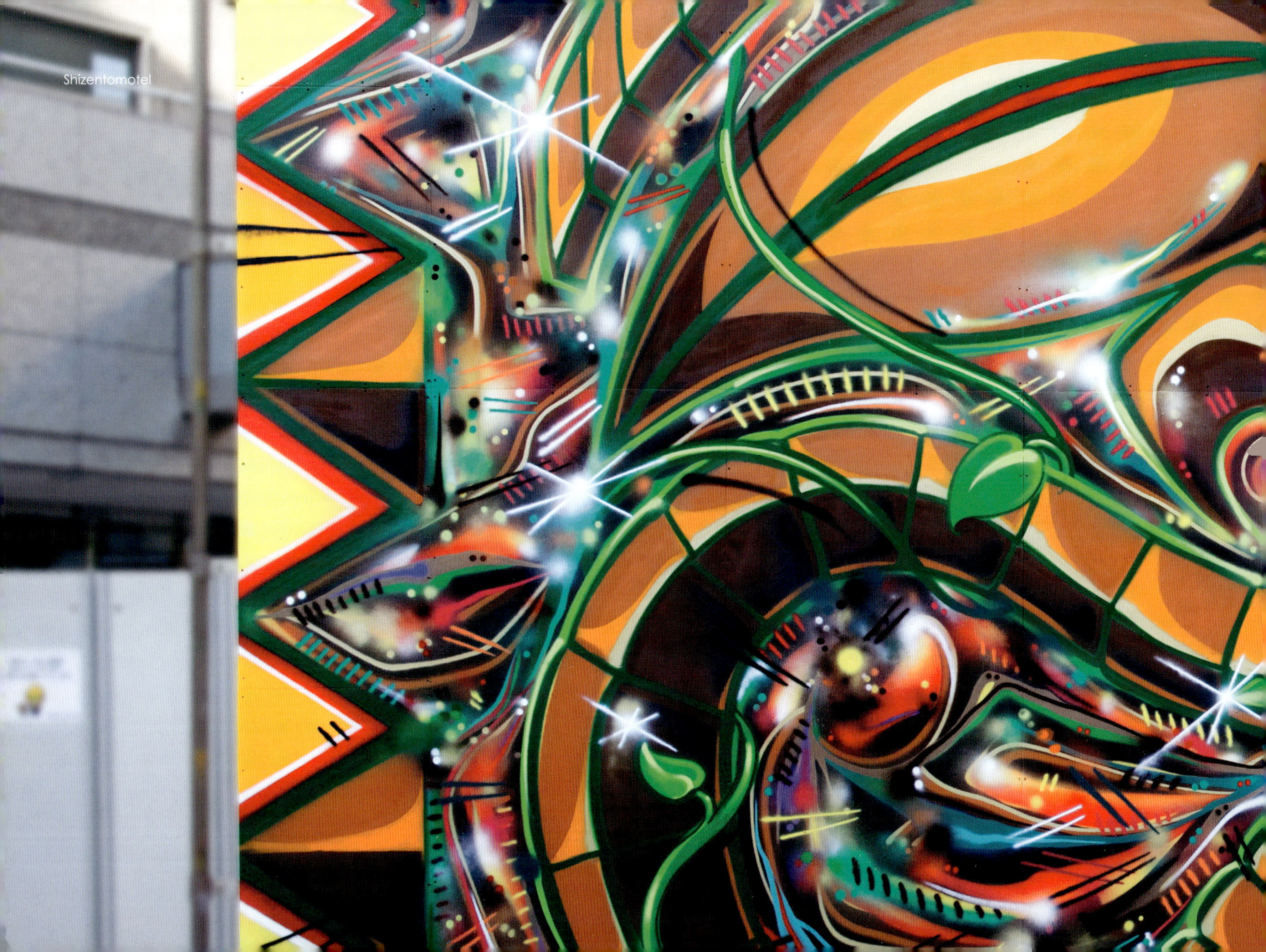

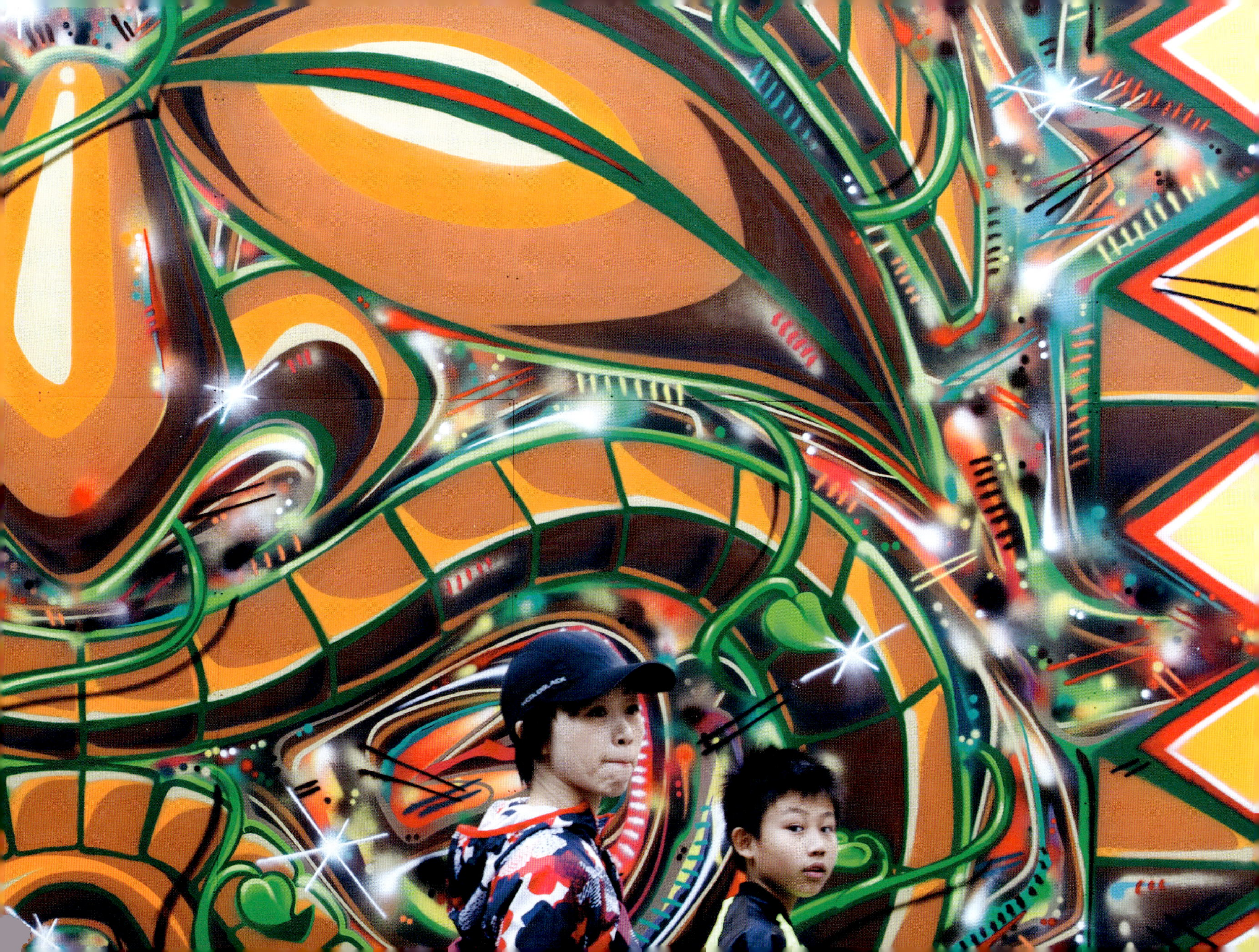

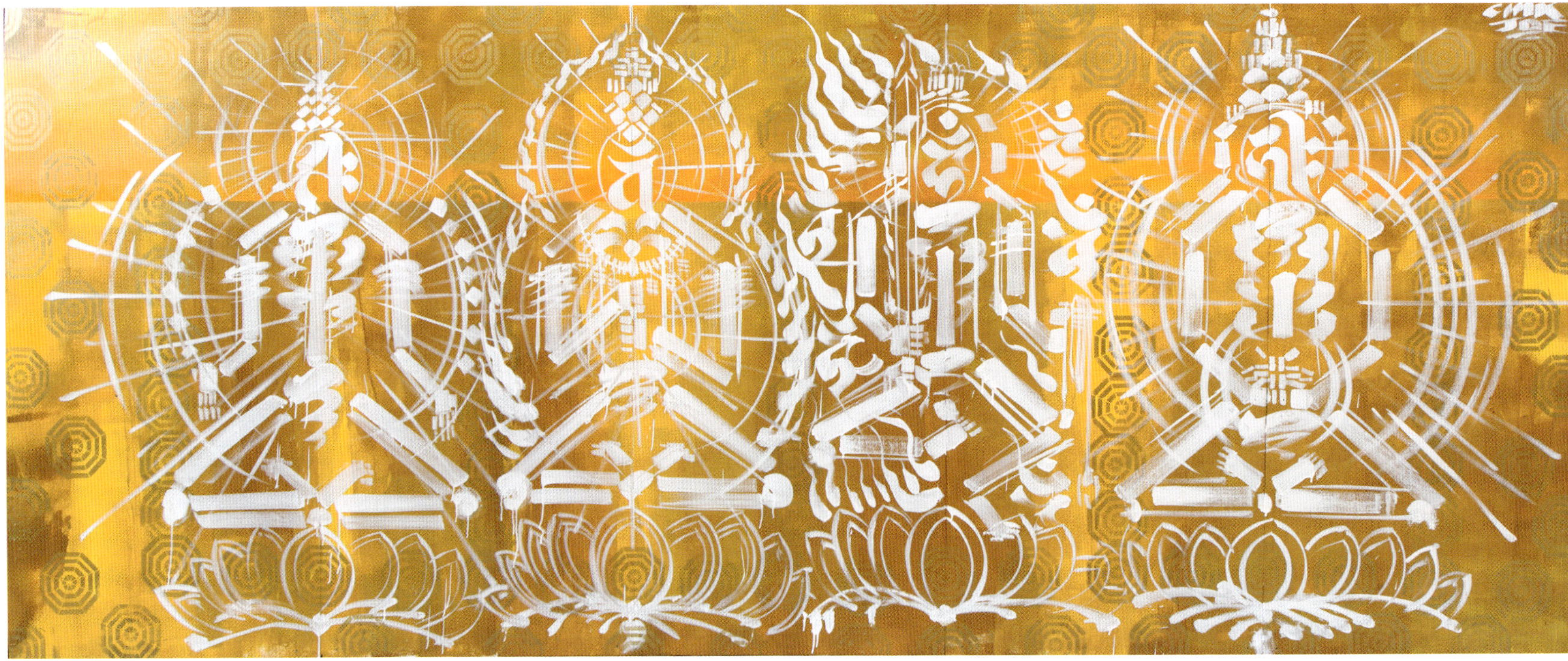

CMK Joe

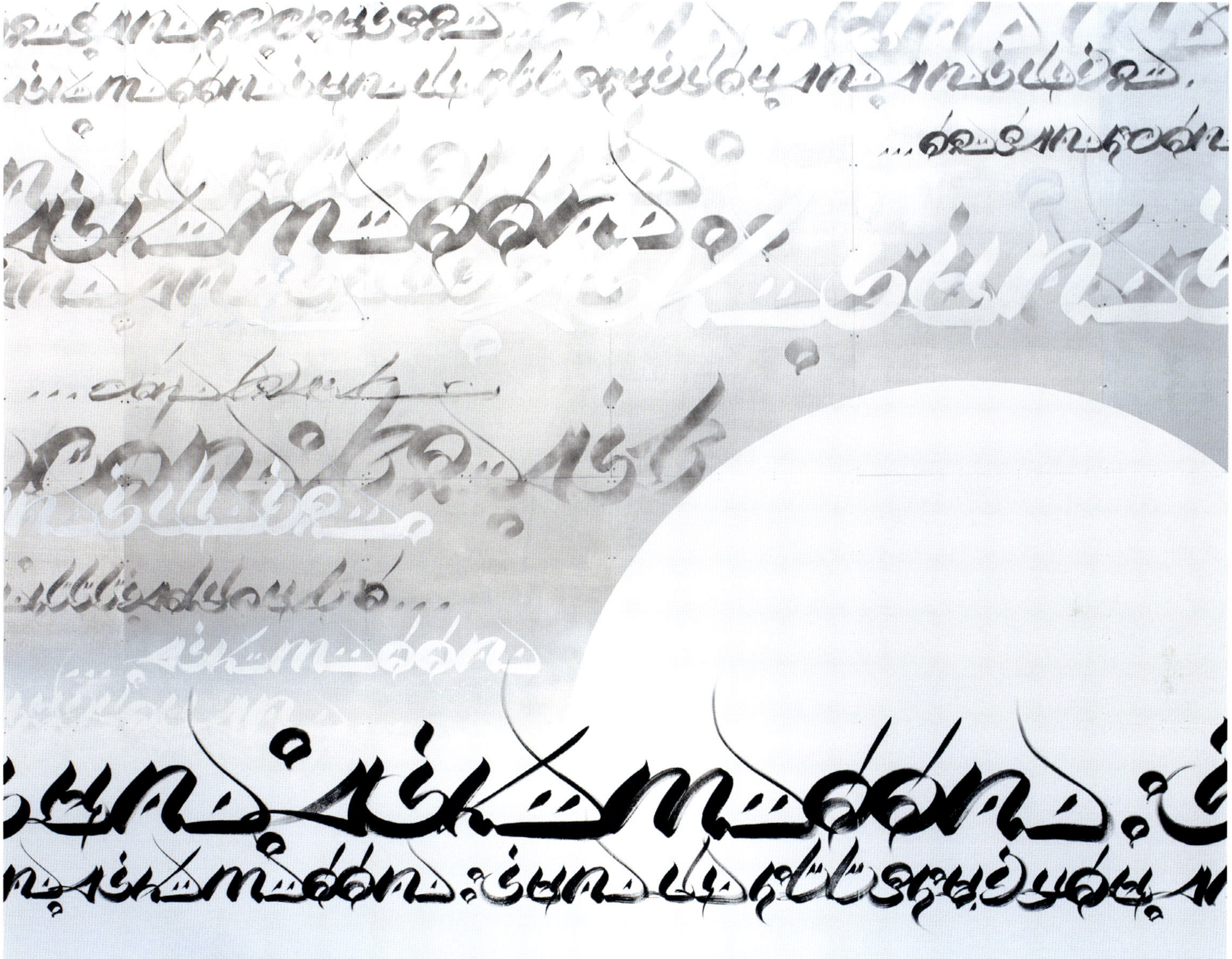

Usugrow

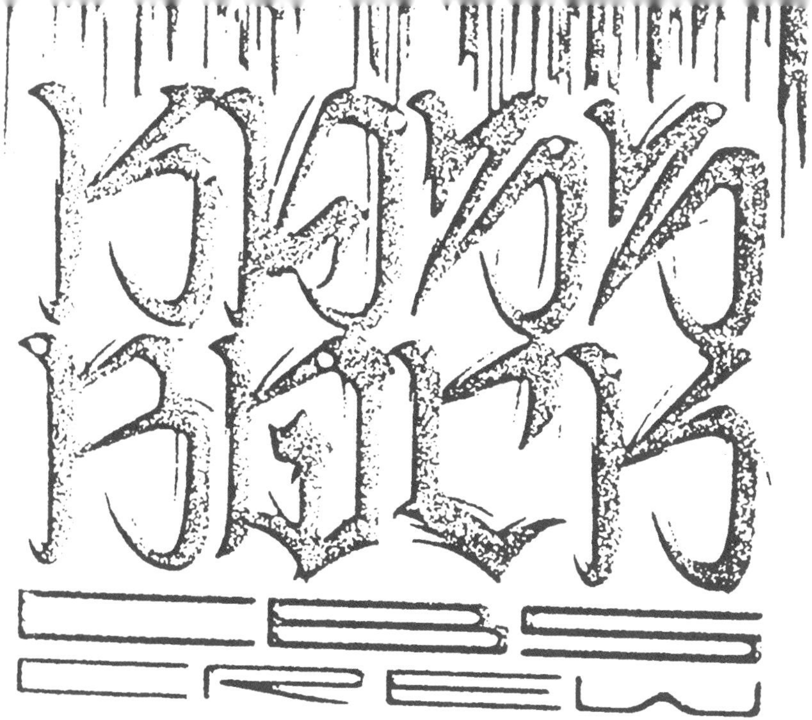

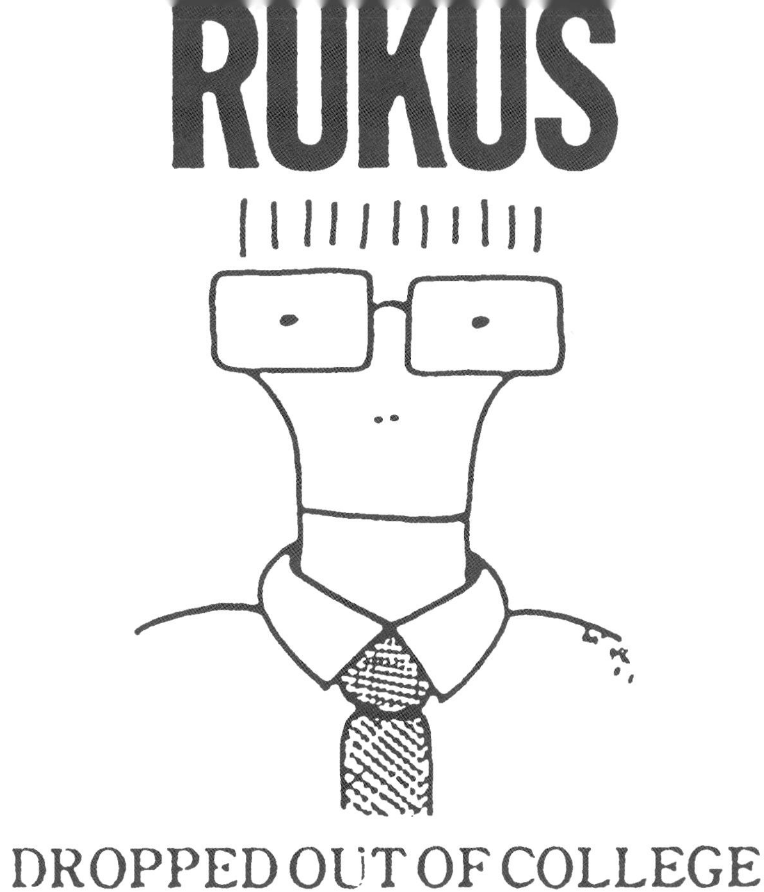
RUKUS
DROPPED OUT OF COLLEGE

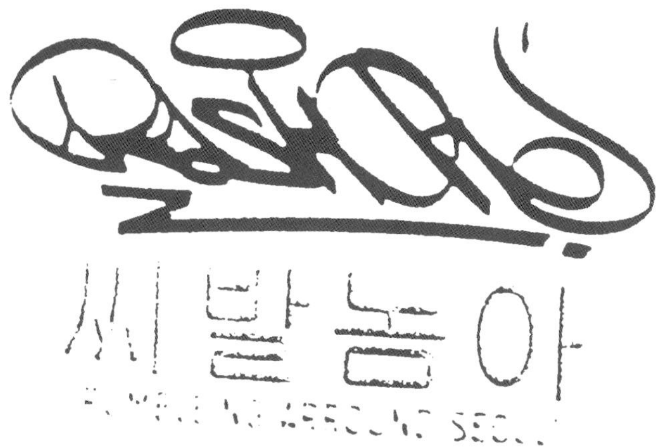
씨발놈아

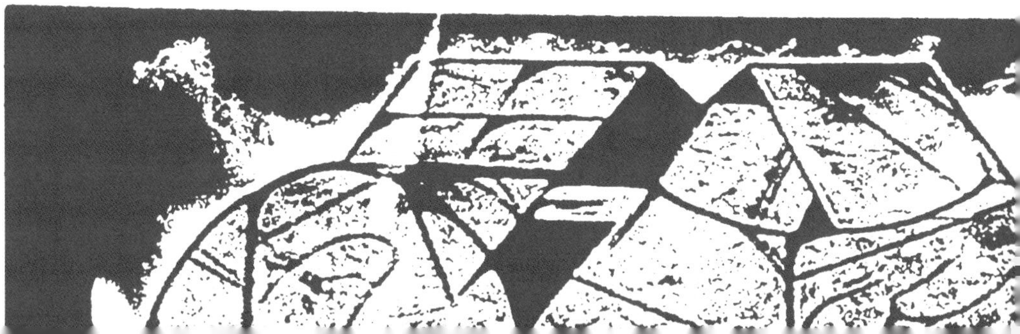

Indoors

It is common for artists with roots in tagging and graf culture to create and display works for sale at home décor and indoor shows. Often scaled down to a smaller canvas or framed paper or wood panel, these works are refined versions of illustrative concepts. In Tokyo, the traditional Buddhas, dragons, and geishas of old are reworked and remixed, creating contemporary imaginings of compelling mythos. The inclusion of street styles indoors is perhaps indicative of some steps towards a more open-minded, artistically open-bordered Japan—it optimistically beckons a new phase of a social, creative revolution.

Although the acceptance and commoditization of a style like street art can often signal the end of an era, it also signifies some creative and hopefully constructive shifts in the cultural identity of this extraordinary city. Retaining its duality—calm and thrilling, timeworn and pioneering, guarded but receptive—Tokyo may be the last great city to slowly transform its outdoor skin to reflect the changes beneath its surface.

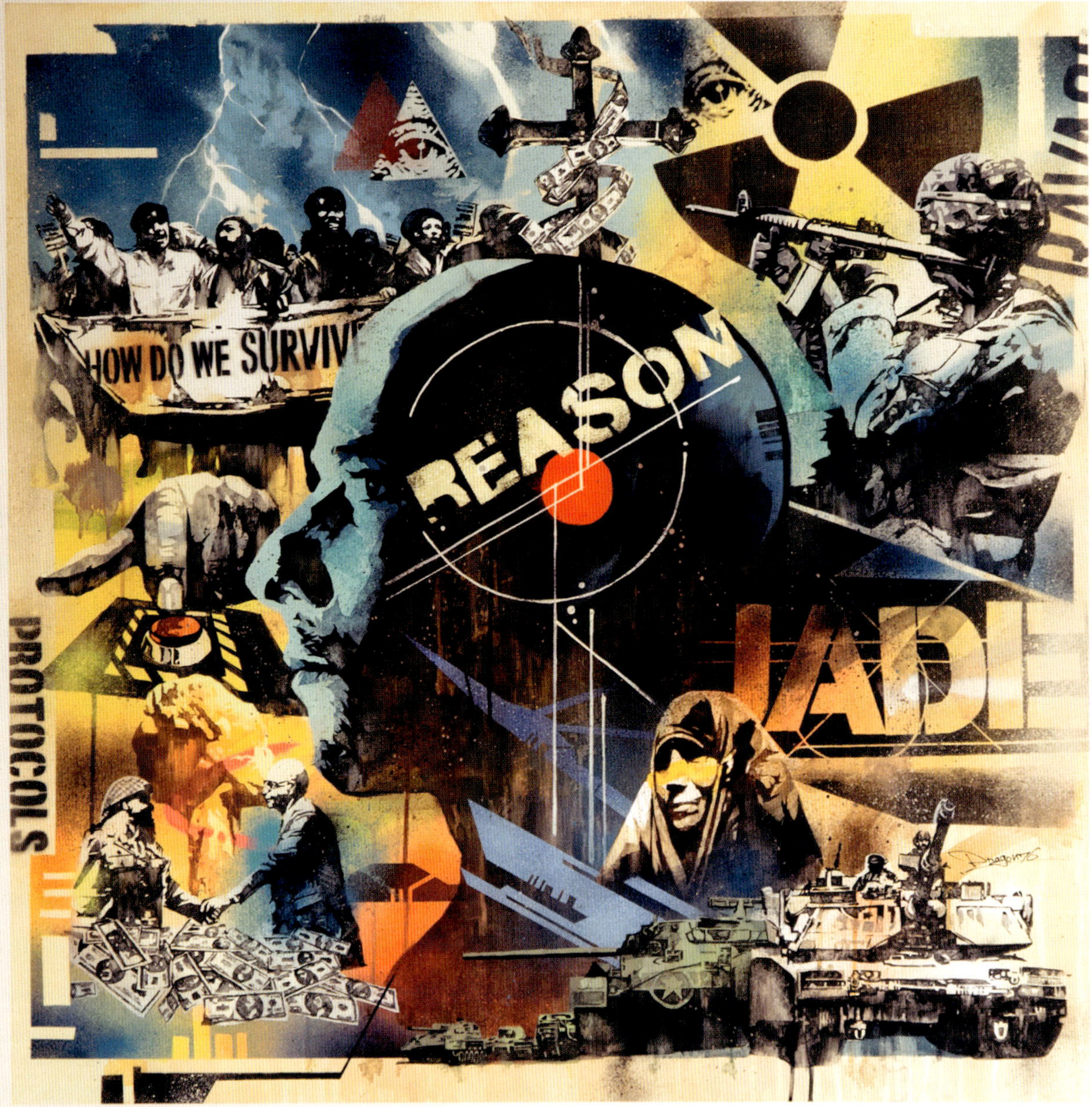

Dragon76

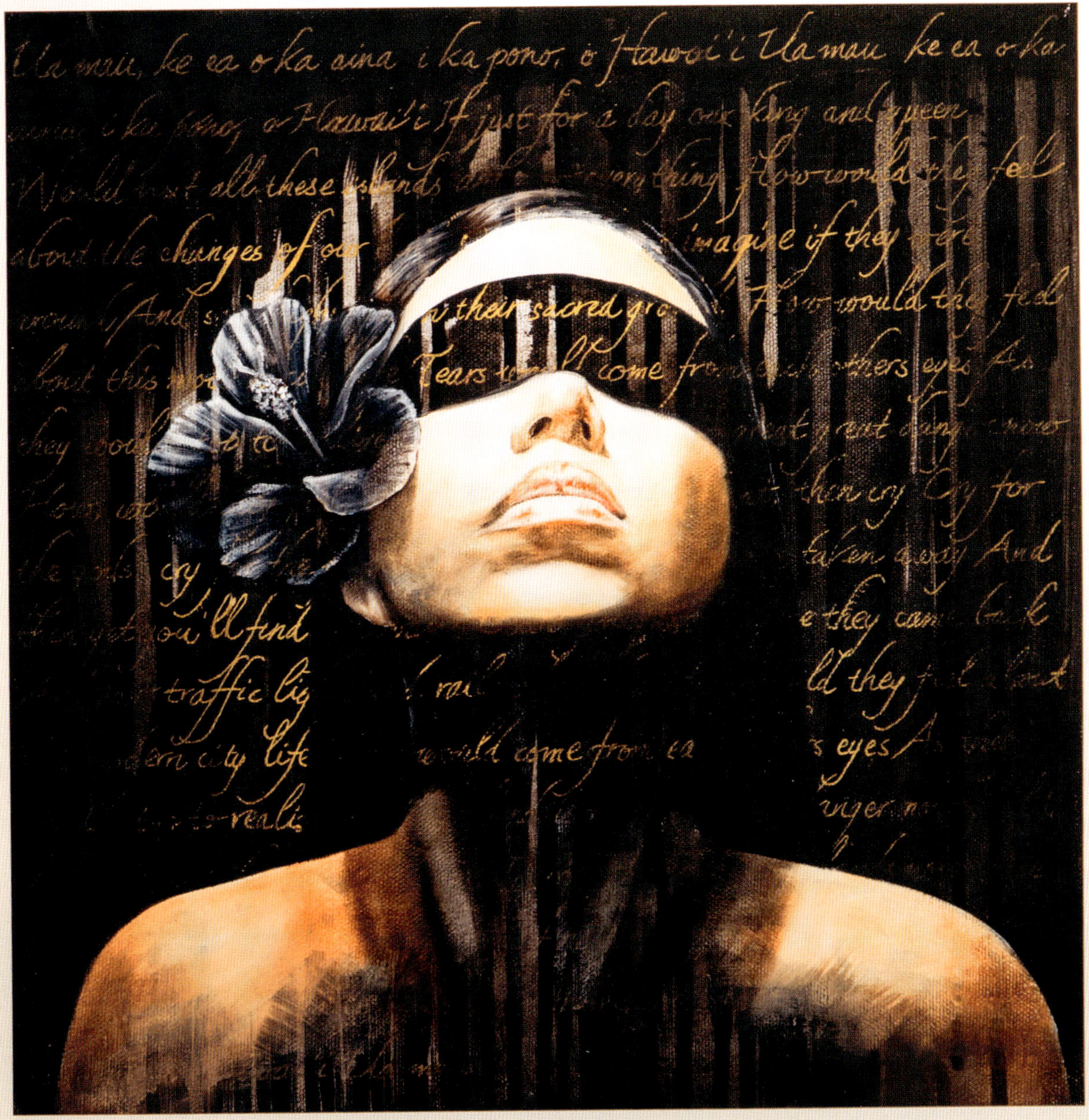

Kamea Hadar

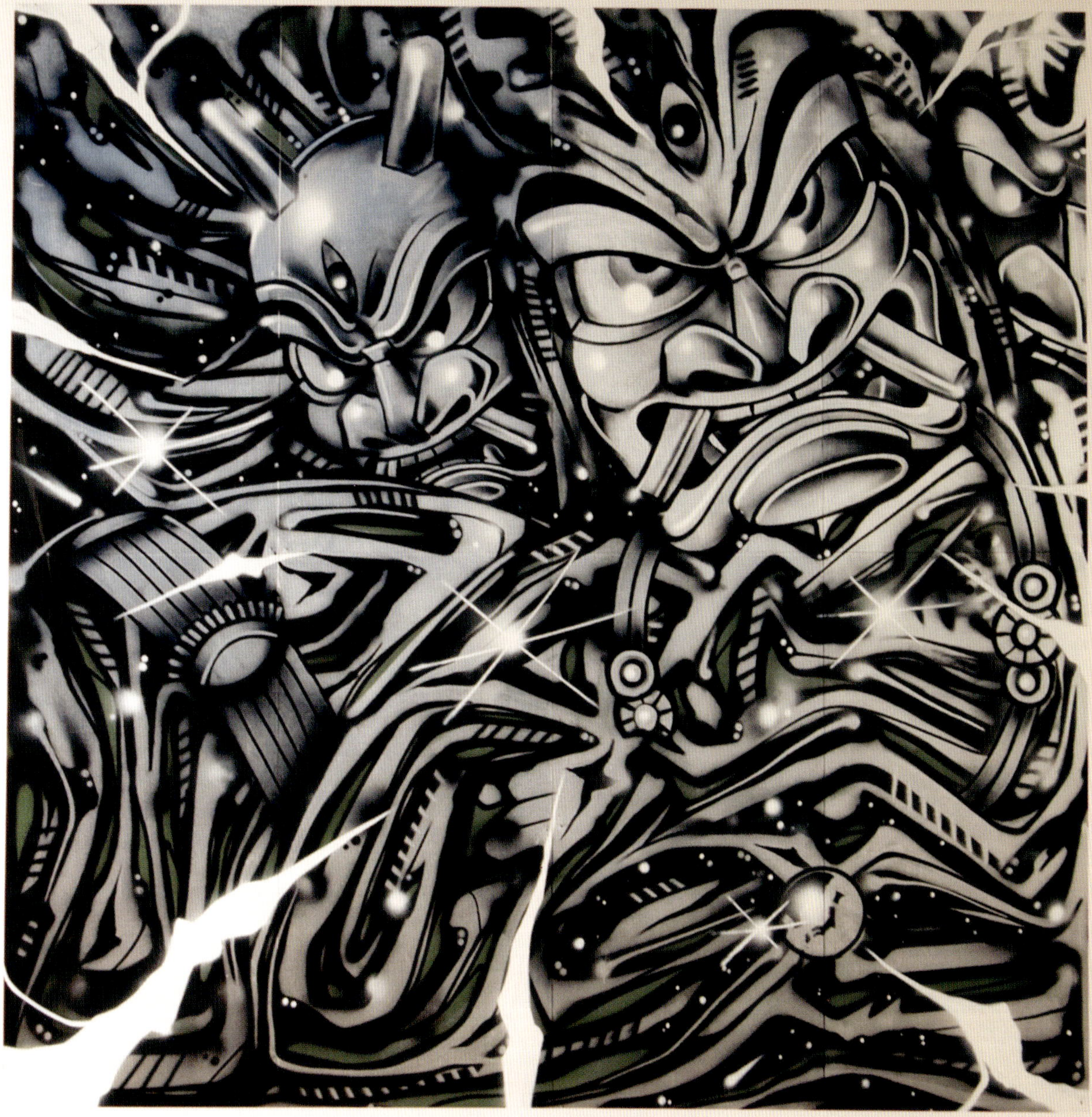

Shizentomotel

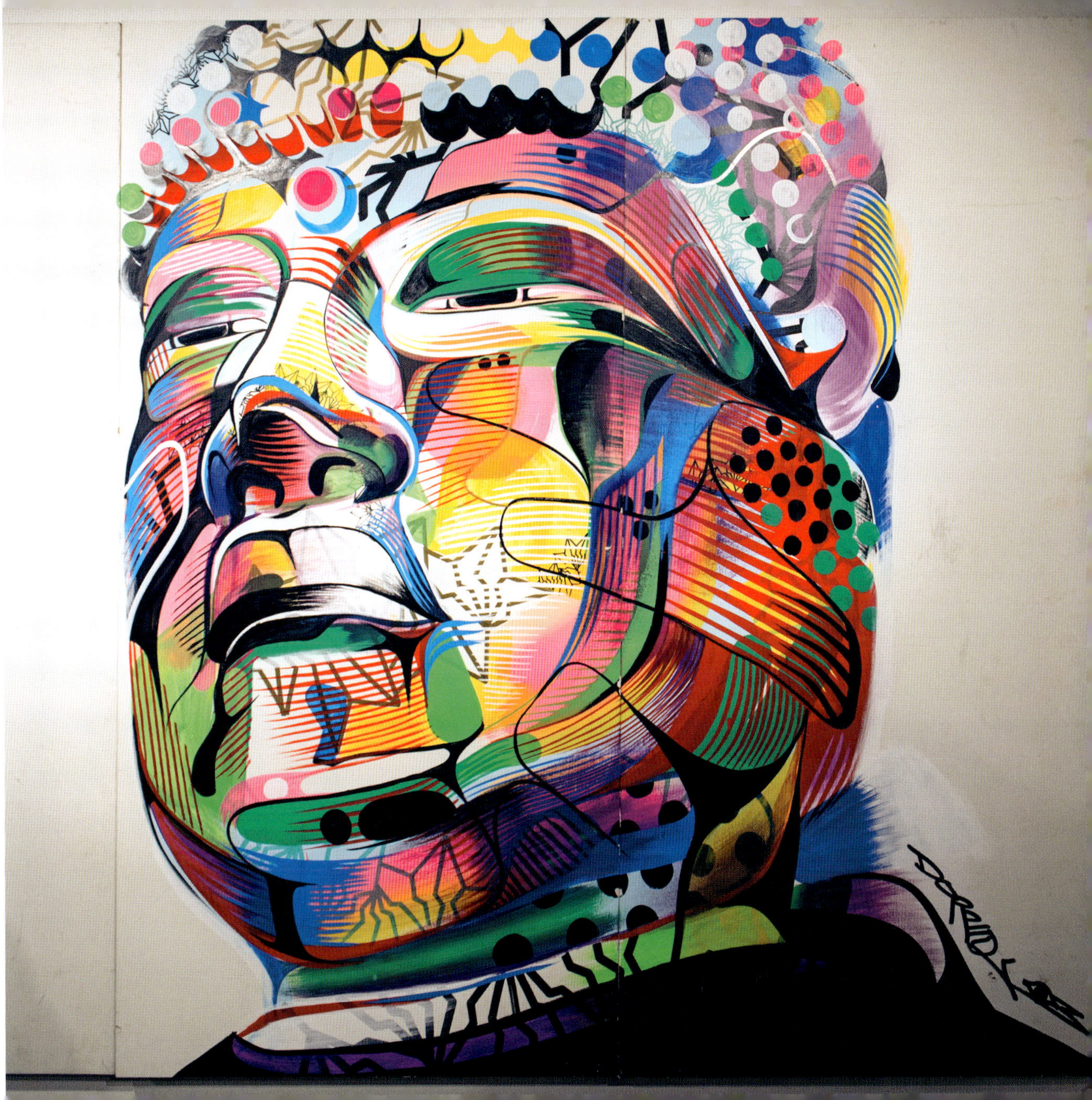

Doppel

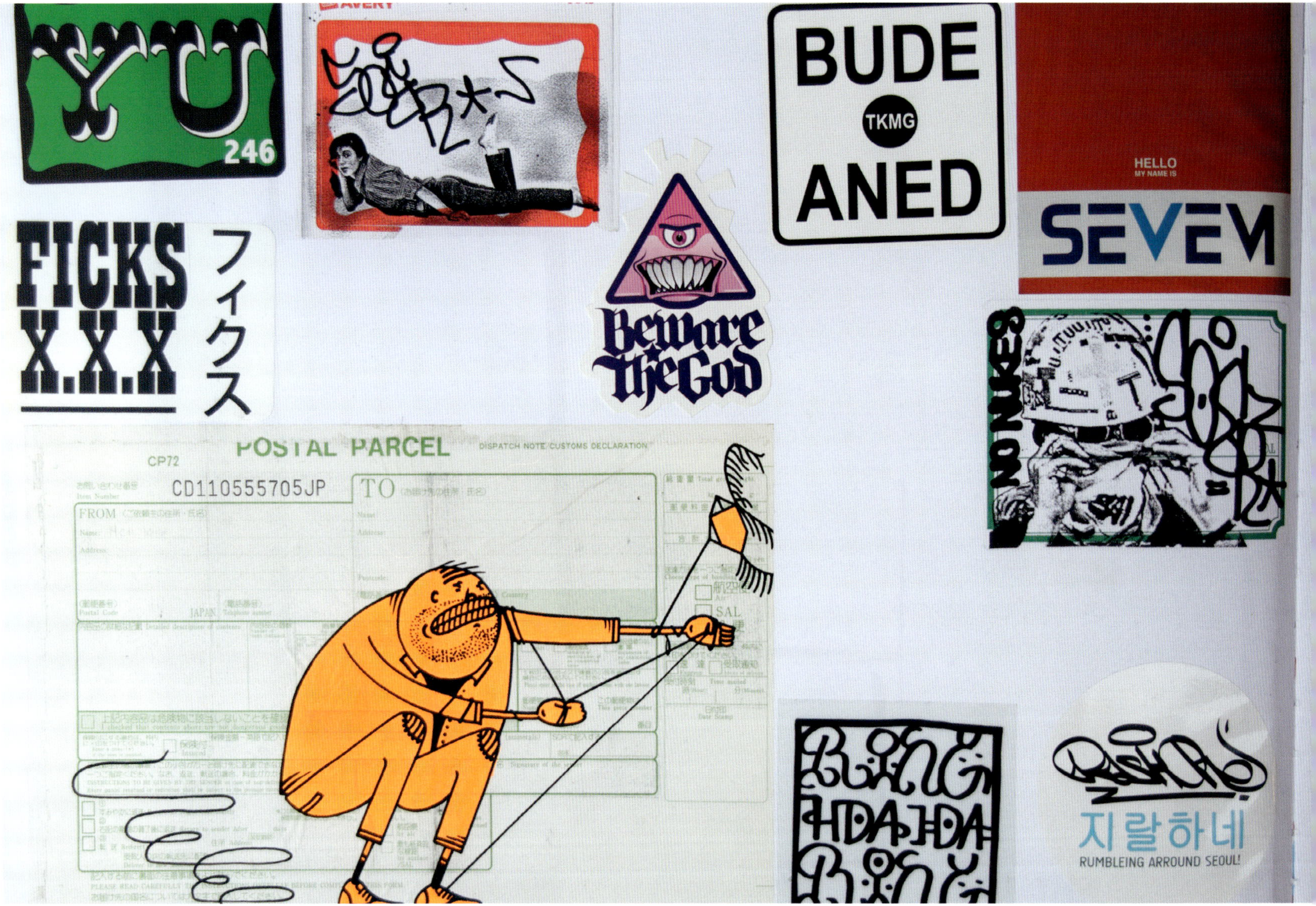

Stickers by various artists on Makoto's black book

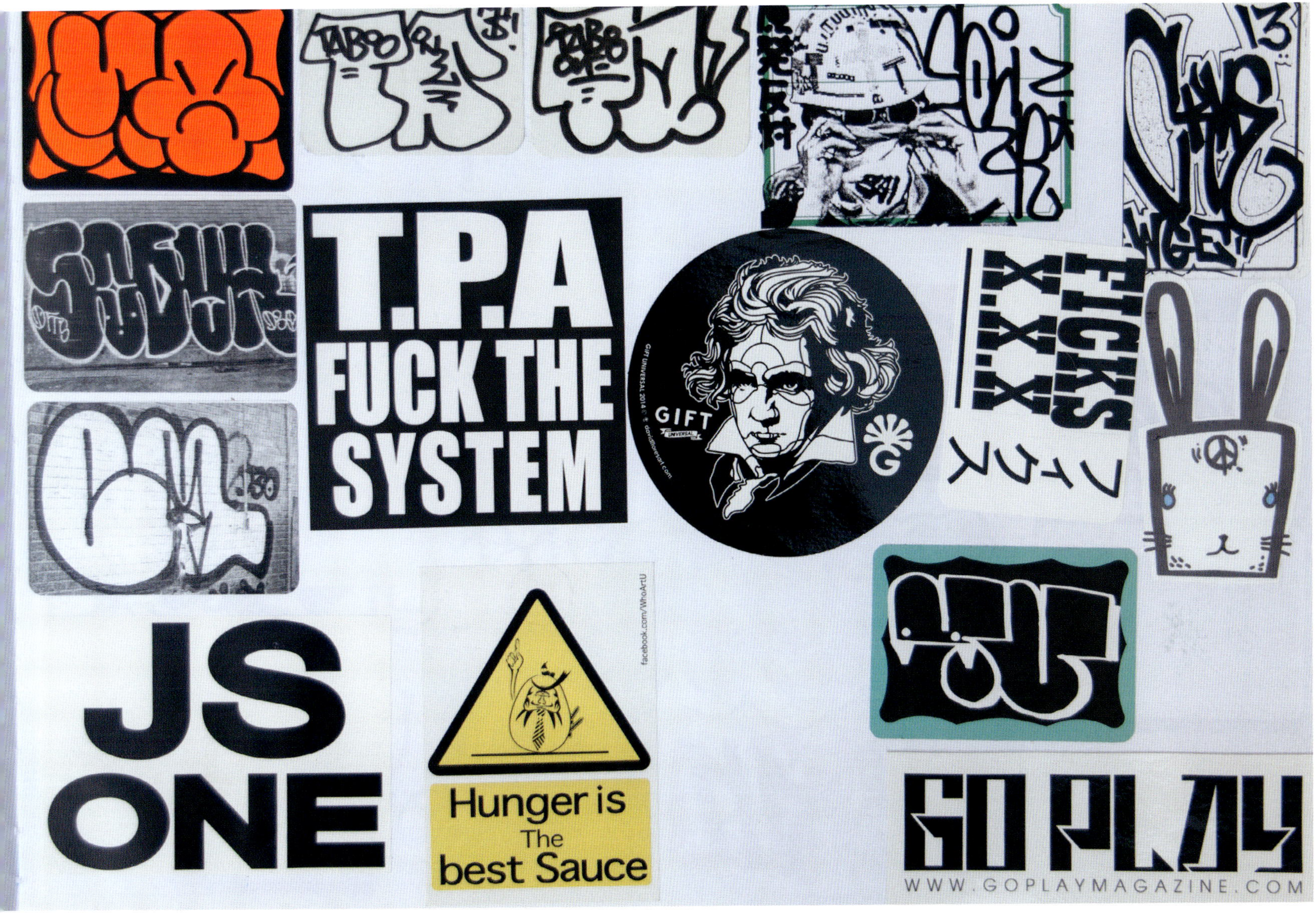

Stickers by various artists on Makoto's black book

Decorative fonts, illustrative figures, cartoons, and logos have all become motifs of the street art culture. It's common to find these on clothing, in commercial advertising, and in fine art galleries. The use of indoor walls for street art is also very popular, and more and more artists are commissioned to do the interiors of restaurants, cafes, and clothing stores. The popularity of the lifestyle as well as the imagery has made what was once simply an act of defacing private property into a methodology symbolic of freedom, individuality, and deviation from the norm.

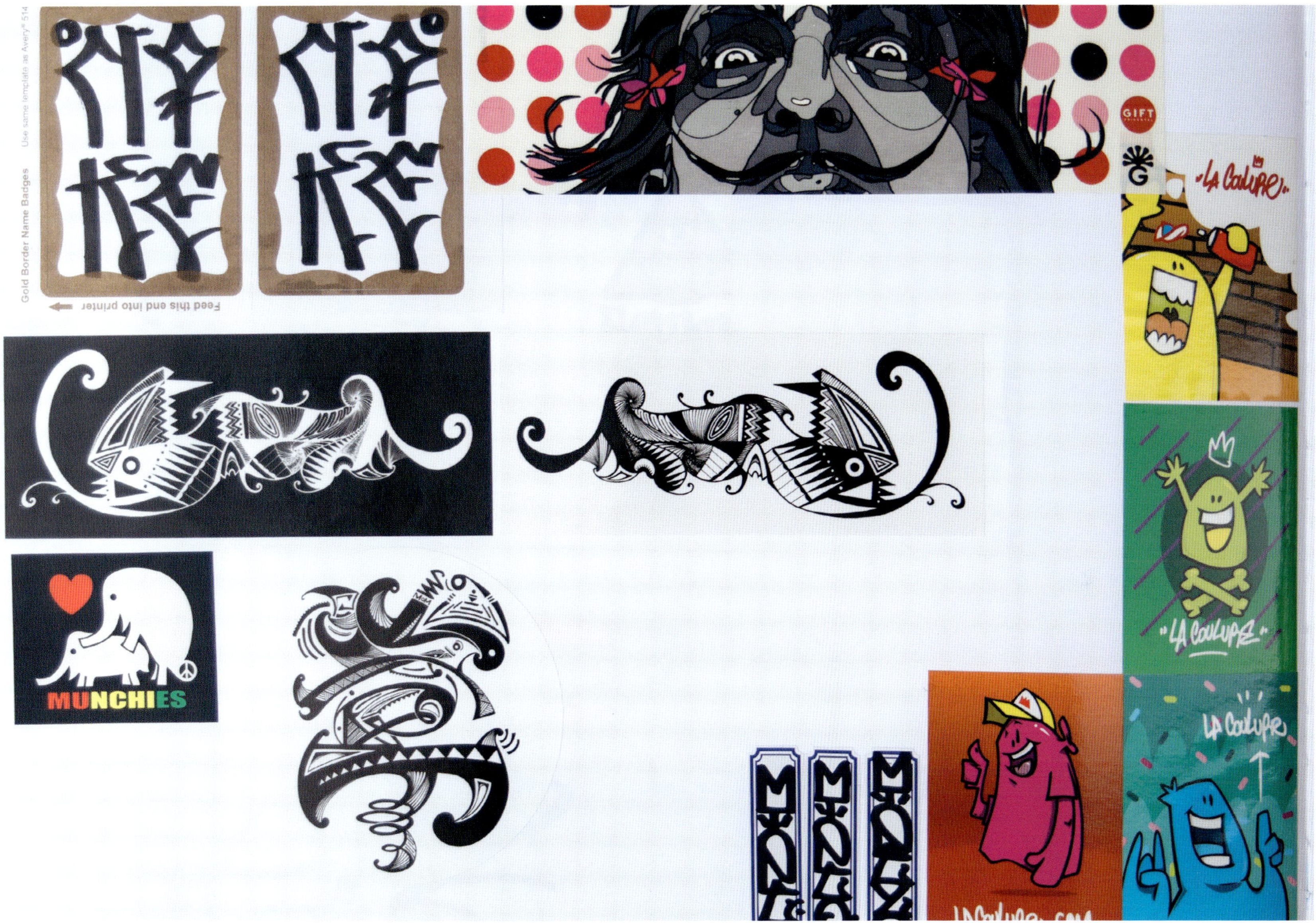

Stickers by various artists on Makoto's black book

Lord K2 (David Sharabani) is a London-born artist known for his photography, as well as his stencil graffiti. He attended the London College of Printing and then moved on to study business. Having spent a large portion of his working life trading stocks from his laptop and traveling extensively, he has had the opportunity to witness how institutions and global economies truly function. This enabled him to make enough for himself to suspend work and move into art. He initially took to the streets to spray paint stencils, having learned his skills in Buenos Aires, and after spending more than two years in Latin America, he continues to travel extensively to pursue his projects. He is working on a number of ongoing photography projects and is currently documenting both the Muay Thai and Sumo cultures in Thailand and Japan respectively.

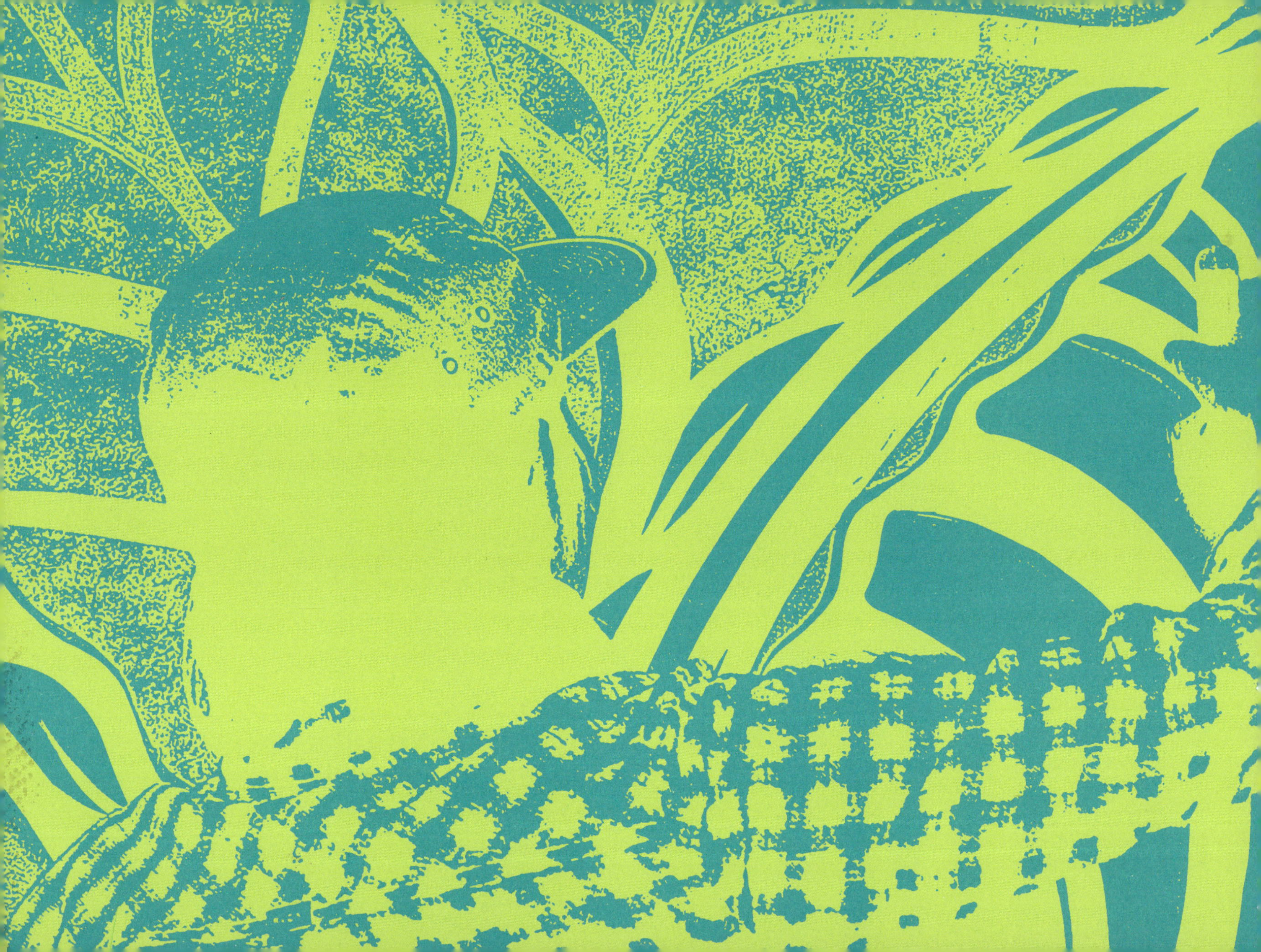